THE LAND WAS THEIRS

JUDAIC STUDIES SERIES, Leon J. Weinberger, General Editor

THE LAND

WAS THEIRS

wish Farmers in the Garden State

GERTRUDE WISHNICK DUBROVSKY

THE UNIVERSITY OF ALABAMA PRESS
Tuscaloosa and London

The paper on which this book is printed meets the minimum requirements of American National Standard for Information Science-Permanence of Paper for Printed Library Materials, ANSI Z39.48-1984.

The research for this work was funded by grants from the National Endowment for the Humanities and the New Jersey Historical Commission. The YIVO Institute for Jewish Research sponsored the work and supervised the grants.

The author wishes to thank the following for use of copyrighted material: Morris U. Schappes, *A Documentary History of the Jews in the United States, 1654-1875*. Copyright © 1950, 1971 by Morris U. Schappes. Used by permission.
Gabriel Davidson, *Our Jewish Farmers and the Story of the Jewish Agricultural Society*. Copyright © 1943. Used by permission of the Baron de Hirsch Fund. Leo Shpall, "Jewish Agricultural Colonies in the United States." Copyright © 1950 by The Agricultural History Society. Used by permission.

Library of Congress Cataloging-in-Publication Data

Dubrovsky, Gertrude Wishnick, 1926-
The land was theirs : Jewish farmers in the Garden state / Gertrude W. Dubrovsky.
p. cm.
Includes bibliographical references and index.
ISBN 0-8173-0544-0
1. Jews—New Jersey—Farmingdale—History. 2. Jews—Colonization—New Jersey—Farmingdale—History. 3. Farmers, Jewish—New Jersey—Farmingdale—Case studies. 4. Farmers, Jewish—New Jersey—Farmingdale—Biography. 5. Dubrovsky, Gertrude Wishnick, 1926- . 6. Farmingdale (N.J.)—Ethnic relations. I. Title.
F145.J5D83 1992
974.9'46—dc20
91-28217
CIP

British Library Cataloguing-in-Publication Data available

For the people of Farmingdale
with whom I have spent
the greater part of my life.

Behold, of the fat places of the earth
Shall be thy dwelling,
And of the dew from heaven above.

Genesis 27:39

He has taken hold in the soil
. . . as if he drives roots into the earth.

I. J. Schwartz, *Kentucky*

The land was ours before we were the land's.

Robert Frost, "The Gift Outright"

My parents always remembered the black soil of Russia
which they were not permitted to plow.

Louis Harwood, Farmingdale farmer

Springtime comes, and the leaves are turning green;
Dewdrops glisten in the sun.
Birds are singing to the rhythm of the stream.
I love living on the land.

Michael Nappa (1944–87),
third-generation descendant
of Farmingdale farmers

Contents

Part 4. Growing Up in Farmingdale

Preface

The poet urged that we "see the world in a grain of sand / And Heaven in a wild flower." In essence, Blake reminds us that by closely examining a small corner of the world, we learn a great deal about the whole cosmos.

I have tried to explore the history of American Jewish farmers through the example of Farmingdale, New Jersey, a community of Jewish immigrant farmers, in which my own history took shape. It is only one of many such rural Jewish communities established in the twentieth century in various parts of the country. That these communities have received scant academic attention does not mean that they are insignificant.

Community histories are the building blocks from which an authentic history of American Jews can ultimately be constructed. They provide a basis for comparative analysis, needed in order to understand how ethnic population groups structure themselves within the larger culture.

On the community level it is possible to see the social, economic, political, cultural, and even the religious acculturation of the Jewish immigrant. But there has been a great paucity of detailed analysis of the Jewish and Judaic experience in small communities and little source material available on the rural history of American Jews.

We have no dependable data on the dispersion of the immigrants in the interior of America, no reliable estimates of how many immigrants left the urban centers for the rural countryside; nor is much known about their communities, many of which already have disappeared without a trace.

If we are ever to construct an authentic and balanced history of the American Jewish experience, a serious effort must be initiated to document how Jews live and have lived in our country's rural areas and small towns. We need to identify people who have had the experience, tape their stories, and collect whatever documents they are willing to share. It is imperative to initiate this work immediately. Rural communities are undergoing radical change; many already have disappeared, and the people who lived in them are aging. Heirs and descendants have little sense of the historic value of the memorabilia they discard when they settle estates.

In the area around the small town of Farmingdale, in central New Jersey, Jewish immigrants without previous farm experience established small family farms and made New Jersey one of the leading egg-producing states in America. It became known both as the egg basket of America and as the cradle of the Jewish farm movement.

Without other community studies to compare, we cannot know how typical Farmingdale is of rural Jewish communities in America. What can be said is that it shares certain similarities with some others in New Jersey, with Perrineville, Flemington, Toms River, Jackson, and North Brunswick, to name a few.

Like them, the Jewish community in Farmingdale grew gradually as individuals who previously had not known each other settled and then created the institutions and organizations they needed to sustain their Jewish life. Although social interaction between the New Jersey enclaves was limited, particularly before the automobile, the isolated settlements appear to have developed similar internal structures. And they all enjoyed a substantial history in time; Farmingdale had a life span of more than fifty years.

Today, it appears that the American economy can no longer support small family enterprises of any kind. The small family farmer, like the small enterprising shopkeeper or craftsman, is displaced. It is "up or out" for too many, and a way of life is vanishing. Experiencing the strains of transition, people try to find their own human places in a technological, industrial world in which they do not feel comfortable. The easing out of the small family farmer left many with a sense of displacement, alienation, and frustration.

The Farmingdale farmers who went through the pain of transition are now either retired or in vastly different types of economic endeavors. Their Community Center and their organizations are no longer in existence. A few individuals have become inordinately wealthy in their new lives off the farm. Yet, none of those interviewed regret the years they spent in Farmingdale. As seen through their memories, the farm enriched them in every way except monetarily. And the community life provided that which no amount of money could buy. It gave them an extended family, a vibrant intellectual community, and a sense of connection to both. They consider these as the important aspects of their experience. They hardly speak of their other achievements.

The Land Was Theirs combines documentary sources, personal experiences, and life histories from over 120 people interviewed. My work began with a realization that the New Jersey community in which I grew up, Farmingdale, was in a state of demise and its history in danger of being irrevocably lost if I or someone did not make an effort to preserve it. I began by interviewing the oldest settlers. All the interviews cited were conducted and taped between 1975 and 1980.

Each interview was a remarkable experience for me. I connected with people who, during the course of the session, shed masks and restraints and tried to be as honest as possible. I cannot say that their accounts of events were entirely accurate. Memory of the past is often romantic and always biased. Who among us can be totally objective about our life experiences? Some memories were often so painful for the speaker that I felt as if I was intruding on forbidden territory. Sometimes I became merely an ear, an innocent reporter needing instruction from a witness who had survived purgatory. Holocaust survivors insisted on speaking English because they wanted to make things easier for me. They talked briefly about their farm experience and then, almost without awareness, slipped into Yiddish and into the dark world they carry with them on a daily basis. On two occasions, I asked if I might return to get the rest of the story, because I could not bear to hear more.

Because I grew up in the community, I had some basis against which to check the answers to my questions. When I recognized a fanciful interpretation of events at which I was present, I rephrased my question, asked another, and then came back to the original subject. Often the speaker was as artful as I was and insisted on his or her answer, which may not have had any relationship to my question. I also knew that there were those who wanted to please me by telling me what they thought I wanted to hear. Such are the problems of oral history.

Regardless of how the subjects interpreted the past, they are worthy of being heard, and there is a level of truth in each account. This I know. Admittedly, I was skeptical when an individual told of a singular event— it may or may not have occurred. If several people reported the same incident, I became confident it happened.

I researched newspapers, analyzed letters and journals, and looked at farm documents, seeking support of remembered events. However, these traditional sources, although in print or manuscript form, are not always accurate or complete either. For example, half a dozen informants told me of seeing the Klan in white robes march past homes of new settlers and of the Klan's burning a cross opposite the Jewish Community Center as soon as it was completed in 1929. Reviewing local newspapers from 1920 to 1940, I found no mention anywhere of the Ku Klux Klan. Nor did I personally ever see the Klan in action. But enough witnesses have corroborated the testimony to convince me it took place.

In abstracting the interview material, I have tried to select typical incidents and words which reflect general sentiments and convey the unique personality of the speaker. But words on a page are a far cry from those originating in a soul and expressed through the body of the speaker.

Rural America stretched the farmers' imaginations and presented opportunities barely dreamed of before. The idea of land—ownership, stewardship, and potential—was voiced so many times that it was hard to miss the significance of it for a people born in Eastern Europe with no possibility to own land. During an interview I caught their excitement, and when, days or months later, I wrote their words, I could hear and see the person in my mind's eye. When Louis Bially, for example, reported his reaction—"The land was mine. Everywhere I stepped, my strawberries, my corn, my tree, everything I planted with my hands"—he was animated, emotional, his eyes full of pride. The reader of the words, far removed from the man and the place, does not have my memory to fill out the picture.

If the readers can grasp some of the poetry, it is a credit to the people interviewed; if the words on the page seem devoid of life, it is because of my limitations.

The tapes were reviewed and analyzed for patterns of responses. I have not attempted a detailed analysis of the process by which individuals became farmers, or of the economic success or failure of either this community or of farming in New Jersey generally. It is sufficient to say that the Jewish farmers in America and particularly in New Jersey were active in every branch of agriculture and developed poultry farming into a major branch of U.S. agriculture, mechanizing the industry, taking the chickens out of the backyard, and making eggs another cash crop for farms.

In the pages that follow, Farmingdale farmers tell who they were, where they came from, how they lived, what they valued, and how they remember the experience. Their testimony offers a perspective on the pressures, problems, and satisfactions of rural Jewish life in one community.

Just as I have tried to look at the history of American Jewish farmers through the example of one farm community, so do I explore my own life as one who grew up in Farmingdale. My remembered experience is a resource I drew upon in my work, and I have included my own story, as an extended case history of the family I knew better than any other.

In telling my story, I tried to choose anecdotes which illustrate the preoccupation and mores of the larger community and how they impinged on my personal life. It was impossible for me to get such material from the informants whose life histories I taped.

In some way, the life of the community and the life of my family are parallel. Growing up in Farmingdale, I yearned for another world and vowed to leave as soon as I could. Instead, I married a farmer's son, settled on a farm, raised chickens, and participated in the institutions and activities of the community. I remained, witnessing the death of friends, family, and community. I saw the farm economy collapse, watched as neighbors moved, and ultimately left myself. I returned to record the history.

In doing my work, I was fortunate in having the support of many friends and acquaintances. First, I thank all 120 families I interviewed for opening their doors, hearts, and minds to me. They were welcoming, kind, and generous in sharing their memories and memorabilia. Some people I had known practically all my life; others became friends after the interview. Sadly, at least a quarter of my sample has passed away since I spent time talking to them. For some, I was the last person they spoke to about a significant chapter of their lives. One man died the day after I interviewed him.

I wish also to acknowledge the support of a few other individuals among many who helped. Linda Oppenheim worked on this project from the beginning. She organized the material in the Farmingdale Collection and indexed all the tapes and this volume. Not a farmer, she became a friend of all the farmers interviewed. Lillis Caulton made a coherent archive out of a vast jumble of papers and documents. Sylvia Orr, who was also raised in Farmingdale, read through the entire manuscript, made many helpful suggestions, and contributed family memorabilia to the Farmingdale Collection. Fannie Peczenik read and critiqued parts of the book. Shirley Stein, a psychologist and a wonderful friend, helped me understand some of the layered meanings in excerpts from my interviews. And by insisting that my work had great value, she helped me through lonely and discouraging periods. Benjamin Dubrovsky, my youngest son, has been a strong supporter of this work and has experienced some of the ambience of his former community through it.

Sally Davidson helped organize an exhibit of photographs from the archive. Abraham Peck, executive director of the American Jewish Archives, has maintained a vital interest in my work, mounted an enlarged exhibit of photographs called "The American Jewish Farmer," and published an accompanying catalogue. Bernard Bush, executive director of the New Jersey Historical Commission, was one of the first to recognize the importance of the work and has consistently been a strong supporter.

Finally, I want to thank a working committee of DOCUMENTARY III, a nonprofit organization established to track rural ethnic history in New Jersey: Allen and Arianne Kassof, Sidney Troy, Barbara Sassone, Mindy Berman, Marion Munk, Peter and Lisa Cziffra, and, of course, Sidney Gray, my husband. We have all enriched our lives by the work we have done, and we hope that others also will be enriched.

THE LAND WAS THEIRS

Introduction

Jewish Agriculture in America

J ewish agriculture in America is a story of tenacious striving and struggle, of failure and success. The early efforts made by Jewish immigrants and well-meaning Jewish institutions, organizations, and individuals who wanted to help them establish farm colonies were largely failures. Thus, many who came to America with dreams of becoming farmers were forced to abandon the idea. Yet the dream persisted among small numbers who persevered and eventually succeeded.

The twentieth century saw Jewish farmers successfully integrated into American agriculture and influencing its practices. They pioneered in poultry farming, making it an important element of American agriculture; they experimented with genetic breeding of livestock; they developed vaccines against animal diseases; they grew new strains of wheat and other grains; they had model fruit orchards, vineyards, and vegetable farms. Few in America are aware of this history.

Writing about the immigrant contribution, American agriculture historian Theodore Saloutos says that "for various reasons historians have played down the role of the immigrant in our agricultural development. Our provincialism and ineptness with foreign languages may account for part of this, but our attitudes probably have more to do with it."[1] In his overview, Saloutos himself fails to include the Jewish farmer.

If the role of the immigrant farmer in America has been played down, that of the Jewish immigrant farmer has virtually been ignored, and the communities they established in rural America are for the most part unknown. Although it is not generally understood, attempts and plans to "colonize" Jews have been advanced in the United States since the end of the eighteenth century. In the nineteenth century, urban American Jews worked hard to establish farm colonies that would absorb new Russian immigrants. While the efforts were largely unsuccessful, the short-lived colonies that resulted provided models for later immigrants who settled on the land and created small Jewish communities across the United States.

Early Efforts to Encourage Jewish Immigration

The first mention of a Jewish farm colony in America came in 1783, when an anonymous letter to the president of the Continental Congress proposed settling two thousand Jews on the land. Thought at first to have been written by a German Jew, it has since been proved "an attempt by a Christian author to demonstrate to his fellow men the necessity of granting full emancipation to the Jews."[2] The suggestion in the letter remains more puzzling than its authorship, because in 1783 the total number of Jews in America could not have exceeded by much the two thousand proposed for settlement.

In 1819, another attempt was made to encourage Jewish emigration. William David Robinson, a baptized Presbyterian of Philadelphia, circulated among the wealthy Jews of London a document entitled "Memoir Addressed to Persons of the Jewish Religion in Europe, on the subject of Emigration to, and settlement in, one of the Most Eligible Parts of the United States of North America." Presented as an investment proposal, the memoir contained a plan for establishing Jewish agricultural settlements along the Mississippi and Missouri rivers as a way of encouraging Jews to emigrate from Europe. What effect the plan had on the London Jews is not known, but the plan itself offers an example of how American Christians tried to induce Jews to come to America. Promoting the sale of land, the author exploits an old stereotype of the Jew as an urban dweller who shuns agricultural pursuits.

> The education and general habits of the Jews, throughout Europe, have fixed them in commercial cities and towns. . . . Some few of them have acquired great wealth and live in luxurious magnificence, but even these few have been so much accustomed to manage the monied transactions of Europe, that they consider this the only proper theatre on which they can exist and flourish. . . . A certain portion have, however, overcome this

prejudice, and hence those Jews who have emigrated across the Atlantic, have in general have been of the opulent class, and in the United States have been led to pursue the same occupations they did in the land from which they came. . . . Very rarely do we find an artisan among them, and still more rare it is to see any of them following the labours of agriculture, or rural occupations.

. . . However wretched the situation of the poorer class of Jews in Europe, there we behold them carrying on the most menial operations . . . in preference to tilling the ground. This . . . seems to be the effect of the uncertainty of their social and political existence, and the consequent habits in which they are unfortunately reared.[3]

Robinson acknowledges the "imperious difficulties" which have deterred the Jew from agriculture, but he cannot quite hide his missionary zeal in suggesting that agriculture would elevate Jews "to a rank in society which for many ages they have not enjoyed. The only difficulty in the realization of the present scheme, is the habitual propensity of the Jews to follow other pursuits than those of agriculture." However, Robinson predicts that if the Jews were conveyed to another land, "a smiling country," they then would be able to eat the "fruits of the trees planted with their own hands and the scene is changed."[4]

Robinson's plan called for conveying emigrants from Europe to New Orleans free of expense, settling each on "a certain number of acres, on a credit of a specific number of years," and providing them with implements of agriculture. In this way he foresees that "both the political and moral situation of the Jews will be bettered, for they will enter on the enjoyment of civil rights, and to prevent crime, there is no safer means than to remedy misfortune." Finally Robinson envisages "Jewish agriculture spreading through the American forests; Jewish towns and villages adorning the banks of the Mississippi and Missouri, and the arts, commerce, and manufacture would advance with the same rapidity in this new settlement, as had been exemplified in all other agricultural regions of the United States." A further inducement for investment by London's Jewish financiers is offered by Robinson in a footnote: Jews would help America as they had helped other countries. As Brazil "is indebted to them [the Jews] for its first harvest [Jews were the first to cultivate that colony]," so will America be.[5]

American concern with the moral condition of the Jews, or efforts to explain Jewish moral lapses, betrays a curious ambivalence toward the Jews, who were being encouraged to immigrate here. In an 1820 editorial of *Niles Weekly Register*, the writer argues for the need to eliminate office-holding restrictions from the Maryland constitution that significantly affected Jews and other minorities. While he urges a more liberal policy, he also wonders in print why most countries deny Jews the rights granted others. Resorting to the old stereotype, he concludes: "There must be some moral cause to produce this effect. In general, their interests do not appear identified with those of the communities in which they live . . . they will not sit down and labor like other people—they create nothing and are mere consumers. They will not cultivate the earth . . . preferring to live by their wits in dealing, and acting as if they had a home nowhere."[6]

During this same time, missionary societies were formed in Europe and America to encourage Jewish emigration. The Nordamerikanische Kolonizationgesellschaft was organized in Stuttgart in 1818.[7] In America, an organization addressed an appeal to Christians for funding to settle emigrating Jews on the land. The ostensible purpose was to make Jews better and more moral by giving them "tools of husbandry" and all necessary instruction. Initially named A Society for Evangelization of the Jews, the organization was denied a charter by New York State because "proselytizing of citizens is prohibited by the Constitution."[8] Changing its name to The American Society for Meliorating the Conditions of the Jews, it was chartered on April 14, 1820, and had the support of some distinguished Americans. John Quincy Adams was one of the vice presidents.[9] Accepting the stereotype of the Jew, the society stated in its constitution that its aim was to help Jews become "intelligent, respectable, and useful members of Society" and to turn them from the "unsettled and commercial habits" responsible for their "rapacious dispositions." This goal was to be accomplished by establishing agricultural settlements in America for Jews from Europe. On the farms, they would receive instruction in husbandry and in the Gospels of the New Testament, which would lead to conversion. Not only would the Jews become better and more moral persons, but also their souls would be saved. That was the return the Christians could expect from their investment.

By 1823, the society was in full operation. Its director and chief fundraiser, Joseph Frey, a baptized Jew formerly of London, was busy crisscrossing the country, preaching sermons about Jews from Georgia to Maine, and raising money. Yet the first published report, in 1823, shows that "they could not commence their operations for the want of Jews."[10] Eventually the society set up two farms in Westchester County. The first, in 1825, was abandoned a year later; the second, established in 1827, lasted until 1835. By 1855, the society had attracted less than fifty converts, and its work was discontinued.[11]

Perhaps the clearest statement made regarding encouraging Jewish immigration is in an editorial of the *Commercial Advertiser*, October 16, 1822, which expresses the hope that "the wealth and enterprise of the Jews would be a great auxiliary to the commercial and manufacturing, if not agricultural, interests of the United States." The editorial also points out the advantage America offers to the Jews.

> A new generation, born in more enlightened times, and having the benefit of education, would be free from those errors generally imbued to the Jews, and participating in the blessings of liberty, would have every inducement to become valuable members of society. That toleration and mildness upon which the Christian religion is founded, will lend its influence to the neglected children of Israel. We shall not be surprised if the views which shall be spread before them should lead to a valuable emigration of these people. [12]

The *Commercial Advertiser* tried to enlist the aid of Mordecai Manuel Noah for the purposes of encouraging immigration. In a letter sent to Noah, the writer states, "You would . . . oblige us by proposing such a number of persons who may be able to be members of our society . . . who . . . would form a perpetual correspondence with us about the means of promoting the emigration of European Jews to the United States, and how such emigration may be connected with the welfare of those who may be disposed to leave a country where they have nothing to look for but endless slavery and oppression."[13]

Noah was a colorful, even flamboyant, American journalist, statesman, dramatist, and Jewish congregational leader. In 1825, following the defeat of Napoleon and new outbreaks of anti-Semitism in Europe, he conceived a plan to establish a Jewish state on Grand Island, New York, as a refuge for persecuted Jews where they could both farm and develop the real estate. The plan never went beyond the laying of a cornerstone for Ararat, the colony-to-be. For years the stone remained as the only memento of a dream, until it found a home in a Buffalo museum. Noah subsequently urged the Jewish return to Palestine and has been called the American forerunner of Zionism.[14]

The first Jewish farm colony in America was actually started in Alchua County, Florida, in 1820 under the direction of Moses Elias Levy, and by 1832 fifty families had settled there. But the lack of proper facilities discouraged the settlers, who returned to their previous homes in New York, New Jersey, and Delaware.[15]

In 1837, thirteen Jewish families attempted a farm colony, named Shalom, in Warwarsing, New York. After five years of struggle, they sold their possessions and moved. In that same year, an agricultural project was initiated by a group of recently arrived German Jewish immigrants. An organization known as Association Zeire Hazon solicited community support in order to establish a farm settlement in the western prairies, whose vast territory provided unbounded opportunities for pioneers.

Jewish farming in the West subsequently became a theme for American Jews. In 1843, William Renau encouraged the formation of a Jewish colonization society. An agent sent out west to find a suitable location for a Jewish colony bought a tract of land at Shaumburg, near Chicago, and reported back to New York, "Chicago opens a vista into a large commercial future, and the land around it, which is flowing with milk and honey, is particularly adapted for tillers of the soil."[16] The few Jews who responded settled in villages around Chicago, where they combined farming with small-business interests. The businesses succeeded and improved at a much faster rate than the farming, and eventually the would-be farmers were absorbed into urban Chicago.

These early efforts on the part of Jews to farm, however small, illustrate that almost from the beginning of their arrival in America a percentage sought to settle themselves on the land. Yet the stereotype of the Jew as an urban dweller persisted. A generally complimentary editorial in the *Washington Sentinel* of 1854 lauds the Jewish character for its self-sufficiency but voices the same sentiments as others. "The habit of acquisitiveness which seems to be natural but which may be the result of oppression, still clings to them. They seldom enter the professions. They seldom turn their attention to politics. They seldom till the soil. They seem to prefer trade and commerce."[17]

American Jews were sensitive to the stereotype and, almost as if they had a moral imperative to prove to the world that it was not true, began urging Jewish agriculture in America. In 1843, the same year that William Renau encouraged the formation of the colonization society, Julius Stern of Philadelphia wrote to the Reverend Isaac Leeser, editor of *Occident*, stressing the necessity of settling Jews on the land in the West. New immigrants without a trade were in the onerous business of itinerant traders or peddlers, he said. The only way they could earn a respectable livelihood and attain happiness was to turn to agriculture. He therefore proposed the purchase of a vast parcel of land in one of the western states. An agricultural community of Jews would have the opportunity to prove "that their aptness and intelligence would produce also in this branch of human industry useful inventions and salutary improvements." There "excellent men and worthy women might spring up, who would deserve to be called an ornament to Israel and an honor to mankind."[18] Although the

Stern plan received no popular support, Reverend Leeser continued to promote Jewish agriculture in the columns of *Occident*.

In May 1855, a circular written by Dr. Sigmund Waterman was presented to a committee of the B'nai B'rith. Entitled "A call to establish a Hebrew Agricultural Society, to encourage agriculture amongst the Israelites of America," it begins with an admonition to the Jews.

> The necessity to direct the attention of the Israelites of America to agriculture has long been felt. The exclusive pursuit of commerce and its cognate branches by our people, is often used as a reproach and it must be confessed with some good show of reason. . . . A few trades have been entirely monopolized . . . the agriculturalist however is entirely wanting. It is on this account that we are looked upon as transitory inhabitants, having neither the desire nor the capacity to settle as permanent citizens.
>
> This view . . . is justified by the exclusive pursuit of commerce, which permits the accumulation of wealth without the acquirement of permanent interest in the soil of the land.
>
> . . . In order then to change this undesirable state of affairs, in order to create a taste for and encourage agriculture amongst our people, a calling so honorable and ensuring the greatest degree of independence and happiness and finally in order to employ the newly arrived immigrants . . . and to wean them from beggary and from becoming a burden to our charitable institutions, it is proposed to organize an association under the title "American Hebrew Agricultural and Horticultural Association."[19]

The newly formed society promised to "persons of proper age and good character" all the necessities of life on a farm and the building of houses, schools, and synagogues in agricultural communities. The support for the venture, however, was not sufficient, and nothing further came of the work of the committee. However, Reverend Leeser resumed his plea for the establishment of agricultural colonies, arguing in *Occident* that this was the best way of combating anti-Semitism and uplifting the Jews spiritually. A corollary benefit, he suggested, would come from removing immigrants from the dense masses of the cities.

The Effect of Increased Immigration of Russian Jews

Although the early discussions concerning Jewish farming in America were often abstract and theoretical and most of the plans for agricultural colonies went no further than the planning stage, the proposed projects did provide the groundwork for the later efforts made at the end of the nineteenth century, when large groups of Russian Jews immigrated to America following the outbreak of new hostilities directed against them. But their plight put the American Jews in a curious and uncomfortable position.

After the Civil War, America simultaneously was expanding its frontier westward and moving in the direction of increased industrialization. The rural areas were hard-pressed for human resources, particularly in the South, whose fields had been deserted by large numbers of blacks, and in the West, which sorely needed settlers in vast areas. Foreign labor was aggressively wooed, pursued, and encouraged by government, business, the press, and even religious institutions. From the 1870s until the early 1890s, immigrants were urged to come to America and people the land.

In contrast, American Jews, largely of German origin, were actively engaged in discouraging Jewish immigration.[20] They tried to convince government officials to place more restrictions on immigration as a way of limiting the numbers of Eastern European Jews arriving. In spite of the news filtering through of increased persecution and oppression in Eastern Europe, America's representative Jews from 1870 to 1890 were not eager to welcome their kin from abroad. Not only did they propose limits on the number of Jewish immigrants, but they also devised schemes to control the destinies of the new arrivals. They were instrumental in seeing that a number judged unfit to care for themselves were sent back to Europe. Since 1870, the Board of Delegates of American Israelites strongly advocated a careful scrutiny of the immigrants for evidence that they will not become "a burden and an unjust tax upon our large cities." At a period when the political reality of the Jews "threatened to be more than ordinarily vexatious," the board sought "to check the dispatch of poor emigrants to America" by urging that only those who demonstrated a capacity for taking care of themselves in a strange country be allowed to come. The board took dubious credit for success in convincing the U.S. consul at Bucharest as to "the wrong of permitting indiscriminate emigration." By their own report, the "representations thus made were not without effect."[21]

Those who showed the capacity to take care of themselves found the vast regions of the West and South open to them. Advocating colonization as a way of dealing with the Jews who did manage to emigrate from Eastern Europe, the board was instrumental in sending sixty-five emigrants from Romania to dispersed places in the West. Urging the "adoption of some system throughout the United States and Europe whereby it would be possible to supervise the settlement of such emigrants to sections of the country deemed suitable as to climate and prospects,"[22] the 1870 Board of

Delegates nevertheless left the ultimate decision of colonization in America or elsewhere to its successors.

While American Jewry was divided over the question of supporting immigration, the B'nai B'rith picked up the suggestion made in 1855 by Rabbi Waterman and, joined by other voices, urged the establishment of agricultural colonies. All generally agreed that the new Jewish immigrants should settle on land in one of the western states badly in need of settlers: Iowa, Kansas, Nebraska, Colorado, or Dakota. The Board of Delegates of American Israelites agreed to forward money to Europe to help immigration efforts, with the condition that the immigrants must settle in "the hitherto unoccupied regions of the West and Southwest," justifying their demand by claiming that "immigration has been so steadily on the increase and so commonly of the pauper class that the charities of the large cities are overburdened."[23]

As the numbers of immigrating Russian Jews increased, more organizations in American cities were formed for the dual purpose of regulating the emigration from Europe and assisting the immigrants in America. Instructions were sent to European Jewish agencies to limit the emigrants to those capable of withstanding the hardships of agriculture. In view of the difficult situation of the refugees, however, the European agents found the instructions impossible to follow.

In America, committees assumed the responsibility of rendering assistance and providing immediate relief to the immigrants. In 1882, the Hebrew Emigrant Aid Society of the United States was organized in New York. Although the society made its priority the "receiving, sheltering, temporarily maintaining and distributing the refugees," it did recognize that "agricultural colonization is the best means of securing the future welfare of the refugees." In a study of the society, Gilbert Osofsky makes the point that

> from the very first signs of a mass migration to the United States, the colonization scheme was proposed as the means by which the immigrants should be cared for. . . . The American West was thought adequate to contain the entire Russian-Jewish population. That there were other than altruistic motives behind the promotion of colonization projects was evident throughout the writings of the officials of the Aid Society. Often it seemed to be the most practical way to disperse the immigrants without injuring the prestige of the Jews already established in the United States.[24]

Implicit in the plans for settling the Russian refugees in the West was the effort to prevent the formation of ghettos in New York and other urban centers.

Colonization: A Means of Dispersing Russian Immigrants

While immediate relief for the Russian immigrants claimed most of its attention, the Hebrew Emigrant Aid Society was willing to participate in plans for colonization in the United States and in Canada. It actually helped to establish one colony in Cotapaxi, Colorado, and it influenced the formation of agricultural societies in other cities. The Cincinnati Society promoted agricultural pursuits among immigrants and issued an appeal "to aid the poor in Israel, so as to enable them to become tillers and owners of the soil to live on broad fields instead of living in crowded tenement houses."[25] The immigrants in Cincinnati were helped to settle in Kansas. In Philadelphia, a society favoring colonization proposed settling Jewish immigrants in Florida and then helped to establish a colony in Clarion, Utah.[26]

On April 23, 1882, an International Jewish Conference was convened in Berlin "to direct the dispersion of refugees in transatlantic places" and to reorganize the relief procedures.[27] There was widespread endorsement of the idea that colonization was essential to the dispersion of the Russian refugees.

That the effort to disperse the immigrants in America was at least initially successful can be seen from the census figures of 1880 and 1890. According to the census of 1880, the greater part of the Russians living in this country were in agricultural pursuits. Students of Jewish demography have concluded that the Russian immigration at the end of the nineteenth century consisted almost entirely of Jews.[28] In the breakdown of foreign-born population, distributed according to the country of birth by states and territories in the 1890 census, we find a total of 182,624 Russians in America.[29] Of these, 58,446 settled in New York, while 34,430 settled in other states in the North Atlantic division, and 89,748 settled in the rest of the United States. In other words, less than a third settled in New York. From these figures, then, it is possible to hypothesize that a substantial number of Russian Jewish immigrants in 1890, like those of 1880, were in agricultural pursuits.[30] However, there are no reliable statistics or studies reflecting the rural experience of Jews in America. How many Russian Jews continued in agriculture, how many migrated to nearby cities and towns and were there absorbed, and how many pursued dual careers as farmers and tradesmen and for how long are questions we presently cannot answer.

But we do know that when the Russian Jews began arriving in great numbers after 1881, Jewish organizations became passionate over the need to settle the immigrants in agricultural colonies. Seeing a possibility in land grants, the *American Israelite* urged its readers to contribute money for the cause. "Send us funds and you will be astonished how fast we will settle on government land every able bodied Russian immigrant. We think the long-deferred project of teaching our people agricultural pursuits can now be speedily realized, and the problem of what to do with the Russians can at once be solved."[31]

While creating the machinery to help the immigrants, American organizations and their leaders betrayed a contempt and condescension toward the Russians that was "akin to anti-Semitism," according to one of them. The final report of the Board of Delegates of American Israelites includes a statement indicating a total lack of confidence in the people they were trying to help. "Very few were mechanics or accustomed to labor of any kind. And some were encumbered with large families and were not the persons to be instructed in American usages and modes of work."[32]

Augustus Levey, resigning as secretary of the Hebrew Emigrant Aid Society, wrote in the *Jewish Messenger*: "The mode of life of these people in Russia has stamped on them the ineffaceable marks of permanent pauperism. Only disgrace and a lowering opinion in which American Israelites are held . . . can result from continued residence among us of these wretches."[33] A group of rabbis in New York, urging colonization out west, advanced the argument that the Russians had an opportunity to fight the old stereotype and to prove to the world at large, and specifically to Americans, that they could be loyal citizens.

> Here are the means to refute the oft-muttered calumny that our people are unfitted by habit, nature and sentiment for honest toil. . . . In colonizing [the Russian immigrants] and settling them as agriculturalists, we feel . . . every moral assurance that they will become worthy American citizens repaying the protection and rights they here receive, by becoming faithful and loyal denizens of the soil and forming a class of useful and honorable men who, adhering to their religious convictions, will also be imbued with the spirit of American institutions.[34]

While Americans saw in the Russian immigrants an opportunity to disprove "the oft-muttered calumny," young intellectuals and idealists in Russia also wanted to prove to the world that "the Jew can live from the produce of mother earth."[35] Although they had no experience in farming, they were committed to the idea of cooperative agricultural settlements. In 1881, they formed two groups: Bilu and Am Olam. Bilu prepared for immigration to *Erez Israel*, Am Olam for farming in America.[36]

Upon their arrival in America, the young idealists of Am Olam were greeted by anti-Russian prejudice they had not anticipated, which considerably dampened their enthusiasm for farming. Their frustration expressed itself in an assault on the New York offices of the Hebrew Emigrant Aid Society. In August 1882, three hundred newly arrived Russian immigrants, temporarily housed in crowded quarters on Ward's Island in Manhattan, demanded the assistance that had been promised them in Europe.[37] Among them was Dr. George M. Price, whose diary offers many insights into the American experience of the Russians in 1882. Of that incident, he wrote, "Part of the immigrants . . . were sent to Vineland and Carmel, New Jersey, to establish them on a colony; part was deported back to Russia; part they actually drove to New York." Price went to "a farm where we learned to know the American type of work and language."[38]

The history of Am Olam in America is sketchy. Estimates as to the number of colonies in which its members were involved vary from four to twenty-five.[39] Most of these were short-lived, victims of an unwise choice of location, inadequate farm experience on the part of the colonists, lack of sufficient funds, and the haste with which the colonies were established. Disease, fires, floods, extreme poverty, insufferable physical hardships, and internal conflicts all took a toll of the once eager and enthusiastic idealists.

Organizations anxious to settle the Russian immigrants on the land were not reliable in the manner in which they settled them. They sent representatives who were not farmers to the South and West to choose locations for colony sites. New Yorkers, working with an organization in New Orleans, chose the totally unsuitable semitropical site of Sicily Island, Louisiana, for one of the first colonies. The colony lasted barely a year until malaria claimed its toll in deaths and the flooding Mississippi River swept away all the possessions of the colonists.

The Hebrew Emigrant Aid Society sent Dr. Julius Goldman, a nonfarmer, to investigate opportunities for agricultural settlements in the West. Goldman cautioned the society that while a great majority of the Russian immigrants had expressed a desire to become farmers, only a limited number were sincere, and still less had any idea of what farming in America, and specifically in the Northwest, entailed. He reminded the committee of its grave responsibility in settling the immigrants, considering the consequences which might result. Although Goldman limited his investigation to Minnesota and the Dakota Territory, which had proved to be good farming land for Scandinavian immigrants, the Hebrew Emigrant Aid Society established a colony in Cotapaxi, Colorado. Why they did so is not clear. Of that colony, a Denver committee who visited the struggling colonists wrote:

We know of no instance where quality was so sacrificed to quantity. We do not exaggerate when we say that a beast could not subsist on these lands. It is a mean narrow strip of land extending a few yards on either side of a creek, which runs dry in the winter and contains no water in the summer, except when the snows melt in the mountains above and suddenly come down in a flood terrible in its devastation, inundating the whole valley, sweeping everything before it and leaving deposits of sand, huge boulders and drift wood to tell of the remarkable action of water and the freaks of nature. . . . There are not 100 acres fit for cultivation. As an illustration we only tell you that one of the colonists who sowed 14 bags of potatoes reaped a return of 15 bags—of a poorer quality than he had planted, and this with the most favorable wet season that Colorado has had for twenty years.[40]

The settlers endured winter cold, blizzards, summer drought, marauding bears, and Indians. A report of the activities of the Russians in the *Denver Tribune*, February 7, 1883, offers eloquent rebuttal to the stereotype that Jews are "unfitted . . . for honest toil."

Under the unfavorable circumstances they have done more than could be expected; only one who knows what it means to break up virgin ground with a common shovel can appreciate the industrious work of the Refugees. They have broken up the ground with a shovel, they have done the hardest part of the work required to make a wagon bridge; they have filled the ditches with big rocks which they were compelled to cut and hew from the mountains; they went up to their throats in the swift Arkansas River to make a float bridge to enable them to reach their lands; they worked in dark damp mines as well and perseveringly as trained miners; they worked on the railroad, giving entire satisfaction to their employers; they carried lumber on their shoulders to speed the erection of their houses; they walked often twenty miles a day to chop wood in the forest for the purpose of erecting fence posts around their farm.[41]

But their heroic efforts were rewarded by increasing failure. Finally, the Hebrew Emigrant Aid Society recommended relocation of the Cotapaxi colony to some other place.

The Cremieux Colony in the Dakota Territory was established four miles from the nearest available water source. In their eagerness to settle on the land, the colonists had not reckoned how far four miles could be for drawing water; nor had they anticipated the intense summer heat and dryness. They knew very little about controlling prairie fires, which almost wiped out both the colonists and the colony, and they were not prepared for the severity of the winter. One survivor recalls a snowstorm:

"Some of the colonists used ropes, one end fastened to the door post and the other end tied around the body, to prevent losing themselves in the blinding sheets of ice and snow."[42] The Cremieux Colony also was abandonded, leaving its precious toll of dead behind.

The personal hardship of settling on the North Dakota prairie is described in the 1882 journal of one of the settlers. "In the spring our baby was taken ill. I wanted a doctor so badly. There was a terrific storm and when it cleared the snow was ten feet deep. . . . He died unattended. I never forgave the prairies for that. He was buried in a lot with Mrs. Seliger and a child of the Mendelsons. For many years we kept up the lonely graves. In time the wolves and the elements destroyed them. They are unmarked in all save my memory."[43]

Very few of the colonies lasted more than a few years. Added to the hardships were the patronizing attitude and the criticism which the colonists continued to receive from their American benefactors who had set out to help the Russian immigrants improve "their spiritual well-being."

The Reverend J. Wechsler of St. Paul made a tour of the Dakota and Oregon colonies and, in the *American Israelite*, expressed his growing dissatisfaction with the colonists. Although he found the Painted Woods Colony in the Dakota Territory to be more compatible with his tastes than the "totally corrupt" New Odessa Colony in Oregon, his condescending view of the farmers and his displeasure with the Russians is clear from the report he sent back. "Intellectually speaking, the settlers are of the most inferior class. They possess not the least gratitude for all that has been done for them; they do not cooperate together as they should, and are never satisfied, but press their claims as urgently as ever before for assistance. Yet, it is a fact that no other colony has been as liberally assisted as this one."[44]

As critical as he was of Painted Woods, Wechsler had no complaints with the moral character of its members, such as he had about New Odessa, near Portland. This Am Olam colony under the leadership of William Frey, a non-Jew, followed the positivistic philosophy of Auguste Comte.[45] Wechsler writes about them:

> I am sorry to say that I was sadly disappointed. . . . I reasoned with them to show them the absurdity of such a course of life, and urged that our blessed Judaism was the only foundation upon which their future happiness can be permanently secured, but it seemed to me that I made no lasting impression to convince them of their folly. . . . I regret exceedingly that this otherwise intelligent community holds not steadfast to the principles which are generally accepted, and are led astray by many views which sooner or later will be an obstacle in their way to promote their welfare.[46]

Wechsler's criticism is based primarily on the radical life-style of the members, the nonobservance of traditional religion, and on the communal structure of the colony. He admits that "if it were not for their communistic and religious ideas . . . these colonists would have a prosperous future in store, for they are all very industrious and are willing to do any kind of work which is required." Editorially, the *American Israelite* agreed with Wechsler. "The improvements which they have added to the place are of the most limited character. . . . Their present interest as a society is found in the singularity of their social life. They have no religion, they have hardly a political organization for the management of their affairs, and they have no definite code of morals."[47]

The human despair and disappointment of the settlers, both at the way they were treated by their benefactors and by the loss of their dream for farming, are poignantly expressed in letters they wrote to Russia. One letter writer tells how in Europe the emigrants received assurances that they would be helped to become farmers, but they were misled.

Encouraged by these assurances, we departed for New York, but there we met with total disappointment. The committee looked upon us as paupers and refused to listen to suggestions. We asked to be sent to Kansas [where a group of Russian colonists had previously settled] but they sent us to Louisiana. We left for the colony with high hopes, but after having spent a few months there, we found conditions unbearable. The heat affected most of the colonists, and malaria has stricken the women and children.

The secretary of the colony wrote to a friend in Russia: "The aim of the first colonists was to do pioneering work. We wanted to pave the way for those who would join us or establish agricultural colonies elsewhere. We wanted to show them what we have accomplished, so as to make it easier for others. We wanted to show them how to become successful farmers. This, however, we could not do under the existing conditions."[48]

A letter from Painted Woods clearly expresses both idealism and despair.

Our unmerciful enemies across the ocean broadly proclaim that we are unwilling to do any kind of manual labor and live only on the products of others. Our aim is to prove to those anti-Semites that their statements are false fabrications of the vilest nature. We are willing to work and we do work hard whenever and wherever we are given a chance to do so. . . . Ever since we settled in this country, we had to fight many difficulties. We have conquered most of them—and were on our way to prosperity, when a great misfortune happened to us and our course is stopped entirely. Our crop this year proved to be a total failure. . . . Now the land having produced nothing, our hopes are entirely broken and starving threatens most of us. We are all men with large families, the sufferings of which will be impossible to witness.[49]

In 1887, Painted Woods was abandoned; the settlers left, their hopes sorely disappointed.

Social Life in the Colonies

In spite of the hardships, traumas, frustrations, and disappointments endured by the pioneering Jewish immigrant farmers in the last quarter of the nineteenth century, the settlers provided themselves with a social and cultural life in the tenuous colonies they established. According to Gabriel Davidson, who tried to preserve a history of these colonies, the meeting house or meeting room was high on the list of any building plan. Often this room housed a library, chorus, or dramatic group and was the central point for nightly discussions or study sessions. In torpid, semitropical Sicily Island, in a climate to which the Russian Jews were not at all accustomed, the Jews managed an active social life, even while fighting mosquitoes, rattlesnakes, disease, and loneliness. They issued a weekly bulletin and gathered almost nightly for debates and discussions. One of the settlers sums up his memory thus: "Work—mostly useless—hope, despair, love, song, poetry, happiness and misery. Life as we lived it there in Louisiana."[50]

In Bethlehem Yehuda, an Am Olam colony in South Dakota, the colonists worked very hard and lived on the edge of starvation. Yet every evening they gathered for discussions, dances, and entertainment. Like their Louisiana counterparts, they published a Russian newspaper. In Cremieux, South Dakota, the colonists had their own theatrical group and chorus and staged plays and concerts from time to time. In New Odessa, Oregon, they worked out a regular routine that included working hours and evening hours devoted to study, discussion, and recreation. Davidson provides an idyllic picture of social life derived from interviews with the original settlers.

Imbued with the loftiness of their ideals these youthful "intelligentsia" did their work, manual and menial, with joy in their hearts and songs on their lips. Their diversions were largely intellectual. Nightly they gathered in the assembly hall to discuss, debate, and to argue. They expounded the theories of positivism. The more learned delivered lectures in their special fields of study. One night a week was devoted to a "self criticism" meeting at which the members were encouraged to pass judgment on one another's actions and to suggest means of improving the affairs of the Colony. The thirst for knowledge was unquenchable. The books in the library were read and studied with avidity. . . . Their religion was the "Religion of Humanity." The moral life of the colonists was unimpeachable. . . . A spirit of brotherhood reigned. This was so striking that a wandering farm expert, a non-Jew who lived in the Colony a year or so, remarked that in all his wide experience among many classes of farmers in many parts of the country, he had never come across so remarkable a group of young people. . . . The Colony, though composed of newly arrived immigrants, and Jews at that, commanded the respect if not the admiration of the Christian neighbors. . . . Staid American farmers travelled long distances to spend a social evening and brought their wives and daughters to the dances given at the Colony's assembly hall. Harmony reigned for two years. Then the serenity became disturbed by the intellectual bickering of the colonists.[51]

In terms of social living, the hardships were justified by the rewards. But the odds against these small groups of pioneers were too great. Emotional hardships, especially feelings of isolation, intensified the reaction to physical deprivation. The secretary of the ill-fated Sicily Island Colony in Louisiana blamed its failure not on the unfavorable climate or on the infertile soil or on onerous work but on the fact that the immigrants could not endure so entirely isolated from Jewish life.

Learning from the Failures

None of the colonies survived beyond six years—most lasted less than two. The failures of these often-misdirected efforts had a most depressing effect, and the general interest in agriculture for the Jews began to decline. In addition, the country seemed able to absorb the immigrants in any number of ways, while the immigrants seemed to have an infinite capacity to adjust themselves to new conditions.

While a detailed analysis of the failure of the early Jewish farm colonies is not intended here, a few observations are in order. Cultural isolation, as claimed by the Louisiana farmer, cannot be sufficient reason for the failures. Jews did succeed as isolated merchants in small American towns and hamlets, often the only such Jews in the town. And they remained, often growing with the town and contributing to its growth. There are also numerous examples of isolated, successful Jewish farmers. The isolated farm colonies, however, especially those in which larger Jewish organizations were involved, failed.

The early Jewish farmers came to America with very few financial resources and were dependent on the social organizations for their direction and support. Many of the immigrants also came with unrealistic and romantic notions about farming. For example, the Am Olam members and those attracted to that movement were basically young Russian urban intellectuals who decided that through farming they could prove to the world something about Jews. If in Europe they had been a cohesive group, in America they became fragmented in their ideology, their commitments, and in their numbers. Abraham Cahan, an enthusiastic member of Am Olam in Russia, writes in his Yiddish autobiography, *Bleter fun mayn leben*, that he became so enthralled by the dynamic energy of New York when first he stepped foot on it that he could not possibly think of leaving it for the dull countryside. Thereafter, his tone concerning the Jewish farmers, about whom he writes occasionally, becomes condescending.[52]

In America the immigrants received the help of Jewish organizations responsible for helping them become established on farms. However, the objectives of the organizations and of the prospective farmers were different. Basically the immigrants wanted to farm; the benefactors wanted them out of the cities. The faraway farm lands—especially the free land under the Homestead Act of 1862—seemed a likely place to initiate colonies. The selection of sites seems to have been done in a haphazard way; proper farming instruction was not available; suitable shelters had not been built; and there was barely enough money for meager food supplies. In addition, the parent or sponsoring organizations were remote, physically and psychologically. When representatives of the organizations came to visit the struggling colonists, they found fault with the way they were managing or with the life-style they observed.

The collective living arrangements which the Jewish farmers attempted apparently did not work for them. Nor did they have the means, for the most part, to sustain themselves on farms outside the collective. Many of the early Jewish farmers began to gravitate to the closest towns and cities where they could earn some money. Some put on peddler's packs and moved through the countryside, selling to the natives. Others took whatever jobs were available in trades they might have known before or in new trades which they had to learn. They experienced more success in commerce than on the farm. The crucial difference is that they had previous experience trading and almost none farming.

Only 4 percent of the total Eastern European Jewry had any connection with farming in Europe. Restrictive laws forced 94 percent of the Jews living in Russia to reside within a specified area known as the Pale of Settlement, where their occupations were limited to certain specified trades and commerce. There they were not permitted to own land, although they may have scratched out a little garden. For the most part, the new Jewish farmers in America had no experience and no models from which to draw.

Other ethnic groups—Germans, Scandinavians, Italians were more successful. Having been farmers in Europe before immigrating, they were more adept at picking suitable land for their crops. They either grew the same crops as the Americans among whom they settled or looked for land on which they could grow crops they had grown in Europe.

Like other immigrants, the Jews also had language and cultural differences to overcome. However, whereas the Germans, Scandinavians, Italians, and other ethnic groups had a common religion with the native population, the Jews were much more alone. The church, an important institution offering strong support for integration in rural America, was unavailable to them.

The New Jersey Colonies

At the turn of the century, the only viable Jewish colonies were those in South Jersey: Vineland, Alliance, Carmel, Rosenhayn, and Woodbine, all established between 1882 and 1892.[53] In some measure, the colonists profited from the experience gained by the previous failures. Certainly their geographic locations, between easy reach of New York and Philadelphia, made it easier for the settlers. They had nearby markets to sell their produce and friends, relatives, and Jewish institutions to sustain them emotionally.

The Alliance Colony in South Jersey was founded in 1882 by a group of Russian Jews fleeing persecution. They were helped by the Alliance Israelite Universelle, a French Jewish defense organization committed to helping Jews under attack, encouraging the pursuit of useful handicrafts, and providing relief for Jews in trouble. As a tribute to the organization, the early colonists named their community Alliance. The name also carried an optimistic hope that an alliance would be formed among the small scattered Jewish communities in South Jersey. In 1892, the Baron de Hirsch Fund took over the Alliance Land Trust, putting the Alliance community on a more solid financial footing.

In 1889, a renewal of persecution in Russia made immigration to the United States swell again. By then the Baron Maurice de Hirsch had decided to devote his energies and his fortune in the service of his co-religionists. Firmly convinced that the "Jew, so long denied the privilege of owning land, could win for himself peace and independence, love for the ground he tills and for freedom; and he will become a patriotic citizen of his new home," the baron financed colonization projects in Argentina, Canada, and the United States.[54]

In 1891, the fund purchased a 5,200-acre tract of wooded land in Woodbine, New Jersey. In its New York offices, the fund planned and created the first totally Jewish municipality in the country. Since the mission of the fund was to relocate Jewish boys from the unhealthy environment of the city slums and train them to be farmers, the Baron de Hirsch Agricultural School, the first secondary agricultural school in America, was established in Woodbine in 1894.

The school provided a model in 1897 for the National Farm School, established in Doylestown, Pennsylvania, under the leadership of Rabbi Joseph Krauskopf of Philadelphia's Keneseth Israel.[55] Unlike the Baron de Hirsch Agricultural School in Woodbine, the National Farm School declared itself to be nonsectarian, although its intention was also to educate Jewish boys from city ghettos. Both schools provided an avenue of escape from the degradation of poverty and an option for a new life in America.

Farming began in earnest in Woodbine when the settlers were allowed to get mortgages for $180 each on individual tracts, which had to be cleared by hand. Helping the farmers earn an income before they could realize money from their crops became a top priority for the Baron de Hirsch Fund.

The Jewish Agricultural and Industrial Aid Society, incorporated in 1900, received its base financing from the fund and assumed the same mission: to remove immigrants from the city, to help establish them on farms or in trades, and to provide them with the training and the means of earning money in a variety of occupations. The JAIAS subsidized the relocation of small business and manufacturing operations near the homes of the Jewish farmers so that they or members of their families could work during the winter months. Small manufacturing plants were established in Woodbine, Alliance, Brotmanville, and other South Jersey communities. They produced such items as brooms, children's clothes, men's hats, shirts, buttons, rubber heels for shoes, and hand-rolled cigars.

By 1921, the words "Industrial Aid" were dropped from the Jewish Agricultural Society, which then concentrated on helping immigrant Jews who showed a strong inclination for farming to establish themselves. The previous experience of collective farms and colonies which Jewish immigrants attempted indicated to the society that in America, where individual enterprise was highly valued and encouraged, collective farming had little chance of success. Thus, the society disengaged itself from colonization experiments and evolved a program designed to help settle individuals who wanted to farm. For about forty years after that, the JAS provided subordinate or supplemental loans to would-be farmers, who were required to borrow what they could from conventional banking or government sources before applying to the society for additional funding.

In contrast to the ideological communities which were supported and subsidized by charitable organizations, the JAS treated its loan applicants as businessmen rather than objects of charity. By structuring loans so that repayments could be made over an extended period of time, the JAS gradually made farmers rely upon their own resources.

The society provided a necessary support system to help the novice farmers succeed. The society's Yiddish-speaking agents traveled through the states where there were clusters of Jewish farmers, giving advice and instruction in farming techniques, bookkeeping, and necessary sanitation methods. The work became the model on which the later Federal Extension Service was patterned. From 1907 to 1957, the JAS published *Der Yiddisher Farmer*, a farmers' monthly magazine written in both Yiddish and English, which kept the farmers informed of the latest agricultural advances and provided information about Jewish farm communities and farmers from coast to coast.

In 1948, an article about the Estomin family in Toms River brought the following letter from a New York City woman who wanted to meet a Jewish farmer. She wrote to Mr. Estomin:

> I am a young Jewish girl of 22 who is very interested in farming and agriculture. I've attended the JAS evening course. I'm taking my second home study course from Cornell University. But I find it quite difficult in meeting young men with ideas about farming as a future. I read about you in *The Jewish Farmer* [*Der Yiddisher Farmer*] and I thought that you may be in a position to help me. Perhaps you know some young fellow who is interested in meeting a girl with my ideas? Please try. I shall indeed appreciate any aid you offer. Thank You.[56]

Because the Jewish Agricultural Society understood how important an adequate social life was to the success of the new farm communities, it provided building and maintainance loans so that they could have community centers. These centers served as synagogues, social halls, cultural centers, and forums where Jews could work out their ideas for creating the better world they envisaged. When communities were ready to start feed and marketing cooperatives, the JAS provided start-up funds and guidance.

Indirectly the JAS helped communities become established, but the process was evolutionary. The communities grew as Jewish individuals or families settled. With few exceptions, then, the new farmers early in the century, with the help of the JAS, settled in several counties of New Jersey, New York, and Connecticut, and eventually in many states across the country. However, as word spread, as friends and relatives settled on farms, and as nascent communities grew, many others found their own ways to join them without the assistance of the JAS.

The Jewish farm movement in America became a theme in popular contemporary Yiddish literature and films. Articles about Jewish farmers and the activities of the JAS appeared in the Yiddish press, particularly in the *Forward*. Whereas, in 1948, an urban woman wanted to meet a Jewish farmer, in 1909, a letter to the editor of the *Forward* from a young Jew in North Dakota complained that as soon as young women learned he was a farmer, they were no longer interested in him. The editor, Abraham Cahan, who came to America intending to be a farmer but changed his mind in New York City, responded: "There is certainly nothing to be ashamed of in living in the lap of Nature. Many people dream of becoming farmers. The cities are full of many diseases that are unheard of on farms. Tuberculosis, for instance. . . . People in urban areas grow old and gray at forty, but most of the farmers are healthy and strong and live to be eighty and ninety."[57]

In 1916, Isaac Raboy wrote a popular Yiddish novel about a Jewish cowboy in the Midwest, and in 1918, I. J. Schwartz wrote his classic *Kentucky*, about Jews settling in a rural area around the vicinity of Lexington. The Yiddish films *Grine felder* (Green fields), *Tevye der milkheke* (Tevye the dairyman), and *Fishke der krumer* (Fishke the lame), all set in Europe, were filmed on farms in New Jersey and New York. By 1940, the filmmakers were using American settings. An elderly Jewish couple on a poultry farm in Connecticut was the subject of the Yiddish film *Eli Eli*.

From 1946 to 1952, the JAS settled between 2,500 and 3,000 families, so-called displaced persons, survivors of the Holocaust, on small family farms in New Jersey. They granted these new farmers second, third, and fourth mortgages to help them get started. About a thousand immigrant farmers in the Vineland area formed a self-help organization, the South Jersey Poultry Farmers Association, which made interest-free loans to its members.[58]

Jewish farm communities in New Jersey endured and spread from South Jersey to Central Jersey—to Toms River, Farmingdale, Lakewood, Freehold, Englishtown, and Hightstown. Subsequently, they spread further north to the areas near Somerville, Flemington, Bound Brook, Morristown, and even further.

The scattered Jewish farm communities appear to have had a similar history and apparently evolved in the same way.[59] In New Jersey, they were geographically close to each other, but there was little contact between them. Except for occasional meetings of the feed or marketing cooperatives to which they belonged, the farmers and their children rarely saw each other. All had ties to New York City or Philadelphia but very little connection with a neighboring Jewish farm community. Transportation no doubt was a problem; in their insular life-style, however, the Jews were very much like the native farmers among whom they lived, in spite of their cosmopolitan background.

Jewish farmers, of course, were not limited to New Jersey, nor were they solely poultry farmers. They were dairy and cattle farmers in New York, New Jersey, and Connecticut; grape growers in Ohio; produce farmers in Florida, Texas, and California; grain farmers in the East and Midwest; orchard growers in Michigan; and so on. But it is in poultry and egg production that they made a significant difference. According to Richard Chumney, former director of natural resources, New Jersey Department of Agriculture, "Jewish farmers made New Jersey the white Leghorn capital of the world."[60]

Although few became wealthy from their farm labors, most found farming a very satisfying way of life. The contributions these farmers made to American agriculture are barely acknowledged, but their agricultural experience had far-reaching implications. It influenced the lives of their children, providing them with easier access to the mainstream of American life and helping them retain, at the same time, a strong sense of Jewish identity. On a parochial level, it provided Jewish-grown food and vineyards for urban Orthodox Jews, whose dietary and religious needs required them. In a larger sense, farming gave new Jewish immigrants an identification with America that made them part of the land. Rural living allowed the best of their values to flourish: a strong sense of family and community, a belief in cooperation, and a strong commitment to human rights for all. Indeed, their ethical values and impulses for social justice melded with American values of democracy. The Jewish family farmers persisted, like their counterparts across the country, as an economic and cultural force in the American communities in which they settled until they could no longer sustain themselves by their farming efforts.

Their history in America presents a vivid example of the persistence of ethnic cohesiveness and "cultural pluralism."[61] While the Jewish immigrant farmers tried to acculturate and assimilate into the larger community of rural dwellers, they could depend only upon each other for support. An early farmer described it thus: "In the beginning, when there were so few of us, we huddled together like baby chicks under a stove."

Afraid that their children would lose their identity, they worked hard to maintain their own cultural distinctiveness and created the institutions they needed to help them carry on a Jewish way of life.

In a sense, farming represented the fulfillment of a dream the immigrants carried with them to America of owning their own piece of land, a privilege denied many in Eastern Europe. It also represented a romantic return to nature and to a familiar environment. Many had lived in small rural communities in Europe.

Furthermore, settling on the land represented to the immigrants a significant way of becoming rooted to the new country. Benzion Trachtman of Carmel, New Jersey, said: "We wanted to be Americans. We wanted to become a part of the country on a farm." Others spoke of the land as something tangible to pass on to future generations. "I wanted my sons to inherit these fields," said Harry Sokol.

But the motivation to farm was more complex, involving layers of feelings about the immigrants' native homes. Farming in the United States represented at once a break with the past and a re-creation of it. It presented Jews an opportunity to prove they could succeed on the land, in other than the commercial and artisan trades to which they had been restricted in the Old Country. At the same time, rural communities, with their economic cooperation and intimate social ties, represented a kind of reconstruction of the towns they had left behind.[62]

The new and developing communities provided their settlers with opportunities to create the institutions and organizations they needed. Working together in small groups brought out in people leadership qualities that would have gone unnoticed in the cities. In addition, the cooperative efforts fostered strong bonds between the families, individually and collectively. "If a farmer was sick, we all took turns taking care of his chickens. We couldn't let them die," said Israel Friedman, who settled on a farm in 1919.

This book presents a detailed picture of the Jewish community of Farmingdale, New Jersey, in whose history the Jewish Agricultural Society played a leading role. The community grew around the town of Farmingdale, from which its name comes. It had its beginnings in 1919, when two Jewish immigrant families pooled their resources to establish a farm. By 1945, it was one of the leading egg-producing communities in the United States. In its evolutionary development, Farmingdale is typical of other such communities, all of which had a similar mix of settlers: immigrants born in Eastern Europe, German Jewish refugees, American-born settlers, and, in the last years of small poultry farming enterprises, Eastern

European–born immigrants once again—survivors of the Holocaust. With them, history came full circle.

Characteristically, the early settlers were in their thirties, married, with young children who had started school in New York. By and large, they were strongly individualistic. Their very choice of leaving a city where family and friends lived was a radical one. In choosing farming as a life work and life-style, they were going counter to the urban life of their coreligionists and the trend toward urbanization in America. Removing themselves from the security of organized Jewish institutions in the city, they settled in what was then a remote place, among people whose rural ways and regional dialect and mannerisms they did not understand. Among alien Christians—Methodists, Presbyterians, Catholics—who periodically manifested hostility toward them, they maintained their ethnic identity.

In the late 1930s and early 1940s, German Jewish refugees from Nazi lands arrived and formed a subgroup within the larger Jewish community. They were older and better educated and, in their native Germany, had lived middle-class lives. Unlikely farmers, they rolled up their sleeves, worked hard, and succeeded. After World War II, a number of American-born veterans with young families became poultry farmers. Many had been trained for other professions in New York or elsewhere but sought instead a way of life more in tune with values tempered by their experiences in war. Finally, in the late forties and early fifties, Eastern European survivors of the Holocaust arrived to become farmers. They settled on the farms as the farm economy was beginning a serious decline. Children of the first group of settlers became farmers themselves in the area, while those of later groups generally did not.

The mid-1950s marked the peak years of prosperity for New Jersey poultry and egg producers. Shortly thereafter, however, the market took a nosedive from which it never recovered, resulting in a forced exodus from the family farm. Although isolated Jews are still farming, few, if any, Jewish farming communities remain in New Jersey.

The Jewish community of Farmingdale has changed radically. The farms, whose owners work elsewhere, have either turned into suburban housing tracts or have evolved into horse farms or nursery operations. The community life Jewish farmers remember with nostalgia was lost for most of them when the farm economy collapsed, and they needed to find other means of earning a living. Their sense of displacement and deprivation can be understood universally by those forced to abandon satisfying occupations and leave familiar communities and cherished homes to seek new employment in other places.

Part 1
Beginnings

1

The Place

Farmingdale

Farmingdale is a small town in central New Jersey, seven miles west of the Atlantic Ocean, fifty miles south of New York, and sixty miles northeast of Philadelphia. In 1919, two Jewish families settled on a farm on the outskirts of the town, which then had a population of about 600. Today, it has little more than twice that number; the 1980 census gave the figure 1,348.

Years ago, the Jersey Central made several stops each day at its small, charming railroad station, and buses running regularly between Trenton and Asbury Park would stop at the corner of Main Street and Asbury Avenue to pick up or discharge passengers. Now, there is no more public transportation in Farmingdale; the railroad station has been abandoned, the buses diverted to other routes. Nor is there any particular reason why one would seek out this place unless to visit relatives or friends.

It is a clean, neat one-steet town with no distinctive architecture, no historic monuments, no unique shops. It is like hundreds and thousands of others in America. A bank, a post office, a supermarket, a drugstore, a liquor store, three churches, two doctors, two dentists, and a firehouse are the tenants along Main Street.

Once there was an old-fashioned brick-oven bakery whose immaculate glass cases and shelves displayed crusty bread and fresh pungent gingerbread cookies. The proprietor would often give a child staring through the glass at the shelves a cookie as a gift. It is gone. The supermarket sells the packaged and wrapped products that inspire neither awe from the children nor gifts from the manager.

Farmingdale used to have a general store where one could find everything and anything, from pins and fabrics to flour and sugar to garden tools and working shoes—a marvelous store that avoided becoming a plastic department store. That is gone too, just disappeared. The owners died, bequeathing the property to the town with the stipulation that a small park be established on the place where the store once stood and providing money for that purpose. Two stone benches on a spot of grass and a marble stone with a legend are all the furniture of the bequest.

The town has grown slowly; its population has remained small. People in Farmingdale have watched each other grow old. Each night they put the town to bed at eight o'clock.

In spite of the small population, at one time its Main Street was busy—very busy. The people in surrounding Howell Township,[1] living in their various communities, came to Farmingdale to shop, usually on Saturday nights. In the first quarter of the century, Saturdays were so busy that it was often difficult to ride down Main Street. Horse-drawn buggies and wagons competed with cars for parking space. Now shopping centers, liberally located off the surrounding major highways, have claimed the trade from a good part of the farm and rural population that at one time depended on Farmingdale for its commerce and its staples.

The heart of the social lives of the various communities in the township was the Grange and the church, which served also as the meeting places and social halls. The nine schools in Howell Township—one- and two-room structures—were not used for evening meetings as schools often are now. In 1932, the year my family moved to a farm near Farmingdale, the schools had electricity but no central heat or plumbing facilities. Furthermore, the rows of seats, rigidly fixed to the floor, did not permit any flexibility for groups.

The communities in the township had other gathering places. At the blacksmith shop next to the school in West Farms,[2] for example, a man could always find others with whom to talk and a warm fire in the wintertime. Farmers had plenty of time for socializing in the winter, when neither tree nor field bore fruit.

Across from the blacksmith's was Wooley's General Store, another gathering place. Like the general store in the town of Farmingdale, Wooley sold everything. One lifelong resident of Farmingdale describes it as "a department store. Flour and sugar in big barrels. Shoes. Socks. We could get everything there. There was a little pot-bellied stove, and customers came from all around. It was the only store in quite a big area."

Wooley also sold penny candy. Every day during the lunch recess, the children from the West Farms school across the road arrived with pennies in their fists to shop among the jars of brightly colored candies on the counter. The whole Wooley family came from the back of the store to help the thirty or so customers.

When the children left, the men went back to their checker games or their gossip. Mary Peskin, daughter of pioneer Benjamin Peskin, has the impression that the men sat around and smoked and exchanged news. "This is where they would get all the news, so they'd come down and sit around the stove, and they'd warm themselves and talk and catch up— 'What happened here?' or 'How are you doing?' . . . because . . . well, we didn't have a newspaper." While the men socialized, the farm women who lived within walking distance shopped and left. Wooley made the rounds to the outlying farms with a horse and wagon, and later with a truck, to take and deliver grocery orders.

The families living in the various subcommunities of Howell Township had well-established roots, most having lived for generations on the same farms where potatoes and tomatoes, corn, berries, and fruit orchards were the primary crops. Almost all the farmers had milking cows, and a few ran dairy operations.

Most of the Farmingdale natives lived all of their lives on their farms. Few had ever ventured much beyond the neighboring towns. One man, in his eighties, summed up the experience of many when he said: "I've never lived anywhere else, and my wife has never moved but once. She was a farmer's daughter, and she moved here with me when we married. And neither of us has moved. We both stayed here until now, until the end."

They had planned a honeymoon to Niagara Falls when they married, the first time either was to go so far away. They got as far as Albany and then were filled with anxiety about returning. "We were all day getting to Albany. . . . By golly, we thought, we'd never get back home. We got that far away from home. . . . So we came back to New York City and spent the rest of the week in New York." Thirty-five years later they finally visited Niagara Falls.

If the parents did not travel far from home, neither did the children. They regarded New York City or Philadelphia as another world, and Europe was as far away as the moon. The children attended the public school nearest their homes, to which they walked or were bused, and went to Sunday school in the local church.

Like the town of Farmingdale, the adjoining farm communities of Howell Township were insular, provincial, and poor. The people worked hard and took good care of their fields, orchards, and animals. Innovations were very slow in coming and not quickly accepted. The school system stubbornly resisted change; the precarious economics were a way of life, and the politics reflected the conservatism. It almost seemed as if the whole area were in a deep sleep. But that was its charm. Not only was the area free of the tensions and tumult of the nearby cities, it was totally unaware of them.

Beginnings

2

Pioneers
Peskin and Friedman

The peacefulness and serenity of West Farms, one of the farm communities for which the town of Farmingdale served as the central business district, appealed to Benjamin Peskin and his brother-in-law, Israel Friedman, when, in 1919, they made a tour of central New Jersey looking for a farm and a new home. They arrived in the late spring when white mountain laurel covered the roadsides and fresh green carpeted everything else. Although the houses they saw for sale seemed run-down, the grounds surrounding them were beautiful. They found exactly the location for which they were searching. Within two months, they had relocated their families.

The two and their wives had crossed a continent from Eastern to Western Europe and then crossed an ocean to settle in New York City, where they lived for a number of years. They were fluent in five languages, their children in two: Yiddish, the language of the home, and English, which their parents had not yet mastered.

Like most of the other Jewish immigrants who had come to America, the Peskins and the Friedmans had left close family and reliable traditions in their small Russian villages near the cities of Smolensk and Vitebsk. When they moved out of New York, they left behind another community, composed of Jewish immigrants like themselves, and a network of *landsmanshaften* (societies of landsmen, or people from the same European town or region) and other social institutions with which they had become familiar.

BENJAMIN PESKIN, ON
THE FARM, AROUND 1925

In their new home in Farmingdale, they maintained significant ties both to the old world of Eastern Europe and the new world of the lower East Side. Such connections set them apart in Farmingdale; no one else received mail from Russia and visitors from New York, or newspapers with strange print.

The families had no intention of starting a Jewish community when they settled on a farm in the midst of strangers. Their primary motivation was to leave New York. In spite of the helpful social organizations there, they found the city neither congenial nor compatible with their European vision of America.

Living in congested apartment houses with no free space anywhere, working sixteen hours a day in their New York hand laundries, they had begun to think of America as a pile of dirty linen. When Peskin became seriously ill in the influenza epidemic of 1918, his doctor advised him to leave New York as soon as possible. It was the impetus the brothers-in-law needed to make the move.

They had read in the Yiddish press how the Jewish Agricultural Society helped Jewish immigrants settle on farms. But when they appeared at the New York office of the JAS, instead of getting the encouragement they expected, they were advised to consider certain cold facts carefully. They were told that rural America was lonely and alienating, that farm life would be hard, and that their families might feel lost in a place without the structure of a Jewish communal life.

The young men were adamant. Both the Friedmans and the Peskins felt that the city offered no future for their children. Furthermore, Friedman, who had absorbed and internalized socialist ideology in Russia, felt that farm life offered him an opportunity to live in a way consistent with his principles. As a farmer, he would not be in a position to exploit anyone, nor would he be exploited himself. The determination of the two young men gained the respect and the cooperation of the JAS, who sent them to central New Jersey to scout the area.

They arrived in Farmingdale, looked around the town, and found in West Farms a pretty countryside and a farm of fifty-three acres, with a farmhouse large enough for two families. Outbuildings provided the options needed for livestock. They made an immediate decision to buy at the price of $6,000. Friedman contributed $1,000, and Peskin $2,000; the owner took a $2,000 mortgage, and the balance came from a loan by the JAS which carried a liberal repayment schedule of $200 per year plus 1 percent interest.

The men hardly noticed that the primitive house was in very bad repair. It had no running water, no central heat, and no electricity. None of this seemed to be much of a problem in the summertime when they purchased the property, but during the first winter, the snow actually came through the cracks of the windows and the walls.

Mrs. Friedman tells how the cries of her eight-month-old baby awakened her one night from a deep sleep. When she got to the baby, she found that his diaper was frozen stiff. At times, she reports, it was so cold that the families all slept close together in one room. But even as Helen Friedman remembers the hardships, she remembers how much she loved the farm. "It was just like Europe," she said. "Things were growing, the air was fresh. It was beautiful."

Primitive as the house was, they were among the very few people in Farmingdale to have a telephone. When a child was sick, they called the town doctor, who gave instructions on the phone and sent medication with the postman. Mrs. Friedman remembers him arriving with medicine for her son who had the measles. Because of the language barrier, the postman could not communicate the doctor's instructions, so he did the next best thing. He mixed the prescription, stirred it with his index finger, and gave it to the sick child. "He recovered," said Helen Friedman, laughing.

Since neither Peskin nor Friedman had any experience in farming, they consulted neighbors about crops and methods of planting. Mr. Van Brunt gave them advice about planting potatoes. Early in the spring they set out the seeds and eagerly waited, but not long enough; the potatoes they dug up were the size of walnuts, and there was no market for them. Rather than throwing away the fruits of their labor, they stored the potatoes in the barn to be used by the family during the winter. Instead the cows and horses got into the bin and ate their fill. Helen Friedman relates how the animals "blew up like balloons with gas" and ultimately had to be destroyed. It was a severe blow to their shaky economy. "That was the worst thing that happened to us on the farm, when we didn't make a success that first year." Sixty years later, the memory was still painful to her.

A PESKIN FAMILY PICNIC, FARMINGDALE, 1921. (LEFT TO RIGHT: VERA PESKIN BENSON, BENJAMIN, SOPHIA, ROSE, AND MARY PESKIN.)

It was decided that Mr. Friedman would continue operating a hand laundry in New York to provide a source of income. There, he lived alone looking forward to the weekends, when he came to the farm. But he grew increasingly unhappy with the arrangement, and it was clear that it would be years before the farm could support one family, let alone two. Three years after they had settled on the farm, the Friedmans returned to New York City, much to the regret of Mrs. Friedman, who cried when they left.

"I really loved it," she said. In 1936, they returned to Farmingdale and remained until their retirement in 1972 to nearby Lakewood.

Peskin persevered. He supplemented his farm income, what little there was, by taking house-painting jobs or selling farm goods in Lakewood, a much larger town than Farmingdale. The six-mile journey by horse and wagon to Lakewood was an all-day affair, starting before dawn. Once, midway home, the horse keeled over and died.

Gradually, the farm expanded from produce (potatoes and corn) to animals (pigs and cows). Peskin sold the milk to a local dairy, the pigs to a butcher. In the early 1930s, he paid for his older daughter's tuition to Georgian Court, a Roman Catholic college in Lakewood, by selling vegetables and milk products to the nuns.

A gregarious and sociable man, Peskin was creative in his efforts to earn a living, and he was in contact with many different people. But for Mrs. Peskin, life was very different. After the Friedmans left the farm, she felt very much alone with her children. Not having a common language or a shared experience with her neighbors, cut off from the Jewish life she had come to know in New York City, she was lonely and unhappy. According to her daughter, she threatened to leave her husband if more Jews did not settle in Farmingdale. Her daughter, Mary Peskin Weisgold, vividly remembers her mother's unhappiness at her isolated life and her very hard work.

> Momma said to Poppa, "If you don't get Jewish people here, then we're going back, because I've got to talk. I have to talk to somebody." . . . Being the only Jewish woman in the community for several years was very lonely and isolating for her, as well as for us. She had absolutely no one to talk to. Even if she did feel comfortable with the English of her Christian neighbors, they did not have a common experience or background to share. . . . And she worked very hard. I remember her taking water out of the well in the wintertime, and her fingers sticking on the chain.

Peskin knew that if they were going to stay on the farm, he would have to encourage people actively to settle in Farmingdale. He obtained a real estate license and was in constant communication with the Jewish Agricultural Society to send prospective settlers to him. He helped many of the early farmers get established. Abe Dobin, an agent of the JAS, remembered Peskin as being integral to the development of the community. "If ever one person can be said to be responsible for creating a community, that person was Benjamin Peskin. He was the pivotal man in getting people to come to Farmingdale and settle on farms."

Peskin met prospective farmers at the railroad station, housed them in his home free of charge, and showed them farms. Once the new farmers arrived, he helped them make the adjustment, instructing them on procedures. He taught them how to put the chickens to sleep at night and how to regulate room temperatures in the winter. So important did he become to the new farmers that they also called upon him to mediate inevitable tensions between husband and wife.

The increasing numbers of Jewish people made life more tolerable for Mrs. Peskin. But her work remained strenuous and became more so when Peskin went into the summer-boarder business, by which he tried to augment the family income.

From the very beginning, friends and relatives from New York City visited in the summertime and on holidays. Finally, it occurred to Mr. Peskin to charge money. For Jewish immigrants living in New York City, the farm offered an inexpensive vacation, wholesome food, and sorely missed contact with nature. The relatives and friends brought paying guests with them, and the family was launched in a new business. It was the first really successful "crop" for the Peskins and established a pattern later followed by other farmers.

Peskin converted his barn into sleeping quarters and his home into a gigantic dining room. Mrs. Peskin cooked all the meals herself, and the children waited on the tables. Within two years, the business grew until the farm accommodated as many as sixty people. Some of those early guests later became chicken farmers themselves. But success brought its troubles. Mrs. Peskin could not keep up with the work and suffered complete exhaustion. The boarding business was forced into early retirement.

The JAS then advised Peskin to raise chickens. The first batch of baby chicks thrived on the top floor of his own home, while the family confined themselves to two rooms on the lower floor. The following year, Peskin reconverted his barn-hotel to a chicken house and even later into a hatchery. Eventually the real estate business grew large enough to support the family.

Like the later farm women, Rose Peskin worked hard alongside her husband to build a future. Typically, the men often receive star billing as architects of communities, while the women fade into the background. Such was the case in Farmingdale. It is Benjamin Peskin who is known as a pivotal figure in the history of the Jewish farmers in Farmingdale. But behind him was the force of his wife's need for a Jewish community to which she could relate and her threat of leaving if more Jewish people did not settle in the area. If Benjamin Peskin is the father of the community,

Rose Peskin, whose role is more often forgotten than acknowledged, is really the mother who made it happen.

By 1926, approximately forty Jewish families had settled on farms around Farmingdale.[3] People heard about the new community from friends or relatives who had firsthand experience as guests at Peskin's summer "hotel."

Peskin grew with the community and was involved in all aspects of its life. He donated the land on which to build the Community Center and retained his membership there for his lifetime. At his death, his daughters were given life memberships as a tribute to their father. And Howell Township, in recognition of the contribution the family made, named the road on which he lived Peskin's Lane.

Part 2
The People

3

Eastern European Settlers

Eastern European Jews and their families continued to settle as farmers throughout the fifty-year history of the community, but the majority came between 1920 and 1940. The typical pattern of migration was from Eastern Europe to New York City. There the immigrants remained for about ten years, spending youthful energies in the shops of New York's needle trade or related industries. They spoke of working "by luggage and bags," "by hats," "by raincoats"; or they reported that they were small shopkeepers such as grocers, laundrymen, or tailors. Some were in other trades as "payntners," window washers, boiler-makers, or electricians. Few had any formal schooling beyond a few years of traditional Jewish education in Europe. Almost none had any experience in farming.

Their very choice of leaving the city where family and friends lived was a radical one, but perhaps no more radical than their previous decision to abandon their European homes and to search for fulfillment in America. It coincided with the emerging enlightenment of the Jewish world, with the revolutionary and socialistic ideology sweeping across Eastern Europe before the turn of the century, and with the new Zionist movement.

Whatever shape the American dream took for the Jews in their European homes, it was abruptly changed by the confrontation with New York, a city so psychologically alien and alienating that many could not adjust. Nor had they anticipated the pain of separation from supportive family in Europe. Although they lived in the lower East Side in a completely Jewish environment surrounded by Yiddish speakers and familiar institutions, many immigrants never felt at home. The crowds, the noise, the concrete and brick landscape, the collective indifference to personal suffering—all intensified their feelings of distance from the family and home they had left forever in Europe and from the city in which they were unsuccessful in sending down roots.

For the largest number of the Eastern European settlers, the desire to farm was intimately related to a growing realization that the city was not a congenial place for them. Moving out of New York and onto a farm was one way of leaving behind all that was unsettling. Furthermore, a farm offered the possibility of raising children in a healthier environment and, even more compelling, the opportunity for economic independence.

The farm also provided a way of metaphorically going back to a familiar environment, to the atmosphere of the old home they had left and for which many yearned. Helen Friedman compared the farm with the life she knew in Europe. "I liked the farm because it reminded me a little bit of Europe, the way I lived, with the garden and the open spaces, the fields and the horses. I didn't care too much for New York."

Khana Rivkin, who settled with her husband, Alter, in Farmingdale in 1924, talks of her husband's need to be on a farm, a familiar environment to them. "He didn't like the work he was doing in New York, and he decided to go on a farm because he was born and raised on a farm in Russia. . . . No, it was not a farm. In Russia, Jewish people didn't have the right to have farms. He lived in a place like a small town. . . . The people that came to Farmingdale had dreams that they're going to farm like some people remembered from Russia."

Most of the early Jews who settled on farms had limited resources and could buy only marginal, run-down, low-priced farms. Often, in order to survive, they had to generate income from other sources until they could earn money from their farms. Many families like the Friedmans and like ours were separated, as either the father or the mother remained alone, working in the city. For some, like the Peskins, their first successful "crop" was summer boarders.

Instead of experience in agriculture, the Eastern European immigrants brought their experience from the sweatshops, the trade unions, and the small businesses of the city. In place of deep-rooted attachments to the land, they brought firm attachments to their specific Jewish culture, their own Yiddish language, and their ties both to the old world of Eastern Europe, where family and friends lived and with whom they communicated, and to the new world of American cities, where landsmen lived and

SAMUEL STROGER CAME
TO AMERICA FROM
EASTERN EUROPE. LIKE
MANY JEWISH
IMMIGRANTS, HE LIVED IN
NEW YORK CITY
TEMPORARILY BEFORE
SETTLING ON A FARM,
FIRST ON LONG ISLAND
AND THEN IN
FARMINGDALE. HE SENT
THIS NEW YEAR'S
GREETING TO FRIENDS
AND FAMILY IN EUROPE IN
1905.

with whom they remained in touch. Willing to take chances, eager to learn, possessing an endless ability to adapt, they arrived on the farm with their dreams and their children, with the good wishes of their friends, and with staggering debts to relatives, banks, and the Jewish Agricultural Society. It is not clear whether the greater motivation for these Jewish settlers was leaving the city, farming, owning land, or engaging in work they found meaningful.

All the people interviewed were asked why they wanted to become farmers, when the chances of success were not very promising. After all, they had no common language with their neighbors; they knew nothing about rural America, and for the most part, they had no previous experience in farming. Although many people implied that farm life attracted them because it was like the European home they left, none of the farmers interviewed actually said they were looking for a familiar environment.

Rather, they cited a whole range of other motivations for becoming farmers. Behind every reason given lay a complex of other reasons suggested but not articulated. Perhaps the most honest was the simple statement, "We came here because we wanted to farm." Some said things like, "We wanted to leave New York."

Other questions were explored: Why a farm? Why New Jersey? After all, if they wanted simply to leave New York, there was a whole country full of places they might have chosen. One man gave seven reasons for choosing to settle on a farm, including his having been inspired after reading a Yiddish novel by Isaac Raboy, *Herr Goldenbarg*, about a Jewish cattle rancher in the West. One person said she and her husband had come to a farm so they could observe the Sabbath. As grocery store owners in New York, they violated the holy day every week, much to their distress. On a farm they could keep the Sabbath, even though they had to feed the animals. Taking care of living things was a moral obligation superseding the injunction against working on the Sabbath.

Several farmers interviewed cited their increasingly painful awareness of the social injustices they witnessed while working in the shops and factories of New York City. Louis Bially talked of an incident involving a coworker in a luggage shop. "We were both working all day. But he was twenty years older than me and not producing so much. The boss comes over and fires him. I said to the boss, 'What I make takes care of him too.' The boss didn't listen, and I couldn't stop thinking that when I get a littler older, I'll get fired too."

Some people rationalized that economics impelled them. "What do you mean, 'Why did we go on a farm?' We had to make a living." When questioned further about their chances of making a living on a farm when they had no money, no experience, and a huge debt load, they said something like: "But we had to take a chance. We had no choice. We were dying in the city."

Louis Newdow, interviewed in Israel where he eventually moved after leaving the farm, said he settled on a farm to make a living. But he began rethinking his motivation while talking. "In New York I was an electrician, and making a good living. Did it mean anything that every day I got up and went to work as an electrician for somebody else? On the farm I did my own electric work, my own plumbing, my own building. But that's not it. On the farm I was productive. My work meant something. I was producing food for other people. I watched things grow."

Some people spoke of an ancient desire to own land of their own, so long denied most of them in the Pale of Settlement. Restless and rootless, the Jewish farmers looked for "a better, a quieter life" for themselves and their families. In a very real sense, the land, the farm, was a place which could nurture the fragile shoots of an uprooted family. To become rooted to one place in America was to become rooted to the whole of the new country, to make it a home. The farm represented an investment in their futures and in those of their children. The land was something solid and significant, and the farmers were optimistic that it would remain in the family for generations, as it had for the local people. "I was hoping my sons would carry on with the farm," said one farmer. "No one was going to take it away from us here in America," said another.

Owning land was the realization of a dream of an ideal life in America. One farmer describes the feelings of excitement he experienced after he actually settled on the farm.

> Wherever I went, I stepped on my own land. I had my own house. My coops, my chickens, my egg check [from the sale of eggs]. I could do with it whatever I wanted. I planted my own vegetables and ate my own potatoes. I had three acres of strawberries. Those were the happiest years of my life in Farmingdale. I breathed the fresh air. I had a giant tree on my lawn, like a very giant umbrella. I made a bench under the tree and a table. Friends came, and sat under the tree and enjoyed the coolness.

THE BLAINE FAMILY, PHOTOGRAPHED AROUND 1905. ADOLPHE BLAINE WAS RAISED NEAR VILNA (NOW VILNIUS, LITHUANIA). HIS FIRST FARM, PICTURED HERE, WAS IN CARVERSVILLE, PENNSYLVANIA. THE FAMILY SETTLED A FEW YEARS LATER IN FARMINGDALE.

This farmer learned by trial and error, as did most of the settlers. If necessary, they consulted neighbors, books, the county agent, or the Jewish Agricultural Society agent. Some tried to prepare themselves before moving onto the farm. Louis Bially ordered pamphlets from the U.S. Department of Agriculture and studied them in his apartment in New York. "When I set up my farm," he said, "it was a model farm." Almost all of the early settlers read *Der Yiddisher Farmer*, the first Yiddish farm publication in the world. Some took extension courses offered in the evening at Freehold High School. Some regularly consulted with the experts at Rutgers College of Agriculture.

For models they had their own experiences with small garden patches in Europe or the farms they remembered of the Polish or Russian peasants among whom they had lived. Jack Grossman remembers that on his father's farm in 1926, everything was done by hand. "We used to dig potatoes by hand and spade them out with a fork. We had a typical little Russian farm, probably the same as any small farm you would find in Russia in those times."

Professional American agriculturalists such as the county agent predicted that the Jews would not succeed. "One has to go up the agricultural ladder from worker to tenant farmer to farmer-owner," said the experts.[1] Skipping the initial steps, the Jewish farmers became farmer-owners.

The Jewish farmers of Farmingdale were determined to make a living on the farm. Eventually they did, although few realized any substantial amount of profit from their farm operations. They doggedly persevered through traumas and disappointments brought on by their lack of experience, such as those endured by the Peskins and Friedmans, whose ignorance resulted in the loss of the livestock during their first year.

Having made the decision to farm, having committed their energies and hopes to a particular life, the Jewish farmers of Farmingdale were a remarkably stable group. As late as 1952, the Annual Report of the Jewish Agricultural Society notes that of those settling on farms, 90 percent remained for more than ten years, this in contrast to the transiency of their urban relatives engaged in other occupations.

If owning land was an entirely new experience for many of the Jewish settlers in Farmingdale, living as a small marginal group in a Christian environment was not. But there was a significant difference. In Europe, and indeed in most of the small towns of America, the Jews were typically shopkeepers and tradesmen, catering to the local rural people. In Farmingdale, the pattern was reversed. The Jews became the farmers, and the Christians sold goods, provisions, and services to them. Very few native farmers raised chickens and produced eggs, the money crop of the Jewish farmer. When poultry farming became an established branch of agriculture, old-time farmers went into service trades, providing masons, builders, plumbers, electricians, truckers, and haulers for the Jewish farmers.

Many of these older farmers had sold the Jews parcels of land which had been in their families for generations. Some subsequently resented the changing character and landscape of their community, and they did not particularly hide their feelings. One early Jewish farmer related how a neighbor in 1924 showed his fear of Jews. "The minute a Jew came in, everybody wanted to sell their land. They didn't want to live in the neighborhood with Jews. I remember an old neighbor, an old man. He was 99 percent of the time drunk. He says to me: 'How are we going to keep all of *you?*' There were only three or four of us. How was he going to keep *us?* He was as poor as a church mouse, but he was going to keep *us?* This was the situation. I mean, you came into a very unfriendly section."

Another farmer remembers a different kind of incident. He and his wife lived on their farm directly opposite a church. One Sunday, a delegation of Christians visited and informed them that the church found their working on Sunday offensive. The Jewish farmer reports that he answered them simply: "I told them that we were only feeding our chickens. We had an obligation to do that. We were not doing any other kind of work."

In the 1920s and the 1930s, the Ku Klux Klan had an active branch in the Farmingdale area. The Peskins were treated by the Klan to a cross burning opposite their home. A daughter describes the scene. "All I can describe is seeing the cross burning, and there was a lot of big shooting flames. . . . It was dark. Suddenly, we looked out and there it was. I remember how scary it was. What made it even worse was that we never saw the ones that were doing it. Somehow, if you see people, you can understand, maybe. It's not a hidden thing, then."

Harry Sokol, an early farmer, talks of seeing the Klan march past his house. "I saw the Ku Klux Klan march once. We didn't know who was marching because they wore masks. You couldn't tell a face. . . . They were marching on West Farms Road . . . as a demonstration against the few Jews that settled." Sokol's daughter, a very young child then, also remembers the fear that gripped her and the family. They did not understand or know anything about the Klan, but they knew, instinctively, it was directed against them as Jews.

Jack Grossman remembers how his father, who had been in the Russian army in 1917, taught his sons to fire the shotgun. One night the Klan burned a cross on their field, and the boys fired in the direction of the burning cross. The family was never bothered in that way again.

Christian memory of that time is different. None of the Christians interviewed admitted to any firsthand knowledge of the Klan because their parents were not members. But one woman remembers how her father would take the children to watch a Klan march whenever there was one—or better still, she said, to watch a cross burning. It was a real event in their lives, she claims. Asked if Klan activities still continued in 1978, the year of the interview, she said, "They are now much restricted by new fire laws which prohibit fires from being set close to wooded areas."

Living among anti-Jewish feeling was nothing new to the settlers of Farmingdale. Yet, by comparison with some of their previous experiences with the Russian and Polish peasants, those with the Christians of Farmingdale were hardly noticeable. So what if goyim laughed at and mimicked their Yiddish speech patterns or made derogatory slurs, which the Jews for the most part did not understand anyway? The Jews easily minimized the effect of such insults by simply avoiding contact with Christians.

The Jews lived in Farmingdale as they did in many of the small villages and communities of Eastern Europe—as a group unto themselves. There was no social interaction between the early Jews and the Christians. The Jews socialized only among themselves, often around their holidays, and in each other's homes. Although most of the early settlers had rejected organized religion for themselves, they realized they had to do something about holidays "for the children, or they would grow up not knowing who they were." Drawing upon their early religious studies in Europe, where some had attended yeshivas (schools for advanced religious study), the farmers conducted their own services, unassisted by a rabbi.

Some resolved the conflicts created by their personal break with religion through elaborate rationalization. For example, Israel Friedman, claiming that he believed in freedom and not in religion, did not eat bread on Passover. Raised in an orthodox home, Friedman had studied to become a rabbi but then became disillusioned. "I dropped religion before I came to America . . . and I became a revolutionary. By studying, I found out that organized religion is humbug. Absolutely impossible." Leaving the yeshiva, Friedman made plans to continue studying in the secular Russian school in which he enrolled. But his open allegiance to revolutionary ideology landed him in a Russian jail and ended his formal education. He then immigrated to America.

For the rest of his life, Friedman protested that religion was humbug and considered himself a nonbeliever. Yet, he continued to observe the traditional holidays, telling himself that Jewish holidays really celebrate freedom, and freedom is the essence of the morality in which he believes. His ambivalence was characteristic of others who identified themselves as social humanists and continued to observe traditional holidays. Friedman tried to explain the apparent contradictions.

> For me the beauty of Jewish holidays is that . . . you can be not religious and also have the holidays. Passover. It's a holiday of freedom . . . Shevuos. It's a time we got the code how to live. A moral code. The Ten Commandments. The same thing with Sukos. All the holy days of the Jewish people. You can be religious and hold it as a religious man, and you can be anti-religious or a free man and at the same time you can have it. That is my religion. I keep the holidays . . . I don't eat *khometz* [bread or anything made with refined flour] during Passover. . . . I wouldn't touch it. . . . But not as a religion. For me it's not a dogma. I do it, my wife does it, because we feel we have to do it. It's really a holiday. I'm not against God. I don't care if there is a God or if there is not a God. I care for freedom.

The dual pull of religion and ideology persisted in Friedman until his death at ninety-three. Before he died, he made a remarkable admission. "The real thing I would like to be was a rabbi. That's the main thing. That's what's in me." He paused for a long moment's thought. "But I couldn't do it because I didn't want to be false."

Louis Bially came to the farm in 1940 with an ideology diametrically opposed to that of Friedman, although the men were remarkably similar in many ways. Like Friedman, Bially was educated in a European yeshiva. His family, wanting him to be a rabbi, sent him to Brisklatovsk to study, and there he, too, encountered the secular world. He says of his early enlightenment: "Although Jewish life is deeply embedded in me, I did not remain religious. When I started reading Peretz [Y. L. Peretz, 1852–1915, Yiddish writer], I saw there was another world besides the religious one. One has to be a good Jew, a good person, and love all races the same. Although the Jews are my people, I hold that all people are the same. We must not hate one another. If you believe that, you are religious enough."

If freedom became Friedman's religion, brotherhood became Bially's. Although neither practiced rituals, both were committed to a morality superseding ritual observances. When Mr. Friedman was asked how he perceived Jewish values, he answered with one word—"moral." When asked to define "moral," he resorted to his religious training. "Moral, as I understand it, is not to do something that is not already in the Talmud. You shouldn't do something to somebody that you wouldn't like somebody to do to you."

Asked if he could have Jewish values in New York City, he responded, "If a person wants to live in a moral way, he can do it any place where he is." Yet in expressing his motivation for becoming a farmer, Friedman put it into a moral framework. "I just looked for a better, a quieter life. I didn't want to exploit anyone, and I didn't want to be exploited either. . . . In Russia, after I left the yeshiva, I became a revolutionary. . . . And what was the revolution? Not to be exploited."

Bially, reacting to the exploitation of the Jewish laborers among whom he worked, became involved in the labor movement in New York City. By choosing to become a farmer, he looked forward to being able to work and retain his values. "I came on the farm to live like a *mentsh*, to be a responsible doer [as contrasted to merely being human], to help other people, to be involved with everything that happens *oyfn Yidishn gas* [in the Jewish world]."

Much later, when "nonbelievers" Friedman or Bially were called upon in the community to participate in traditional or ceremonial Jewish occasions, neither of them could refuse, although both objected strenuously to religious dogma. Friedman, who lived next door to the Community Center, which also served as the synagogue, was frequently called upon to serve as the tenth man for a Saturday minyan. He said he agreed because it gave him an opportunity to practice his ethics. By participating, he could help those who needed the synagogue. "I had pleasure because I felt I gave them pleasure." But he insisted that he not be asked to participate religiously by being called to the Torah or requested to wear a *talis* (prayer shawl). Commenting on his later participation in Torah study sessions, he said, "It was intellectual, not religious."

Bially remembers an incident on the farm when a neighbor asked him to be present in a minyan at a house where people were in mourning. Bially protested that he was not religious and had not *davened* (prayed) in years, but his neighbor's pleading broke his resistance, and he went to the house. He put on a *talis* and a yarmulke, or skull cap, which he had not worn in "many years," and as he started to read, the memory of how to do it and the melodies of the ancient prayers quickly returned. "And you know," he said softly and reflectively, "it didn't hurt me one bit. I felt good. I enjoyed it."

In spite of their personal religious conflicts and ambivalences, the first cooperative purchase the Jews made for their community was a Torah scroll. Before the Community Center was built in 1929, the Torah was carried from home to home for religious services.

In addition to depending on each other for religious and social occasions, the Jews also needed the psychological and emotional support they received from their fledgling community. Although the distance between their farms was considerable and they had no telephones or cars, they maintained an informal information network which kept all its members in touch with one another.

Harry Sokol, who settled in Farmingdale with his parents and young wife in 1925, organized a welcoming committee. "When a new farmer settled, we were overwhelmed when they were Jews. We were so happy, so glad to see them, that we organized a new group right away. There were three of us. . . . We went as a committee and welcomed the newcomers. I met everybody that way."

Not only did they welcome newcomers, but the established farmers assumed the responsibility for helping them get started. They gave instructions to novices and helped in physical work. Alter Rifkin, one of the earliest settlers, tells of early cooperative efforts among the farmers. Needing building materials, the farmers pooled their money and bought a chain saw. They planned to convert their woodland into lumber for chicken houses. "We figured out . . . we are going to buy a saw. I had woods and Peskin had woods. . . . We were going to make lumber. So when the saw came, everybody got together. We were eight, nine, ten people. We worked and worked and worked, you know, a whole day. And we pulled down two trees." His wife, not intending a pun, offered the explanation: "Nobody, nobody was farmers. They was all 'cluckmakers' [cloak-makers]."

Just as the new farmers shared their labor, they shared their newly gained farming information—or misinformation. One bizarre incident involved efforts to move brooder houses, floor and all, because one farmer had heard that land on which a brooder house stands becomes infected in a year and must be changed.

They said each year we have to move brooder houses. So how to move a brooder house? We take it all together, you know. Sokol had a horse. I had a horse, and there was another. I forgot his name. He had a horse, and Peskin had two horses. We worked a whole day . . . from the morning till the night, and we moved one brooder house with Peskin's horses. If not his horses, we wouldn't move. . . . We had to change around. Change around they said. If there was chickens on this ground, this ground is infected already. You have to move on fresh ground. . . . And the goyim, you know, they used to sit and watch us. And they were laughing. The next day I got a man with a tractor, and it took him an hour. He moved all the brooder houses.

Although the early cooperative efforts, when everyone was learning how to become a farmer, were often amusing, even if occasionally frustrating, cooperation was an important part of the community experience and con-

ADOLPHE BLAINE IN
FARMINGDALE AROUND 1917.
THE HANDWRITTEN CAPTION
SAYS "ADOLPHE DER FARMER"
IN YIDDISH.

tinued through the years. People now remember the sharing of heavy seasonal jobs as one of the most satisfying of their experiences of the farm. Extra help was needed for vaccinating the chickens against diseases while they were on the chicken range; bringing the chickens in from the range; and shielding, specking, or debeaking the chickens to prevent them from pecking each other to death.[2] When the call went out for help, families, couples, or individuals responded. At a later time, some of the more affluent farmers hired vaccination crews of young farmers looking to supplement their income by providing the service. But others continued the early tradition of helping each other because they enjoyed the socializing. During the work, there was an opportunity to carry on the inevitable political discussions, a very important part of their lives. And when the work was finished, there was a large breakfast for the workers. "Work and social activity was intimately connected," said one farmer. "It's much different today, where people work far away from the place where they socialize."

"I loved Farmingdale," said Louis Bially, "because *s'iz geven a briderlekhn lebn* [it was a brotherly kind of life]. . . . When there was a problem, poor people or a farmer was sick, we had to help out. We couldn't let his chickens die. We shared the work among several farmers and took turns to help."

In addition to the satisfactions of such cooperation and the feelings of mutual concern and responsibility, there was another kind of satisfaction. Farming was totally noncompetitive. It was in everyone's interest to see that their neighbors did well, that the neighbor's flocks were healthy. "After all," said one, "if his chickens were sick, chances are that mine would also get the same disease." The farmers were not competing for the same customers as shopkeepers or professionals might have. Morris Troy, Toms River farmer in 1943, put it this way: "In Brooklyn, if someone has a store and a man opens up a store across the street, he is a competitor. But on a farm, when someone buys a farm across the road, he will be my neighbor. That makes a big difference." Higher egg prices and lower feed prices benefited everyone. People gave advice to each other freely, and whether it was accepted or not, their motives were not suspect. "Your neighbor didn't feel that if he advised you and offered you some help and suggestions that you were competing with him."

In spite of the satisfaction of owning land, the positive values of producing food, being close to nature, and working cooperatively, many of the early farmers found that the work itself was not particularly interesting. Yet Israel Friedman, comparing his life on the farm with his previous work in a hand laundry, said: "The farm work wasn't so interesting. . . . But between the laundry and the farm, I liked the farm a thousand times more." His wife added, "From the beginning, we really liked the farm for one thing: we didn't like to deal with people. The chickens never complain. They died if you didn't take care. But they wouldn't give you any argument."

Louis Bially needed more stimulation than the farm offered him, and he became very busy creating a richer cultural life with like-minded friends. "Farming didn't satisfy me. Not entirely. A cultural life was missing. I started to go to the Jewish Community Center, and there I met many other farmers and we spoke about forming a cultural club. We organized three reading circles. One in Farmingdale, one in Lakewood, one in Toms River. I was on the executive. We had lectures in Yiddish and English . . . and we lived a cultural life."

Lacking Jewish institutions, the Jews created them. If the demands of the city were enervating, exhausting, and devitalizing to some, the demands of the community, if not of their new occupation, were the opposite: stimulating, inspiring, and fostering all sorts of creative impulses. The satisfaction of meeting difficult challenges, the sense of being somehow in control of their own destinies, and the comfort of a familiar landscape and a simpler pace or rhythm of life gave them the feeling of being free. Said one woman, "We worked hard, so hard. *Shver un biter* [hard and bitter]. But we were free." The word "free" was repeated and emphasized by many of the people interviewed, who seemed to share an understanding of what being free means.

For Bially, freedom meant planning his own working hours. As a result of his efforts, Farmingdale became culturally richer. "On the farm I arranged my own working hours. I had the luxury of being able to have a meeting during the day for two hours, for an executive [meeting] or whatever. From two to five we didn't have what to do. We had packed the eggs and fed the flock. So we took the car and met in Lakewood or somewheres else and had meetings during the day. We couldn't do this in the city."

When Bially retired to Florida, he also was involved in its cultural life. He and his wife taught Yiddish to retired Jews and did dramatic readings from Sholem Aleichem and Peretz. But Louis Bially missed the intensity of the Farmingdale experience. "In Florida, there is a bigger group, but the ideology is weak." And Friedman, on the opposite end of the political spectrum from Bially, and also retired but in Lakewood, New Jersey, echoed the same sentiment. "In Farmingdale we existed by means of our farming, but we lived, we *lived*, because of our ideology."

As a rule, the women, like the men, were radical and individualistic. Yet, like their peers worldwide, they often acquiesced in their husbands' decisions and played their roles quietly, if not passively. For all intents and purposes, Fanny Dubnick was an outgoing, assertive, and aggressive woman who built, managed, and ran the farm alone. She reported, however, that when she and her husband began thinking about a farm, she pleaded for his permission to allow her to shop for land, although a heart attack had left him unemployed for a number of years and his wife's income provided the sole support for the family.

A number of the early families settled on farms because of a husband's illness. A doctor would sometimes advise that life on a farm would be easier for a sick man than living in the city, although as life became easier for the husband, it became more burdensome for the wife. One woman reports that her sick husband sat on the sun porch and read all day while she took care of all the farm operations. At night, she cleaned the house, cooked, and baked. Asked if her husband at least took care of their children, she replied: "Oh, he didn't know anything about children. What does a man know about children?" Too exhausted after her chores to seek any kind of social companionship but needing some outlet from work, she studied Latin by herself because, she said, "languages interest me." And she wrote philosophical Yiddish poems about her dreams for a better tomorrow. Her husband, having rested all day, attended meetings in the Community Center in the evenings.

Another woman came to the farm completely against her will. She loved New York City when she arrived there and wanted to stay, but her husband said that farm life was much better. Once settled on the farm, he became so involved in cooperatives, their formation and management and their educational programs, that he had no time at all for the farm, except to tell his wife what had to be done. He had meetings night and day, and in between he studied the literature of the cooperative movement. She became so bitter that she would not talk to any of the other co-op members, even after her husband was hospitalized with a breakdown. He eventually died in the hospital. Rejecting all offers of help, she doggedly kept on with the work, making all the decisions for the farm she hated, raising her two sons alone until they were old enough to take care of themselves in the world. Surprisingly, the mother's unhappiness was not transferred to her sons. The older, who assumed much of the work of the farm as he matured, looks back with fond nostalgia at the life he enjoyed there. He does not at all regret his experience and wished he could give his children the same. But his mother wept, even in her last years, at the hardships she remembered enduring.

Another woman, claiming that the farm became her grave, left her husband and moved back to the city she also loved. But the family resources were too limited to support her, and she could not support herself and her children. She came back to her husband and the farm and made an uneasy compromise with her life situation. Still another is reported to have left her husband on the farm, gone to her mother's apartment house in Brooklyn, and thrown herself out of the window.[3]

4

German Refugees

According to the Jewish Agricultural Society, in the late 1930s and early 1940s a greater percentage of German Jewish refugees settled on farms than did other Jewish immigrants. Their motivations for becoming farmers were as varied and complex as those of the Eastern Europeans. Certainly, as refugees, they needed the peace and tranquility the farm offered them. Joseph Bienstock settled on a farm with his parents, formerly clothing manufacturers in Dortmund, Germany. He said:

> I had gone through a very, very difficult time, and there was never really any hope. It's hard for somebody where there is no place to go back to. . . . The farm represented stability and tranquility. . . . I had been in New York for a while, but there was nothing really stabilizing. . . . I knew there was nothing I wanted to do the next day or the day afterwards. I just worked at a job. It wasn't anything that I really got satisfaction from. . . . Out here, on the farm, the whole thing became very appealing. I could see I was working towards something. For the first time I found something I wanted to do. And I found reassurance in having my own piece of land.

By the time the German refugees arrived, the Jewish community was integrated and cohesive, with its own social structure and its own Community Center, built in 1929 by the earlier settlers. Poultry farming, already an established and recognized branch of agriculture, promised a good economic return, especially if a settler had a little money to invest. Some of the refugees had been able to channel some of their money out before they fled Europe. According to Ruth Wertheimer, "Word had gotten around that this was a good business to go into if you brought some money with you. It's not a competitive business, you don't have to learn new methods of making a livelihood, you don't have to learn new methods of advertising."

In 1939, when the Germans began arriving, the anticipated profit was one dollar per bird per year. By 1945, genetic know-how and improved conditions resulted in a higher per annum output of eggs, and the profit was calculated at two dollars per bird per year.

The economics were attractive, and chicken farming seemed a secure investment to the German Jews. But even more attractive was the opportunity the farm offered to these uprooted, formerly middle-class people to be their own bosses, to be "masters of their own fates," as one woman put it. They did not have to accept the menial factory jobs, the only ones they could find; they did not have to struggle, in their middle years, to master a new language. "The chickens could understand German as well as English," said Wertheimer, laughing.

The farm procedures were simple enough to learn, and a newcomer could realize a fairly quick return on money invested. But more than this, the idea of owning land appealed very much to people who had been almost exclusively urban all their lives. As it did to the Eastern Europeans before them, land represented a way of quickly becoming rooted, in the most basic sense, to the new country.

The Jewish Agricultural Society was instrumental in assisting the German refugees in their farm efforts. A training farm in Bound Brook gave many an introduction to farming techniques; JAS agents advised them on appropriate purchases. A certain percentage of the German Jews were advised to go to Farmingdale, and others went to Lakewood, Toms River, Vineland, and other established communities in Central and South Jersey.

In the late 1930s, the German Jews began arriving in Farmingdale, which was then a community of poultry farmers almost totally Jewish. Maurice Nappa, born in Galicia but raised in Germany, settled on a farm, took out a real estate license, and became for the German Jewish community what Peskin was for the Eastern Europeans. He was the principal agent to whom the JAS sent prospective customers, and he helped settle many new families.

Unlike the Eastern Europeans, the German Jews did not linger for years in New York City before coming to the farm. Their initial view of the city shocked them. "New York was a horror to me," said one woman. "I saw myself like an insect, being crushed as nothing." It was not a city in which they could easily establish roots, although they were essentially urban people.

Most had been born and raised in large cities in Germany and educated in the gymnasiums and universities. Before the rise of Hitler, they had enjoyed an upper-middle-class life-style in Germany, where they were manufacturers, professionals such as lawyers or doctors, or well-established businessmen. One owned a number of department stores; another had liquor distilleries all over Germany and Europe. Almost all had been individual entrepreneurs, in charge of their own affairs. None had had any experience in farming.

On the surface, one would think that the adjustment to farming would be difficult. But such was not the case. Men who had previously directed large operations and administered huge budgets worked alongside their wives, who in Germany managed retinues of household servants. Hans Neumann, speaking of his father, who had been a prominent lawyer in Mainz, said: "My father was happier as a farmer than he was as a lawyer. He was the happiest farmer I knew." Neither he nor any of the other people interviewed thought farming represented a lowering of status. One woman, who had been a third-year medical student before Hitler put an end to her career aspirations, found the farm to be constantly challenging and creative. But there was a hint of regret in her voice when she related that she used her medical expertise to treat sick chickens. With the assistance of the Jewish Agricultural Society, she and her husband built what she called "a showcase of a farm," and subsequently they were instrumental in helping friends and relatives settle on farms near theirs, creating a subculture of German Jews within the Jewish community.

The Germans were apparently able to transfer their former business experience and skills to their role as farmers and to adapt economic principles they had practiced to the operation of the farm. Eric Nappa, who in his capacity as a representative of a feed company knew almost all the farmers in the area, said: "They almost all did exceedingly well. They seemed to have the German trait that whatever you do, you do it well. You work hard, and methodically. They prospered. They had the best farms going. First of all, they were good businessmen. Second, they were German businessmen. They are very pedantic, very methodical, and very industrious." One of the German settlers pointed out a difference in economic philosophy between the German Jews and the others. "The Americans invest more than they have, the Germans less." According to her, good business practice paid off.

They managed their farms in such a way that they had paid off their mortgages and paid off their loans. They owned their farms free and clear. They didn't hire workers, they worked themselves, and they didn't expand the farms to be too large. Where many others expanded when business was very good, they kept the status quo. They didn't raise more than five thousand chickens, because they could handle that number themselves. If they went above that, it was because they thought it out very carefully, very clearly, and felt they could afford it. They never overreached, and therefore they made out even when conditions were not good. And they didn't lose their farms, not a one.

Like the families of displaced persons who settled later, the German Jewish families on the farm included aunts, uncles, sisters-in-law, grandmothers, and grandfathers—all under one roof, if necessary. Family groups lived close to each other and became even more interrelated through marriage and children.

Ruth Wertheimer's mother and mother-in-law both lived in her home. Both had followed their children to America, via Cuba, in 1941. The two mothers helped on the farm. When the farm income had to be supplemented, one of them, in her sixties, originally from a wealthy family and educated by private tutors, got a job cooking for a hundred students at a yeshiva in nearby Lakewood. Still mentally alert at ninety, she told how she had enjoyed the farm. "Oh, it was beautiful," she said. "I collected the eggs. It was wonderful."

The German Jews soon formed a community within a community. Rarely did they go to meetings at the Jewish Community Center, which were conducted in both Yiddish and English. Although they could understand the Yiddish, they did not speak it. "And God forbid the members of the center should speak German there," said one woman. However, she and her husband, among the first of the German Jews to settle in the area, did attend some meetings at the center when they were newcomers, out of their need for community. She remembers that "at the time, we were so lost and alone. It [the center] was a place to go to, and people were nice to us and helpful. Everyone wanted to help us. I thought it was wonderful. People were not selfish. They didn't give advice for ulterior motives. They gave advice, that's all. They were just plain nice people." The synagogue services at the center presented language problems because all the commentaries and interspersed remarks were in Yiddish. Wanting their children to have a Jewish education but not wishing to burden them with Yiddish, the women organized private after-school classes in their homes for the children, hiring a Hebrew teacher who came from New York on Sundays. The parents divided the expense among themselves.

One German woman who settled on a farm with her family as a young girl and remained after she herself married, said:

> For some, living in a small group was a cop-out. It enabled them to remain in a community that was almost like home, as far as their social activities were concerned. They were not forced to learn a new language, they were not in a competitive business, they did not have to learn new customs of the country that they had moved to. It really was an easy way out for them. The fact that they could live in a sort of pocket of their people also made it very congenial for them. They could speak German and carry on their normal kaffeeklatsches and whatever German-type get-togethers they would have. And they didn't have to make it in New York City.

Denying that the German Jews made any kind of radical decision in moving out on a farm, she said: "They were the most conservative people in the world. There wasn't one radical thing they did. The one thing they had in common was that they were all uprooted in their middle age at a time when they thought they were settled. They had to reroot someplace, so some of them ended up here."

There is some justice in her observation of the conservative nature of the German Jews. Like their counterparts, the refugees who had survived the Holocaust and settled on the farms in the 1950s, they seemed very apolitical. In an intensely political community, they remained totally anonymous, not identifying with any of the hotly debated issues or with any of the factional alignments. It is not hard to account for this silence on the part of people who had been innocent victims of political tensions and murderous ideologies in their very recent past.

The German Jews had more in common, however, than their uprootedness and their political conservatism. They did, after all, have a common language, a common cultural experience, and a certain perspective. And, according to one woman, they had a "prejudice towards Eastern Jews which they brought with them and retained against all reason." Her own father's irrational conviction that his family was safe in Germany because he was a German Jew and not an Eastern Jew prevented the family from leaving when they could do so.

> My parents were absolutely high society in Germany. My father had a million-dollar business and then some, with branches in France and Holland and all over. This is one of the things that dissuaded him from coming here earlier. He had been to the United States in 1933 and then in 1934 to sort of look around, whether he could move his business. Each time, he came back and said: "I'm crazy. Why should I move, when I'm making a

wonderful living here? To move into a new country with different customs, with different language. I'm too old. And besides, Hitler doesn't mean me. After all, I'm a German." I remember when I was a kid in Germany and everybody said, "They mean the Eastern Jews, they don't mean us. We're German first." . . . They brought with them this prejudice. I couldn't understand it. I said [to my father], "How can you bring this with you? After all you've been through?" And they [the German Jews] still have it, they still have it. They may deny it, but it's there. They just never get rid of it, the feeling of superiority. Socially they remained more or less a closed group.

Closed or not, the German-Jewish subcommunity enjoyed an active social and cultural life, generally outside of the Jewish Community Center. Some were active in the organization of the feed and egg cooperatives the farmers developed. The women formed a social group, a *Krenzchen*, which met one afternoon a week in each other's homes. It was, according to one woman, a Jewish institution brought over from Germany, a kaffeeklatsch for women to exchange news and conversation. Elaborate cakes and pastries were prepared in anticipation of the meeting.

The Germans were good businessmen and for the most part paid off their farms. But like the rest of the poultry farmers, they were caught in the economic squeeze of the 1950s caused by high feed and low egg prices. Like the Eastern Europeans and the Americans, they had to supplement their farm income. Typically, they retailed their own eggs—to stores, hotels, and bakeries, or door-to-door in New York City, northern New Jersey, or along the Jersey shore. When they perceived that farming as a way of earning a living had become completely nonviable, the younger ones prepared for different professions or businesses, as most of the farmers did. The older ones retired and, like the Eastern Europeans, chose to live not too far from each other in nearby Lakewood.

The Eastern Europeans and German Jews did not readily mix and socialize, but their children did. They organized a junior discussion group for young Jewish intellectuals aged thirteen to twenty and thrashed out ideological and theological ideas. Adults now themselves, they remain good friends, and their parents continue their more formal relationship.

Cultural differences between the Eastern Europeans and the Germans persist even to the later years. In addition to superficial differences in dress and speech, there are differences in orientation toward history, reflected both in the interview questions they answered and in the manner in which they approached the subject. German Jews presented well-documented facts. They saved their farm account books and knew exactly when and where their parents were born. The Eastern Europeans considered that kind of information trivial. "What difference does it make where my parents were born? They were born in a small village no one has heard of; they died a long time ago, I don't remember when." To the passionate Eastern Europeans, specific details skirted the heart of the matter. They believed instead in the value of their perceptions. However, the two groups shared some similarities. They were both pleased to be interviewed and genuine in their desire to be honest. Both typically invited the interviewer to lunch.

5

American Intellectuals

Farmingdale was settled by four distinct groups whose pattern of arrival was not necessarily chronological. Whereas the refugee groups (German Jews and displaced persons) came to the community either directly before or shortly after the war, the other two groups (the prewar Eastern Europeans and the Americans) arrived sporadically and continually throughout the history of the community.

The early settlers were followed by friends and relatives, some of whom had been born in America. Many settlers came with native-born children, a number of them young adults. These had graduated from city colleges and universities with professional degrees. During the aftermath of the depression, they could not find work in the city.

Louis [Horowitz] Harwood, who moved to the farm with his family in 1933 after finishing City College as a civil engineer, said that the farm represented the best of the choices open to him.

> When I got out of school I had three choices, roughly. I was given an offer to join a kibbutz in what was then Palestine at no pay, but with a great career as a pioneer. Then I had a choice to join a group that was going to the South Seas to live on coconuts and fish. Our alternatives were very limited. And then I was offered a job with a labor union, to join their educational committee. You were supplied with a baseball bat, and you went out and educated bosses. I did have one other choice, which I took for a while. I was

offered a job at a lumberyard, pulling lumber around. The pay was eight dollars a week, six days. The only qualification besides my recognized talents was that I must not be Jewish. So that was easily taken care of. I called myself Lawrence B. Hedley, Jr. I was hired immediately. When my uncle suggested I try farming on a proposition of a partnership, it sounded very tempting to me. It was in the depths of the depression, and very talented and able people were doing almost anything. Fields were pretty well closed, the opportunities were very slim, there was really nothing much you could plan on. And my feeling was that farming was about as good an idea as any other. I simply treated it as one other alternative.

But Lou's friends, all college-educated young men and all unemployed, felt that he had gone out of his mind with his decision to move to a farm. "They thought first it was funny, and then they were very sorry for me. Because from the point of view of college graduates, my contemporaries, going on a farm was a complete confession of total collapse. But I got satisfaction from doing something a little bit different." Ultimately, a few of his friends visited the farm, changed their minds about his sanity, and also moved to Farmingdale.

The experience was duplicated for many of the people settling on farms, whose friends and relatives expressed disbelief and dismay over the decision. One young American woman reported that relatives kept saying: "Where is she going? Out in the wilderness someplace. No houses. How can a young girl from New York City go out to a wilderness?"

If the relatives were worried, the settlers were not. Nathan Deutchman, who was nineteen when he moved to the farm with his father and mother, found the experience exhilarating. "It was the happiest time of my life. I welcomed the challenge of the change." Part of his attitude was conditioned by the city, which offered him very little at the time. "There didn't seem to be anything in the offering. My father was a *shnayder* [tailor], and it didn't look like tailoring would ever be anything at the time we're talking about—1937 or thereabouts. And for myself, all I had to look forward to was some menial job somewhere and no real great hope. That was one part of it. Then there was a second part. None of us liked living in a cluttered metropolis. We'd rather live in peaceful quieter surroundings."

The search for peace and quiet impelled many of the young people who were born and bred in the city to settle in Farmingdale after World War II. For many, the quality of the life-style was the highest priority. Returning war veterans who had confronted dark uncertainties in the war's many battlefronts consciously rejected material comforts for the more enduring spiritual values which they saw in farming.

A stereotype among the Christians of Farmingdale is that the Jews became farmers to avoid the draft. In fact, many of the young Americans who settled on the farm with their parents enlisted or were drafted into the army, and about half of the American Jews who settled in Farmingdale in the mid-1940s were returning war veterans who searched for a quiet pastoral life, "free from sham, free from hypocrisy, and free from the rat race of the city," as one woman put it.

Joe Fox was not born in America but enlisted in the army as soon as he arrived in the country from Europe. He was sent to the Pacific, where he was captured and survived the Bataan death march. He explains how he managed to endure through his incarceration in a Japanese prison during the war. "On the death march from Bataan, and for three years in a prison in Japan, I kept dreaming of a farm. It was the only thing that made life possible—that dream. If God spared me." God spared him; the dream came true. In 1949, he and his city wife and two infant children settled on a farm in Farmingdale.

Many of the Americans had been trained in professions that carried more status than farming and promised a more affluent life. They were lawyers, dentists, accountants, teachers, psychologists, economists, pharmacists. All put their degrees aside. As farmers, a whole new life opened up for them.

Joseph Zelnick, who had spent six years in the merchant marine, felt that farming offered him a greater opportunity for independence than did the teaching for which he had been trained. He and his wife envisaged a rich social and cultural life on the farm and an opportunity to practice, even in a limited way, a cooperative type of life in which they believed. "In seeing other farmers and visiting them, and knowing them personally, we became enamoured of the way of life in terms of the independence, the social and cultural life, and the integrity. Working seven days a week didn't seem any big drawback. It got us out of the economic rat-race—going to work everyday, competing with traffic, competing with someone on a job. The farm fit in with our belief in a cooperative way of living."

George Brick returned to his home in New York City after five and a half years of service in the air corps. He married but could not adjust to the city. Nor could he and his bride find a suitable apartment. They were living with his in-laws in the Bronx; as he said, "I just couldn't settle down. I didn't feel right."

Kenneth Dubrovsky had spent four and a half years in the army medical corps, most of which had been in the war-torn South Pacific. His parents had moved to a farm while he was in the service, and he had visited them only once before being sent overseas. When he returned, he had no desire to become the pharmacist for which he had been trained. It was the farm rather than the pharmacy which represented the kind of life he wanted to lead. He says: "It seemed to me that on a farm you were on your own. You could do things that perhaps you wanted to do, you could say things you wanted to say, you could think things you wanted to think. And you could work for yourself and have close family ties." Ken needed to be with family. Like him, a high percentage of the young men and women who arrived in Farmingdale came because their family and friends were farmers. Most were in their twenties or early thirties, newly married, and ready to start families of their own.

As the Eastern European settlers had denounced their early training and discarded their old traditional beliefs in exchange for new promising ideologies, so too did the American-born settlers in Farmingdale turn their backs on their early training and discard the professional careers for which they had been trained in exchange for the promise of a more meaningful life. They also elected to take "the road less traveled by," as Robert Frost put it.

Like their parents, they were not Zionists. Indeed, they went a step further and disavowed parochial ties to Judaism. Yet, they too were aware of the Zionist dream of returning to the land. Amour Morgan put it this way: "We made a deliberate choice to go back to the soil. There was a need to simplify, and living off the land presented a practical way of life." As farmers, they found that the pace of living was completely different from anything they had experienced before. "It was more harmonious with our needs. We had time for living."

If moving on the farm was a romantic effort by the Eastern European immigrants to go back, to recapture an environment they had lost forever when they came to America, the search for Utopia by the nonconforming Americans was equally romantic. The farm was the answer to their need for personal fulfillment. One poetic person said: "My husband and I settled on a farm in order to get close to the land, close to nature, and close to the strivings of the heart. It was a Rousseauian kind of existence."

These mid-twentieth-century Romantics saw the perfection of an ideal embodied in nature. Nature was free and spontaneous and ultimately orderly. The farm simultaneously provided a livelihood and a way of affirming old ethical and spiritual values: close family living, harmony with one's environment, and honesty in pursuing a life of peace. It offered cooperation rather than competition with neighbors, affirmation rather than aggression, and the freedom to entertain many different ideas.

These ideals were really not much different from those for which the Eastern European settlers searched. First-generation American children might simply have been continuing the search started by their parents. In a way, their settling on the farm was a wish fulfillment of the parents. The children inherited their mothers' and fathers' sense of alienation in the lifelong effort to make America a home. The idea of the land, the attraction of the land, the need to become rooted to the land is a motif repeated so often by the Farmingdale farmers that it must be interpreted in its symbolic and metaphoric sense. The land represented a way to become rooted to a place, to find a home at last. By their work on the farms and in the community, they made the land theirs.

The Eastern European parents wanted their children to make good in the American sense: to work hard and achieve status and material success. But they also wanted them to make good in the Jewish sense: to be, above all things, responsible human beings. Responsibility meant establishing an order of priorities for one's life.

For many of the Farmingdale settlers, the dream of becoming rich was at the bottom of the list. "The last thing we, or any of the people we knew, who came out at that time, thought of was aggrandizement of finances," said Dan Herson, who had been an advertising executive in New York. "When we bought the property, it was at a very poor and unprofitable period. Even the years before were kind of lean."

Few who settled on the farm envisioned a traditional life of luxury. One settler said, "Poultry farming was the kind of business that whatever you finally built up to, it was always just short of making a living." All who settled on the farm knew that the work was seven days a week, sometimes eighteen to twenty hours a day. All knew there was no real money in it.

Like the Eastern Europeans, most of the American settlers came on the farm with very few resources of their own and with many debts to relatives, friends, and mortgage companies. Many settled on primitive, run-down farms with few of the conveniences they had taken for granted in the city. Lou Harwood gives a graphic example. "When we arrived there was no toilet and no outhouse either. So, if you'll excuse the expression, we shared the common pile with the cows. In the bitter cold, we let the cows go first." But he still takes pride in the fact that he and his family were able to adapt. "We adjusted ourselves quite nicely, considering that we'd come from the city and were supposed to have been raised under civilized conditions. We not only adapted very quickly, but were pleased by the fact that we could adapt. I was sort of proud of that."

Some of the American settlers bought land that had no buildings, and they lived with family and friends until they could move into one of the rooms of the chicken house that was being built. They often lived in their chicken-coop apartments with their newborn infant children until they could afford to build a house. In looking back over their experiences on the farm, no one felt that they were in any way deprived because of these circumstances.

In common with their predecessors, few of the Americans had any kind of previous farm experience, except for what they acquired helping friends or family when they visited. Like their European counterparts, they learned on the job, by trial and error. But they had an advantage that the earlier settlers did not have. The newer farmers could ask assistance of those who were already established. They spoke the same language, they trusted each other. Advice was always gladly given, and the recipient could feel confident that the people providing it knew what they were talking about.

Living on the farm was not without its difficulties. The settlers made costly mistakes and suffered from the vagaries of the weather and the epidemic spread of chicken diseases, which multiplied in direct proportion to the growth of poultry farming. One man tells of how, as a young inexperienced farmer, he had carefully prepared for his first batch of baby chicks. He was thrilled by their beauty when they arrived. He tended them all day, nursing them "like a mother." But he did not know that he needed to check the brooder stoves at night. Two stoves went out, and in the morning he found a thousand baby chicks smothered in a corner where they had all huddled together to keep warm. "I cried," he said. "I couldn't get over those chicks dying like that." Another man talks of coming into his coops and finding virtually a room full of mature chickens dying of a disease he did not recognize and did not know how to treat. It became one of his recurrent nightmares while he was on the farm—that all the chickens would die while he stood by helplessly. Another man tells of his automatic fountains overflowing. When he came into the coop, he was in water up to his ankles while the chickens were crowding on the roosts. They then went into a serious molt and stopped laying eggs.

The farmers had to deal with frozen water pipes in the winter and with wells drying up and running out of water in the summer. They were victims of fluctuating egg prices influenced by futures trading in the commodity exchange, which few understood, and with escalating feed prices, which they understood all too well. Yet, in looking back over their experience as farmers, the American-born settlers claimed, when interviewed, that their lives on the farm were completely satisfying. In spite of the reverses, the hard work, and the parsimonious living standard most imposed on themselves, they enjoyed the farmer's life. For a while, at least, the farm measured up to their expectations.

All agreed that the greatest satisfaction came from having their small children near them at all times. Fathers spent as much time with their preschool children as mothers did; children accompanied them in the coops, on the range, on trips to the feed mill, even to meetings held during the day. One couple summed it up: "It was a lovely type of life for raising children. We raised the baby chicks and the babies." The close family ties developed on the farm could not have occurred in the structure of city jobs.

Next to the pleasure derived from watching their children grow, the settlers derived a great deal of satisfaction and pleasure from the cooperative spirit of the community. The social life consisted essentially of visiting friends and neighbors and talking. Occasionally, they would reach into their pockets and pool all the money they found there. If there was enough for everyone to go to a movie, they would go. If not, they enjoyed themselves talking.

As they sometimes pooled their money, so did they often pool their efforts and share heavy seasonal jobs. As one person explained: "Everything we did, we did communally. Everything. That's what made it so exciting. For example, when we had to take the chickens in from the range, we would all come together in the morning, and we would be working at each other's farms, bringing the chickens in from the ranges into the poultry houses. Then the woman at whose farm the work was being done would prepare a huge breakfast. This went on for years. It was a combined social and work experience."

The farm represented a way of life in which economic, social, and community life were inextricably intertwined. Farmers claim that there was very little distinction between living on the farm and living off it. Both were connected, and husbands and wives shared the same experience. One man put it this way: "It was not something you did from nine to five and then went home and forgot about. When you went out with your friends, you would talk about new chicken diseases and what can be done about them. It was not gross or in violation of social ethics. It was part of our living experience. It pervaded our whole life. Twenty-four hours a day, seven days a week. But it was lovely."

Amour Morgan feels that the cooperatives established by the farmers grew out of the shared work they did. She compares the experience in Farmingdale to that in Israel. "It was very, very exciting. There was communal living on all levels. It's almost like in Israel."

Although many shared romantic notions of an ideal life, the common economic and social experience in fact made Farmingdale a cohesive community. And the noncompetitive nature of farming contributed to the cohesiveness. Dan Herson put it into perspective as follows:

We all had the same problems. We all got our livelihood from the farm. Low egg prices did not discriminate. The high cost of feed did not discriminate. The competition with the southern egg did not. Actually, it made the farmers a more cohesive group. They tried to stay on and continue farming. The simple thing is that you were not in a competitive business. If I were selling automobiles, the next guy down the road wouldn't tell me how he sells his cars, he wouldn't tell me how he sets up his bookkeeping system, he wouldn't tell me what he pays his help because we were competing with each other. But here we were not. If my chickens were sick, it was a danger to the whole community. If my chickens were healthy, then my neighbor was happy. If mine were sick, he expected his would be too. It was to his interest to see that my chickens stayed healthy. The man who bought my eggs—it made no difference at all. He could take my eggs, he could take my neighbor's, he could take all the eggs. And if he didn't, then someone else would. We were not competing with each other in sales. If I found a place where I paid lower prices for feed, I would tell my neighbor. I had no advantage in keeping the information to myself. I wanted to see my neighbor prosper, because if he prospered, I was better off. This is why we got along so well in Farmingdale, even if we didn't get along socially. We had much in common. We were all trying to succeed at the same thing.

The sense of shared living and working experience and of a shared economic status created strong personal links among the American-born settlers, as it did among all the Jews of Farmingdale generally. Although most started poor and few became rich from the farm per se, they did become successful farmers. That is, they built up their farms and their poultry capacities, applied the latest techniques and technologies to their operations, and developed their flocks for maximum production. Many expanded their farms by genetic breeding of stock and adding hatchery facilities.

During the 1940s, poultry farming was a fairly sound business; eggs brought good prices, and the farmers prospered. Most of the farmers were able either to modernize their homes or to build new ones. Contrary to a stereotype that Jews were not good keepers of the land and not concerned with maintaining their farm buildings, the poultry farms of Farmingdale were for the most part modern, neat, efficient, and well run.

In the mid-1950s, the industry, composed primarily of small family farms, started going downhill. The recession after the Korean War, the withdrawal of government price supports, escalating feed prices, and the competition of the southern and midwestern eggs shipped by improved refrigerated transportation all contributed to the demise of small poultry farms. The death of the small-scale industry resulted in the disintegration of the community.

The American-born settlers, like the others in Farmingdale, had to consider other ways of earning a living. A few tried retailing their own eggs and poultry. In more than half of the American farm families, either the husband or the wife worked off the farm. In some families, both worked away from the farm at other jobs in an effort to keep the farm going. Joe Zelnick is typical. He said: "When we not only went into debt, but used our salaries to support the farm, we finally decided it was no use. We had to give up."

Of the total sample interviewed, 70 percent paid off their farm mortgages, but most left their farms with very little money. Land prices were very depressed, and what capital had been acquired went into the futile effort of keeping the farm. Although Joe Zelnick's finances qualified him to declare bankruptcy, he refused. "It was probably the American ethic or something. For years, month after month, I paid off the FHA. At the end, I got a letter congratulating me on my valiant effort in paying the debt off."

Some of those who had paid off their mortgages or did not owe much money were able to keep their farms and continue living in their homes. However, they had to find other jobs. Some went back to previous professions, such as teaching, social work, or engineering. Some went into farm-related fields, such as selling feed or real estate. Some took courses and prepared themselves for entirely new professions or businesses, including insurance, real estate, construction, manufacturing, and retailing. Most made more money in their new ventures than they ever could have imagined making on the farm.

When asked which life they prefer, the American-born settlers invariably point out the problems associated with the farm but then ultimately say that the farm life was a better way to live. The following excerpt from an interview with Louis Harwood, who, with his brother Milton, became a successful manufacturer, illustrates the point.

Q. What do you like better, manufacturing or farming?
A. Well, farming is a relatively insecure business. It's pleasant, but it's insecure. The risks are much greater.
Q. As a life-style, what do you prefer?
A. Farming is a simpler way of life. But it's fairly risky in the sense that you are subject to the ravages of the weather, disease, and markets. You can't control your prices. There are variables which you can't control. All kinds of problems. Diseases. Others. Prices were good enough for a while to cover a lot of these problems. From 1950 to 1960 was a miserable, very difficult time. Many farmers became teachers or salesmen. But some of them went to work on the roads, cleaning the roads. Many of them lost their farms.

Q. But most of them stayed in the area.

A. Yes. Very few went back to the city. They had lived here long enough so that they felt they belonged here. They didn't leave. But farming as a way of life is attractive. It is still attractive to me as a life.

Q. In spite of the fact that it is a seven-day-a-week job?

A. Well, I was used to that. That didn't bother me. But the insecurity always bothered me. I always had the sense of insecurity. I came and I was poor, extremely poor. And things got better, but there were so many things you couldn't control that you always had to fear. They [the fears] come back to haunt me again. You always had the fear that if enough things went in reverse, you'd find yourself back where you started from. And that was true of many farmers. They ran into very serious difficulties. Went into bankruptcy, foreclosing. . . . Farming has a romantic sound to it, but it's a tough way to make money. A tough way to make a living. But a good way to live. A healthy way to live. A good way to relax. It makes you feel good.

The Eastern European settlers envisioned their farming efforts as stretching beyond them. They saw themselves preparing something meaningful for their children to inherit. They provided a means for their children to become farmers and to live close to the family. One of the earliest settlers, Harry Sokol, pointed out the fields of his former farm and said: "I was hoping my son would want to take this over. But he wasn't interested." And with some resignation, "Well, what can we do?"

The American-born settlers, who came to the farm in pursuit of spiritual values and a more ideal way of life, were searching for a better life for themselves but did not see life as farmers as necessarily good for their children. Amour Morgan now says that, just as her parents had directed her to be a professional, so too did she direct her children: "I don't think there was anything which my husband and I did for our children that would in any way direct them into farming. I don't think it was anything very interesting. There were other professions. Our orientation from our parents was for us also to be professional. You see, the value system that we gave our children was the same value system we had been given."

Lou Harwood feels that the Jewish farmer was not deeply rooted to the farm. He was not there for a long enough time to have the impulse passed on to the children:

If Jews are on the farm for one generation, they can't very well develop deep roots. If they had been on the farm for three or four generations, then you begin to develop a culture which is based on the farm, and you have generations of children who live in terms of farm life. But one generation of refugees in the depression does not a culture make. It doesn't have enough of an opportunity to take root. And the kids grow up in a situation where the parents are not quite sure whether they can make a living on the farm, and meanwhile these kids hear that you can do well as a teacher or something like that, the tendency is to take off. The normal tendency is to leave the farm, go where you had the most opportunities. Most opportunities were in the educational field.

Still another couple feels that their children would have considered it uncivilized to remain on the farm. "We gave them too much exposure to the cosmopolitan. We always took them to the city," they said.

In evaluating the farm experience and their lives in the community, the American settlers recalled an episode of their lives that occurred some twenty or thirty years previously. Inevitably, there is nostalgia in memory, and perhaps some romanticizing, as time takes the edge off pain and intensifies the feelings of previous joy. The farm experience came to them at a time in their young married lives when worlds were opening up and everything was possible. No one interviewed regretted the time they spent on the farm. On the contrary, they all felt their lives were made richer by the experience.

Amour Morgan, who is now a practicing psychiatric social worker in New York, in evaluating her years on the farm, recognizes that the perspective of time enables her to articulate from a mature reflective point of view what she and her lawyer-husband were looking for as young married people. Asked what her expectations of the farm were, she replies:

> A way of life, a value system, a place where you could live by your own ideals without having to get caught up in a kind of pragmatic, commercial system, where you would have to make basic choices between conflicting values. People are always faced with one set of ethics valid for business, and another set valid for personal living. On a farm, your own individual farm, there was much more of an integration of those two sets of values, an integration where you could set up your own life and live by a value system that had meaning to you.

When asked whether she was consciously looking for a particular value system or life-style at the time, and whether she in fact found it, she replies:

> I don't know. And if you asked us that question at that point, I don't know if we would have been able to verbalize it then. There was something about the experience, the sharing, the being, the doing, and the sense of integrity. I don't think I could have put it this way then. Now, I feel that the experience gave each of us an opportunity to find ourselves in a way that

would not have been possible if we had stayed in the city and gotten into one kind of channel. There was a sense of well-being when we came on the farm—even before that, when we came to visit my parents for weekends. And there was something meaningful, fulfilling, expressive in being out of the pressure of a big city and making it. A sense of freedom, a sense of freedom from tension. I don't know how else to put it. Free of tension. This does not mean that we were free of problems.

Amour Morgan is aware now that she and her husband, Wolf Morgan, were propelled onto a farm by their own search, however poorly they could define it when they were young, and by a restlessness that was in them. Restlessness was a salient feature of the Farmingdale settlers. In trying to account for it and for the insatiable curiosity in the community, Lou Harwood said:

> It's a small community with a lot of interaction. And a group of people with the average intellect on a fairly high level. An intellectual life, such as we had here, is an intellectual life, basically, of people who have a tendency to nonconformity. With all our mistakes here, with all our mad movements developing, there's a basic discontent, there's a ferment—there always was. There's an urge to search, to question, to argue. The Jews who came here to develop farms left all kinds of problems and tried to move out into a new field. They were pioneers. People who are pioneers are far different from people who are settled, those whom you might call the bourgeoisie. It's a different type of personality. You are dealing with a completely different type of person. You see, we came here because we were discontented in New York. We were looking for something. In that sense we were ready to probe, to ask questions. And many other people left whatever they were doing and moved out into the unknown. Farming was the unknown.

In comparing pioneers with immigrants, and Jewish immigrants with other immigrant groups, Lou Harwood feels that pioneers and immigrants have in common a certain aggressiveness and assertiveness that those who remain behind do not have. People move because they are discontented and, having moved, become more aggressive, more progressive, and accomplish more. "The Irish who came here during the famine did remarkable things. The Italians who left Sicily accomplished far more when they left than the Italians who stayed put. And the Russian Jews who left their relatives behind, who were willing to take a chance and plunge into unknown America, were a more aggressive, lively, and stimulating group than the ones who remained. The Jews that left the city were lively radicals."

Whatever the needs and concerns of the American Jews in settling on farms, they had certain things in common with their Eastern European predecessors. They came with limited financial resources, they assumed huge debts, and they lacked substantive experience as farmers. But very few had the anxieties which troubled the others. There was an identifiable and viable Jewish community when they arrived, although many of these modern American Jews felt they did not need the identification.

Most had grown up in the Jewish ghettos of New York City in the 1920s and took their own Jewish identity completely for granted. Their parents had rejected traditional Judaism with its accompanying rituals for secular worldly ideologies but had maintained their cultural identity. Their American children ignored the old cultural ties and interested themselves instead in new American thoughts and ways. In New York City, an accepting, nonthreatening Jewish community, they had no need to affirm, assert, or defend their Jewish ties as did the American-born children who grew up on the farm and attended the rural schools.

Some of the young city Jews, particularly the more radical ones, seem to have had the opposite need—to get beyond the narrow parochialism of the Jewish world and experience America as Americans. They knew Yiddish because their parents and grandparents spoke it at home. But to them, Yiddish was out of tune with the modern world, an anachronism in America. These Americans did not feel a need, in the first third of the century, to identify with specific Jewish institutions. Such identification was not in keeping with the new humanism to which they subscribed.

Settling in Farmingdale, in a Christian milieu, some of these farmers tried hard to fit in with the new world to which they came. Morris Freedman, a friend of one of the farmers, has written about them: "There is a good deal of ambiguity, not to say confusion about their [Jewish] attitudes. . . . In general, the members would like to consider themselves, at least on the broad social level, as typical integrated Americans (in the fullest 'white Protestant' sense) with no distinguishing marks; but their way of thinking and living does stamp them as different, and the fact is that they are rigorously set apart from any portion of the Gentile community."[4]

The farmers described here are admittedly unusual and atypical. Not only were they intellectual and radical, but they were also willing to take risks, to try something new, "to venture into the unknown," as Lou Harwood phrased it. They left the conveniences of the city, the security of their friends and groups, the comfort of familiar institutions, in search of a more satisfactory life for themselves. Whether they found it or created it is beside the point. They say that the farm did, in fact, measure up to their expectations, and no one feels poorer for having had the experience.

6

Displaced Persons

T he term "DP," for displaced person, is one that is often used
to refer to the survivors of the Holocaust in Eastern Europe, many
of whom lived in DP camps set up for them after the war. They
were called DP's in Farmingdale, and I designated them here as
such. Settling in Farmingdale in the early 1950s, when the farm economy
was already beginning to collapse, the Holocaust survivors were not farmers for an extended period of time, as the others were. But they did form a
discrete group of settlers and have to be so considered.

When interviewed, the DP's were asked the same questions asked the
others about their farm experiences: why they chose farming; why Farmingdale; what their expectations were for themselves and for their children; and how well the farm lived up to those expectations. They were all
eager to help, but like the others, they answered only the questions they
wanted to answer and repeatedly dodged others. Questions about how
much money they had when they came onto the farm made them uneasy,
as did questions related to political issues. Telling me it was better for me
if they spoke in English, most insisted initially on speaking the language
that was obviously difficult for some. I replied in Yiddish that I was comfortable in both languages, but they paid no attention and continued in
their efforts to communicate in what they thought was my language rather
than theirs.

The talk about the farm lasted for a very short time, however. Soon, with a remark like, "When I think of what I have been through, I cannot think that the farm was hard," the conversation immediately shifted and centered on the war experiences of the speaker. Without their being aware of it, their language shifted to Yiddish, from which I have translated their quoted remarks.

In interviewing this group of people, I was drawn into a very dark and dismal world as these new farmers relived their experiences for me, or for themselves. Their survival is the most significant fact of their lives, superseding all others. Their memory of the horror is part of their daily lives; their feelings of guilt, an overwhelming burden. Yakob Kawer expressed it for all: "From seven children, I was the only one that remained. I don't understand it. Is it a miracle? I am not smart, I am not intelligent. I admit it myself. I am not educated. I am nothing but a plain simple person, a worker. Why did I remain?"

The DP's talk about their experiences constantly when they get together. They remember them during the day, when they are busy at other things, and at night, when sleep is impossible. I arrived at their homes wanting to learn about the farm experience. Instead, I became an ear, an innocent who had to be instructed. From those who had been partisans, I heard grisly stories of Jews digging their own mass graves, falling down with the others when the guns rang out, crawling out from beneath stiff bodies wet with blood in the dark. And running, running, running in the woods—for years, never seeing the inside of a house or having enough to eat; watching companions and relatives die; leaving them without burial in order to keep on running. Malke Metterman's experience is typical of those who survived this way in the woods.

We ran among the cornstalks. Just where we were running, we did not know, we just kept running. And then we heard the screams of the people gathered together at the mass grave. We kept on running. Finally, we fell down. I must have fallen asleep. When I awoke, it was night, and the whole sky was covered with red flames. I can't forget those flames. . . . We stayed there a whole night. . . . I prayed to God, "Make me a cat. Let me be a dog." Childish thoughts. . . . My brother said, "Better the wild animals should get us rather than those men." We turned back into the woods. . . . We began to get swollen from hunger. . . . The woods were seven or eight miles deep and full of wild animals. We no longer were afraid of the wild animals. We were like them. We learned how to eat wild grass. We had no more strength, we couldn't walk, we crept on our hands and knees. We were in the woods two years. . . . A mother who was with us was killed. We took off her clothes, shut her eyes, and tried to cover her. We waited until her baby died also. Then we tried to bury them together. But we couldn't stay. We left a sign for others to find, and we kept running.

From Yakob Kawer and others who had been in the concentration camps, I heard how human beings felt themselves reduced to the status of animals.

> We had to stand outside on the snow, all together, for hours and hours. We couldn't take care of ourselves. If we had to relieve ourselves, we had to do it right there, one on the other, just like animals. That's the way it was. Completely like animals. On winter nights, it was very cold and we were freezing. We took snow to rub ourselves, because we were dying there. One started to scream, "Shma Israel. Take my soul. Shoot me. Let me go." We stood outside in the cold without shoes, without anything, in a line, and we saw no end.

These were the memories that came to the farm in Farmingdale with the survivors of the Holocaust. Small wonder that nothing on the farm seemed hard after what they had been through.

According to estimates by the Jewish Agricultural Society, 10 percent of the survivors of the Holocaust who came to America settled on farms. Indeed, new farming communities were created whose population consisted entirely of Jewish survivors and they became part of Danielson, Connecticut; Mays Landing, New Jersey; and Fresno, California. The figure contrasts sharply with the estimated .06 of 1 percent of the American Jews who went into farming in 1945.

All of the farmers interviewed in this group hated New York City, where they landed. They could not adjust to its ways and were convinced "it is not a good place to raise children." Like those that came before them, they too were searching for a better life. They left the city at a time when the farm economy was already beginning to go downhill and the prognosis for economic success was quite slim. But on the farm they found the independence they needed, while not feeling pressured to acquire English language skills. Gradually, they became accustomed to America.

No doubt the wartime experiences of the survivors influenced their decision to "go rural." Tina Benson, during an interview, summarized it for the group. "We felt too tired, too sick and disappointed and everything. We had very little energy. We did not feel like starting all over again, especially in a place like New York. New York was shocking to us."

The farm reminded her of the life she had before the searing events of the war destroyed everything for her. She expressed the same feeling expressed by some in the first group of settlers, those born in Eastern Europe, for whom the farms were also a reminder of the homes they left. "I loved the farm life because it reminded me of home. The hard work was balanced by the tranquility I could have. Mine was a choice of going back to a state of life I had over there. It is always a nostalgic feeling with people who are old. We came here old—old in experiences—and very, very tired." Tina Benson and her husband, Harry, were in their thirties when they came to America. She continues: "We wanted our old way of life, a life where *shabos iz shabos un zuntig iz zuntig* [Saturday is Saturday and Sunday is Sunday]. Alright. We have to attend to the chickens. We can do that. But we don't have to put up with the hoo-ha everyday."

One man, speaking for himself and friends who settled on farms after the war, said: "We had to flee New York. We needed rest in our lives. We became farmers, not because of any kind of idealism, but for psychological reasons. The work and the life were good spiritually." Another agrees. "For people who need to rest their nerves, the farm is very good."

None of those interviewed had any experience in farming, although some of their families had been involved in businesses peripheral to agriculture. They were grain dealers, lumber merchants, cattle dealers, and fur traders. Like the other Jewish farmers of Farmingdale, they learned by trial and error once they settled. Some consulted books, but most asked questions of their friends and neighbors. And all were visited by agents of the Jewish Agricultural Society, who advised them.

Few of those interviewed had anticipated leaving their homes in Eastern Europe before the war. Malke Metterman talks of life in her town of Shatsk, Vollin, in Czechoslovakia. "We had a poor life there. OK. But it was a *balabatish* [mature, comfortable, orderly] life. The family was close to each other. No one had it in mind to leave, to go to America. What for? It's true, we had one pair of shoes a year, one dress a year. But whatever we had was all right. We didn't expect to have much more."

None of the DP's interviewed believed that their towns were of any particular interest to the Nazi army, or that humanity could become so debased as to indulge in mass killings of innocents. Tina and Harry Benson came from the small town of Grzymalow, near Ternopol, then part of Poland. In 1939, her family did not know what the Germans were doing because, in her words, "there were no radio announcements about it, nothing written in the papers, there were no TVs. We were not aware of what was going on." When the occupation occurred, they never dreamed that the Germans would be interested in them other than to force them to work. "We thought they will drive us to work. So what's the big deal? We'll work for them until the war will be over." They knew nothing of the mass killings until an eyewitness came back to report to them. And they found it hard to believe.

A man came and told us that Germans shot a group of Jews on the spot. They dug big holes, big graves for them, and they shot them just there. Two or three people ran away, and they came to our town and told us, and we laughed. We said it's untrue. We did not believe them because it was something unheard of. To gather men, women, and children to a mass grave and just shoot them, kill them and cover them with soil. It was something we could not believe. And somebody else came, and somebody else. But by then, we were enclosed.

Like others before them, many of the DP's came to Farmingdale because friends or relatives were already there and because there was a recognizable Jewish community. Many described the community environment as being more Yiddish then either New York, where some had tried to settle, or the later towns to which they moved after leaving the farm.

Max and Bessie Bielory came to Farmingdale in 1948 and had one good year before the economy started to go *barg arop* (downhill). Hard workers both, they made a living from the chickens for eighteen years, renting out other farms and managing fifty thousand layers. Max also retailed his eggs and speculated in real estate. Today they live in what they call a California House in Bradley Beach, a community with many Jewish residents. They feel that their life in Farmingdale was more Yiddish than in Bradley Beach. For one thing, they say, the United Jewish Appeal was much more active and central. And the community was more coherent because of the common experience of its members. "We all shared the same hard work. We came together in the same Community House, and spoke the same language."

Most of the new immigrants had to supplement their incomes and support their farms by other work. Although they continued living on the farms for many years, most gave up the farm operations and concentrated instead on earning a living in whatever way they could.

The Mettermans, however, continued to farm long after most others had abandoned farming. They settled in 1953, after spending four years in Erie, Pennsylvania, where relatives had a junkyard. When they visited relatives and friends in Farmingdale, they "fell in love with the area" and wanted a farm for themselves. They found it to be a very good place to raise children, and they found a congenial group of people that provided the kind of Jewish environment they did not have in Erie. They both worked very hard and by careful management were able to make a living. Indeed, they were among the last settlers to give up poultry farming in Farmingdale. Their farm was in continuous operation until 1979, when Morris Metterman died. According to their testimony, life was hard but pleasant enough. They felt it was too late to do other kinds of work. They needed the quiet, the unhurried atmosphere, and the closeness of the family made possible by working and living on the farm.

Yet, while the DP's expressed the personal satisfactions that they derived from the farm, they expressed surprise when asked if they would have been pleased if any of their children had become farmers. Several said that farming is not Jewish work. "To be honest, it's not a Jewish life," said Malke Metterman. "For us newcomers, it was good. We didn't know the language; we were anxious to come to something, and so we worked hard. But for the children, who have been to college, to settle on a farm? Never!" When questioned about her meaning of a Jewish life, she answered, "Farming is a very hard life. A Jewish life is easier." Another farmer, when asked the same question about expectations for children, said his son is "an intelligent man. He would never become a farmer." The children of the DP's, like the children of the Americans and the Germans, were expected to do other things.

THE WEDDING OF KHAYKE SASS AND YAKOB KAWER IN A DISPLACED PERSON'S (DP) CAMP IN TRANI, SOUTHERN ITALY, 1949. THE SASS FAMILY, ORIGINALLY FROM SKALAT, POLAND, WAS REUNITED IN THE DP CAMP AFTER THE WAR; KAWER WAS THE ONLY ONE OF SEVEN SIBLINGS TO SURVIVE THE NAZI HOLOCAUST.

Like the other groups, the DP's also had their own social organization—the New Americans Club. Although they were dues-paying members of the Community Center and attended the synagogue services with more regularity than most of the farmers, they did not socialize at the center. Like the German settlers, they preferred not being involved in the political wrangling and, at a time when the whole community was polarized, managed to keep neutral. Bielory explained: "We were friends together. Politics is another thing." Another man said: "The Jews of

Farmingdale were Communists. I myself had no connection with politics. I stayed away from it."

The New Americans Club raised money to help its members as needed. Malke Metterman talks about a responsibility the members felt for each other, much like the earliest settlers felt. They both go back for models to the Eastern European *kehile* (community) and to the organizations to take care of Jewish needs. "If a farmer needed a loan, we gave it to him. If someone were sick, we helped. And if we needed more, we made a special collection. Jews are ashamed to ask for money, ashamed to admit their need, but it is a bigger embarrassment not to lend money to someone who needs it. We were very active. We made parties and dances, and we got together three or four times a month." Malke Metterman stresses that the DP's needed to feel independent, but if they needed help, they preferred accepting it from each other rather than from social agencies. "No one went on welfare, no one begged for handouts from others. We knew how to work night and day, if necessary."

THE SASS FAMILY
CELEBRATES A PASSOVER
SEDER IN THE DP CAMP,
TRANI, ITALY, 1949.

Like the other settlers, many bought their farms with funds borrowed from relatives who loaned them money without interest. They take some pride in the fact that they repaid their debts. "We've paid back all our debts, educated our children, made them weddings, and helped them get started."

As in the case of the German-born settlers, generations lived together, and all worked on or off the farm. Salla Silber was in her sixties when she settled with her son Isaac and daughter-in-law, Adele. As a young woman in Poland, her family had been rather wealthy. Unlike many women of her age, she had received an education in Russian and Polish schools and by private tutors. Married to a banker, she had an affluent life-style. Her two sons had attended the gymnasium and were starting careers of their own when the war broke out. In one week, "from Monday to Thursday," she reports, "I lost my father and mother, my husband, and one son. All murdered by the Nazis. I shared my sons with Hitler. He took one and I took one."

Like many of the DP's interviewed, the wartime experience of the Silbers forms the central core of their everyday memories. Yet Salla Silber retains her essential dignity. Not only is her mind sharp and clear in spite of her eighty-plus years, but remarkably, she is still forward looking. Sadness is not her posture, nor does she allow past tragedy to pull her down. In speaking about the traumas of life, she is philosophical. "There are other things, too. I can't forget the past, I don't want to. But yet, I do look forward to the weddings I'll be attending. We'll all get dressed up and have a good time. Life must go on."

Like his mother, Isaac Silber, or Izzy, as he is now called, has a certain serenity and stability about him. He recognizes that their survival was a major triumph. Out of a city of eighteen thousand Jews, they were among thirty to survive. But in the telling of the gruesome episodes connected with their survival, there is place for neither gloating nor bitterness nor even sad resignation. Izzy Silber deeply regrets the poor show of resistance, especially by the young Jewish intellectuals he knew. Yet, he understands that much of the apathy was related to the extreme physical deprivations which they suffered. "We were reduced to a state of animals. We were encased in filth, and starved. We were walking skeletons. We reached a point when we didn't care if we lived or died. We just didn't care."

Interaction with the non-Jewish community was limited in all of the groups who settled in Farmingdale, but it was practically nonexistent for both the earliest Eastern European settlers and the later DP's. Surprisingly, these two groups were also the least sensitive to evidence of anti-Semitism. Perhaps in comparison to what they had experienced, they could dismiss what they saw or heard in Farmingdale as negligible. The DP's were aware, however, of a certain prejudice toward them by the other Jews of the community. They were correct in their perceptions. The following statements by some American-born Jewish farmers concerning the DP's are typical.

- They were not involved with their farms. They were not very good farmers.

- They were not methodical like the Germans were, but they made money.

- Money was very important to them. And they were not afraid of hard work. They worked harder than any of the other farmers. But they were tremendously conniving people. Maybe that's what helped them survive.

- Other DP's would tell me: "Don't listen to any DP. They all lie."

- From a business point of view, they were horrible to deal with. Cheating was typical of them, because in the old country that was their way of functioning.

These remarks are full of old stereotypes about Jews and immigrants, especially about those who become successful. The prejudice that the newest Jewish immigrants to Farmingdale and to America encountered from Jews already established is similar to that experienced by the first large wave of Russian immigrants at the end of the nineteenth century. The DP's do not pay too much attention to the criticism.

Most did very well financially after leaving the farm. All of those interviewed paid off their farm debts. They are now in manufacturing, building, real estate, or small independent businesses. Like the earlier Jewish settlers, they remained in Farmingdale or in one of the nearby towns, close to the people they knew on the farm.

7

Descendants

Second- and Third-Generation Farmers

One of the stereotypes about Jewish farmers is that farming for Jews in America is a one-generational phenomenon. In fact, many children of the early Eastern European settlers became farmers themselves. Their farms were larger than those of their parents, their homes newer and more modern. They stayed on their farms as long as it was profitable to do so. However, they were not as romantic about the farm and the community as some of the earlier settlers were.

Their memories of growing up in rural New Jersey are filled with pain: school was unpleasant, life was lonely and isolating, work was hard, and their adult responsibilities were onerous. They feel they missed the innocent adolescent experiences they are able to give their own children. Warm memories of the community are juxtaposed with their sense that the world they knew was narrow and confining.

These descendants did not make the initial choice to come to the farm; their parents had made it for them. Having started school in New York City, they had to adjust to a drastically different kind of school environment. In school, they felt abused and persecuted.

Herbert Wishnick reports that though he loved learning, he hated going to school because the boys jeered at him and threatened to beat him. "I used to have such fears about going to school. I was all knotted up inside every morning. The kids hated me and Jews in general." When the

teacher invited him to join the Safety Patrol, some boys told him he had better not, if he knew what was good for him. Sophia Peskin said she was singled out for persecution because she was Jewish. "I couldn't tell my father. What could he have done? And besides, he was so busy." Jack Grossman reports that his father instructed him to fight. "They used to call me 'kike' or 'Jew-boy.' I had a lot of trouble. My father told me that the next time I had any trouble, I should pick the biggest kid and just kick him in the stomach. I said, 'That's not fair.' He said, 'Look, it's not fair what they are doing to you.' So I kicked the biggest guy around, and I got the hell beat out of me. But the other guy had a black eye, and nobody ever touched me after that."

Deborah Snyder Kern lived in a religious home and had a different kind of problem. She stayed home on all the Jewish holidays when other Jewish students did not. When the teacher questioned her as to why she was staying out when the other children were not, she always felt on the defensive. Christmas observances, prayers, and references to Christ all made her feel uncomfortable. More than anything else, she resented Jewish children who tried to pressure her to sing Christmas carols.

School difficulties were only part of the problem. The children felt extremely lonely and isolated on the farms. They had only their siblings to play with; no one remembers having any Christian friends. The weekend Yiddish school was their only link with Jewish friends. The parents, aware of their children's loneliness, compensated by sending them to city relatives during winter and spring vacations. It was not unusual for thirteen-year-old children to travel alone to New York City or to the Bronx or Brooklyn to visit a grandmother or an aunt who might have lived with their families in a three- or four-room apartment.

All the children had chores to do on the farm; they had no choice. The family depended on their work. On the produce farms, the girls planted, picked, and graded vegetables, and their brothers worked on the fields. On the poultry farms, the girls packed the eggs with their sisters or mothers; their brothers collected the eggs, fed and watered the chickens in the coops and on the range, and helped to house the birds.

Rarely did these children participate in any after-school activities. There were none for the elementary school children, and the bus schedule of the high school students made it impossible for the older children to participate. Nor could their parents transport them, even if they wanted to. They had no automobiles. But even if they had, it is doubtful the children could have taken part in dramatics or the newspaper club or the school orchestra. Their work was necessary on the farm. Herbert Wishnick grew to dislike the farm intensely because of it. "I always felt a great sense of responsibility. I felt I had to work with Pop. When we were kids, we were always much older than other kids our age," he said.

Jack Grossman also talks of the burden of responsibility he was given. Moving on the farm with his family, who could not speak English, the young boy kept the farm records, wrote the checks, and was the interpreter for the salesmen who came into the yard. At ten years of age, he had to place the orders for feed or explain to the salesmen what the problems were. Every time he was away, he felt uneasy because he was needed at home.

The general stereotype is that Jews encourage their children toward higher education and make any sacrifice so they may have it. Perhaps that was true in urban centers where there was a range of free colleges and universities. But there were no free colleges anywhere near Farmingdale, nor did the early farmers see any particular value in higher education, especially if it implied a sacrifice on the part of the family, which was already sacrificing a great deal for the farm. Jack Grossman lists the jobs his family considered good: "In our family, the best job was a school-teacher, next came a county agent, and then a mail carrier. These were thought of as elite positions." He wanted to be a county agent, and he got a free-tuition scholarship at Rutgers University when he graduated from high school. But he could not go; the family could not spare him. In addition, his father, forgetting what he previously considered as a good job, encouraged him to stay on the farm so that the family could increase the poultry capacity.

Herbert Wishnick finished two years of college, which he attended at night, after his farm work. He felt terribly confined in Farmingdale and on the farm, but his father discouraged further education. Eventually, he enlisted in the army. When he returned, his veterans' benefits would have enabled him to finish college, which he wanted to do. But his father, asking "What do you have to learn in college?" urged him to stay on the farm. Feeling guilty for having been gone for two years, he stayed, disliking the farm and feeling frustrated and constrained. When he married, he moved onto a farm of his own because, he says, "By then, I could think of nothing else to do."

Frieda Metz says her parents could not possibly encourage schooling after high school. "They had barely enough to live on. Their expectation was for their daughter to work, to go out and get a job until we got married." Her feelings about the farm are complex. She feels now that farming develops a certain kind of sensitivity that is lovely. Yet she does not want her children to be farmers. "It's a nothing kind of thing. You lose contact with books and things like that." Although most of the Eastern European parents of the first-generation farm descendants did not encourage their children toward higher education, a high percentage of these descendants returned to school as adults and received some form of supplementary or higher education.

Like so many of the people interviewed, the people who grew up on the farm show great ambivalence toward it. Simultaneously, they say and imply opposite ideas. The first child born in Farmingdale of Jewish parents, Celia Sokol Fisher, looks back on the experience and says it was just a beautiful life—a beautiful, wonderful way to live—something which cannot be duplicated or replicated in this, the "now" generation. "In those days," she says, "we didn't have such essentials as TVs or stereos. And we had fewer problems. Who could afford an allergy? The highs came from good homemade food, not drugs. Nor did anyone worry about gorgeous clothes." Yet, in spite of her idealized look backward, she reveals a sense of childhood loneliness at the isolation, retains painful memories of anti-Jewish feelings, and remembers her embarrassment at the family's poverty.

As a child, Celia said she was happy just to have a friend visit. There were so few people her age. At age ten, she had to assume work responsibility. She washed and ironed all her own clothes, quite a chore in a home that had neither running water nor electricity. Daily living was primitive, and with no central heating, the house was always cold. "The link to the outside world was the Sears Roebuck catalogue."

The most important institution in the lives of the Jewish children was the Yiddish *shule* (school), which met Saturday night and Sunday morning. "We had nothing else. It was like a quicksand," said Celia. This remark immediately was followed by a lovely memory of sledding down a slope on the farm.

At yet another point, she said that as a child she was a prisoner on the farm, "there was so much work to do. The work consumed forty-eight hours in one day." When she started school, she knew only Yiddish, and the other children called her a "dirty Jew." Her childhood memories include seeing the Ku Klux Klan in white sheets march past her home and hiding terrified with her mother under the bed. Although as a child she did not need "gorgeous clothes," she remembers that when she started high school, she felt her clothes had no style. She also remembers how the children—Christian and Jewish—of Freehold (the town where the high school was located) called the Farmingdale kids hayseeds. Having no Christian friends at all, she yet saw the tinsel of Christmas and thought of the fairyland from which she was excluded. She also knew her mother hated the farm and missed the city, while her father loved it very much and was happy, after his chores, simply to sit and read all night.

Like Celia Sokol Fisher, the majority of the children growing up on the farm found life both lonely and creative. At the same time, they still feel frustrated at not having had the opportunities that other young people enjoyed. Yet, most admit to learning invaluable discipline and skills on the farm that could be transferred to other areas.

In addition to providing training for later work, the farm and the community also presented situations which demanded quick thinking and an assertive approach to problems. When chickens had to be vaccinated against diseases, everyone had to pitch in to do it. When a farmer was sick and his farm had to be taken care of, the community mobilized immediately to help. It was very hard to stay on the sidelines and maintain a passive role. This approach to life helped most of the farmers succeed in other occupations when they left the farm. They had to do something else; there were no other options.

Many of those interviewed commented on the resiliency of the Farmingdale Jewish farmers and on their ability to rise again after adversity.

"Nothing could knock them down and keep them there," said one man. "They didn't stay down for long. If something failed, they went on and tried something else."

While this was true of most of the farmers, it was particularly true of the descendants who went into farming almost by default. All went into other occupations after they left the farm; almost all became financially more successful in their new occupations than they could possibly have become on the farm. As do the others, the farm descendants also point to close family relationships as being one of the prime advantages of growing up on the farm. As children, they knew where their parents were, what they were doing, and that both were available in the event of an emergency.

In addition to experiencing the work of their hands and close family relationships, those raised in Farmingdale also had the feeling of the relatedness to the whole community. Going to meetings with their parents, performing Yiddish plays for the community at the center, interacting with the people who came onto the farm, helping with the work on neighbors' farms—all of this reinforced the sense of an extended family which the community provided. The center was a second home, a place where young and old felt at ease and comfortable.

Working on the farm alongside their parents, the young people felt involved in the world of their mothers and fathers. They had a stake in the future, a sense of rootedness to a specific place, a sense of belonging to a community which they knew very well and with which they identified intimately.

Dorothy Friedland Hamburger came to the farm with her parents very early in the community's history, in 1925. As a young woman, she refused dates with local men and dreamed only of the time she would leave Farmingdale for the cultural riches of the city. But she married Aaron Hamburger, who also grew up in Farmingdale. After some years in the city, they came back to their childhood home. She contemplated spending the rest of her life there and then passing the farm on to her children. "This is my place. Here I have lived, here I have grown. It was my parents' place; it'll be my kids' place. It is my point of reference," she said.

The feeling of living on the land and having it as a heritage to pass on made the farmers and their children became a significant part of America. The roots their parents planted took hold in the children, who could belong to the whole of the American experience in a way their European parents and grandparents never could.

Later Descendants

The descendants of later settlers, the children of the 1940s, grew up on their parents' farms amid continuing discussions and growing awareness that the small farm was no longer a viable way of earning a living. They heard stories of farmers going bankrupt and of people being forced to leave their farms. They knew their own parents had to seek supplemental ways of earning money or had to go into totally different occupations. It is not surprising that they were not encouraged to become farmers; small, family-farm operations were no longer a realistic option for anyone.

But even if farming were an option, the chances are that these young people would have received encouragement to prepare for the same professions that their parents had rejected or been denied the opportunity to try. The parents searched for a more meaningful life-style for themselves and, in becoming farmers, took a radical route to attain it. But they expected their children to go to college and become professionals.

"My generation saw farms going under," said one man. Another felt that his parents envisioned a better life for him than that offered on a farm. "There was never any question in their minds but that I would leave the farm and go elsewhere and do something better than farming. Better means not working seven days a week, and not getting my hands dirty."

The views of these later descendants are illustrated by excerpts from the interviews of two of them: Joseph Tenenbaum, now a cardiologist in New York, and Daniel Boyarin, a rabbi and professor of Hebrew literature at Berkeley. Both were born in Farmingdale in 1946 and both left in 1964 when they went to college. Joe is the son of Eastern European parents who moved directly to Farmingdale after arriving in America from Lithuania in 1936 and 1939. Dan is the son of American-born, city-educated parents who settled in Farmingdale after the war and his father's return from service. Joe's father had cousins in Farmingdale; Dan's father is a nephew of the first settlers. Joe and Dan were very good friends in Farmingdale, attending the same schools and belonging to the same social groups.

Joe's views about Farmingdale and growing up on the farm are similar to the views expressed by the generation before his, the children of parents born in Eastern Europe, who grew up on the farm and became farmers themselves. This is not surprising, considering that Joe is a second-generation American. Like those born a generation before, he too felt that the world of Farmingdale was very narrow. Dan's impressions, on the other hand, seem to be colored by the same kind of romantic perspective as that of the American-born settlers. Dan did not stay on the farm and never thought that he would. However, in looking back, he sees the experience as having been ideal and idyllic in many ways.

For Joe, growing up in Farmingdale was restricting. He knew at an early age that there "was another world out there," and he responded to opportunities "to break out of the mold of Farmingdale." He added, "You have no idea how restrictive the life could be." But for Dan and his sister, Janet, the farm meant "freedom, opportunities to explore, no need to be supervised." They both talk of special places to which they could retreat, a spot in the woods, a special path. Dan acknowledges that as a child he was jealous of city children, who had immediate access to a whole group of other children living in the same apartment building. Nevertheless, he says that he was more than compensated by the privacy the farm gave him and which he claims he needed.

Joe became aware of the Christian world in which he lived when he started school and learned for the first time about all the other kinds of holidays. Dan became aware that his community in Farmingdale was unusual when he attended a Labor Zionist summer camp and the other youngsters had never heard of Jewish farmers.

They both appreciate the unique qualities of the community. But Joe perceived differences as a young man on two levels: the personal and the communal. Aware that his foreign-born parents were not in the mainstream, he felt somewhat of an outsider, "an interloper in a different kind of community"—in contrast to Dan, whose parents were American born. "They had grown up in New York and they knew something about American culture. My parents were not rushing to become Americanized. At the same time, I was spared a lot of the crap of American culture by my parents' approach to things. In the end, I appreciate it."

Dan, recalling a provincial New England town where he went to college, sees Farmingdale as a special kind of community.

> In Vermont there was a great deal of isolation, a kind of insularity which was really not true of Farmingdale. We had a special kind of environment both from a Jewish point of view and a general point of view. The fact that it was a farming community set up a certain kind of interaction, both with the land and nature and the community as a whole. In addition, it was a very highly articulate, intellectual community. On the one hand, it was not a typical farming community as we imagine farming communities to be; and on the other hand, it was not typical of a city intellectual community either.

In high school, Joe had his awakening to the fact that Jews were as diverse as everyone else; he met "Jewish jocks and Jewish guys who went to Staten Island on Friday nights to get drunk. I could see that one could be part of the mainstream of American culture and still be Jewish."

In college, both came up against middle-class values in students from "places like Great Neck." Joe was grateful that the people he knew in Farmingdale did not put any emphasis on acquiring material things. Dan feels the Farmingdale life-style provided a full, meaningful life. "My friends who grew up in Great Neck have a sense of their parents' friends as shadows, empties. In Farmingdale, everybody was full, full of some-thing—full of misery, full of pain, full of life, full of humor, full of liveliness. None of them, nobody, was a shadow. Nobody was empty. Life was meaningful, in some way, to everyone around me." For Dan, the people made a community, not just in name, but in feeling. "If a commu-nity is a group of people sharing a common fate, well, this was a group of people sharing a common fate. When the egg prices went down, every-body was hurting. When the egg prices went up, everybody was happy. It was a community with a cultural context, in which ideas and concepts were a very important part. The people worked hard in earning a living, but they were also involved in the world of politics and in the world of ideas."

The community was an important influence both on the lives of these two young men and on their self-definitions. When the old center was vacated and the Torahs were removed in a ritual ceremony to their new home, Joe left a busy schedule as a resident physician in New York to come back to Farmingdale and be a witness to the change. "It meant a lot to me. It was so integral a part of my life, and so symbolic. Because for me, Judaism, as I had grown up, has become in many ways, tradition. And that's what it will be for me for the rest of my life. Tradition. I don't feel I'm the same kind of Jew as I would have been if I had grown up in a different community."

Dan's life was also greatly influenced by the center and by attending the religious observances in the simple, wooden synagogue.

The holidays were really very special and had a profound influence on my later development. One thing that made them so special was the *davening* of Walter Tenenbaum [Joe's uncle, trained as a cantor in Europe but a farmer in Farmingdale]. As he *davened*, I heard the haunting melodies of the com-munity's *davening*. There was a community. It had a *nusekh* [a liturgical form]. One of the very strong influences that led me to eventually become religious were these very strong positive feelings about religion that I gathered from the services in the *shul* [synagogue].

An Eastern European custom of raising money for charity through the auction of *aliya*s, or honors to the Torah during high holiday services, was retained by the Jewish farmers and became a memorable part of the service for the young people who attended.[5] The old tradition appealed to their high sense of idealism and drama. The money raised on Rosh Hashanah invariably went for the maintenance of the synagogue, while that raised during Yom Kippur was reserved for a Jewish cause unrelated to center needs: orphaned Jewish children in Morocco, a poor yeshiva in Jerusalem, an old-age home in New York City, and so forth. Dan describes the *aliya* auction.

> This was a very holy piece of tradition. People were bidding and competing with each other for the right to perform a *mitzva* [good deed], for the right to give money to *tsdoka* [charity]. This kind of competition, this kind of auction, was really something very beautiful and a precious piece of tradition not to be either scorned from a modern perspective or made light of. It's a unique bit of culture. Those men used to sit there and bid up *maftir yona* [the eighth honor] into hundreds of dollars—tremendous amounts of money, and then give the *aliya* [honor] away.

While Joe and Dan share similar views on many issues, they have completely different ideas about the meaning of farming to the Jewish farmers of Farmingdale. Joe feels that the farmers were motivated by their need to make a living rather than by romantic notions of a return to nature.

> To our parents, the return to the earth, the turning back to the communes of the late 60s in our generation is so bizarre. Because it's such a shitty way to live. That is not to say that they knew all the problems associated with farming before they came on the farm. It's not easy. It's not so romantic, getting out as I did sometimes with my father at ten o'clock at night because a water pipe had just burst in the chicken coop and turned the relatively dry manure into a muck, a filthy, smelly manure. And having to dodge huge rats that were running around underneath the chickens was not fun. That's not romantic, it's just plain hard work. I think everyone who got into it realized it as such. Obviously, the fact that they were living in a peaceful country area compensated for the fact that they were working harder, did not have a day off, did not have a vacation. As far as I'm concerned, it was a business.

Dan's perspective is that of the much more idealistic farmers. To him, those farmers had made a choice for a positive quality of life. "Nobody was just making money—getting and spending. Everybody was living. That was a value of the people who chose to live on the farm. They didn't expect to get rich from it, I presume. In other words, the people chose this kind of life. They were choosing a life in which the quality of life was going to be more important than success in the conventional sense."

The later descendants did not experience the same difficulties in school which so troubled the earlier ones. Although a few claim to have encountered some anti-Semitism, the division between the Christian and the non-Christian worlds was much less rigid than it was for others. Christian and black friends were the rule rather than the exception.

The views of the later descendants interviewed coincided almost exactly with those of their parents when they spoke of the advantages and disadvantages of living on the farm. They said life on the farm was often lonely and isolating, especially for those who lived in a remote part of the township. They were aware that their parents worked hard, had no vacations, and never seemed to earn very much as farmers. They were sensitive to the fact that the farmers were at the mercy of the marketplace, over which they had no control. As for the work itself, the young people felt that it was not particularly stimulating. At the same time, they realized that their parents led lively intellectual lives after the farm work.

The advantages of living on a farm, they said, came in the form of a heightened awareness and appreciation of nature and of the outdoors generally. They particularly enjoyed the sense of space they had on the farm. They felt that farming itself is good productive work. All appreciated the fact that they always knew where their parents were, and all enjoyed those times when they worked side by side with them. "We didn't experience the same kind of 'generation gap' in college that our contemporaries talked about," said Dan. Most of the later descendants found the experience of growing up in Farmingdale positive enough so as to want their own children to grow up in a similar type of environment.

Part 3
The Life

8

Living Together

Acommunity is an abstraction; men, women, and children are
real. "Community" implies a group of people who live in a specific place, share similar institutions, and assume some responsibility for each other and their institutions. American
Jewish farm communities have in common the fact that they were isolated
enclaves within a larger and often alien culture. Those that lasted an extended period of time were not communal; their settlers did not necessarily know each other before meeting in the rural byways where they
bought small inexpensive farms and settled with their families.

The new farmers brought with them their Jewish pasts, affiliations, and
assorted experiences. The challenge they faced was to create that which
they needed to make a living and to live a Jewish life. Early settlers
warmly welcomed new Jewish families and tried to help them adjust as
painlessly as possible, because their own futures depended on it.

Although most of the early settlers were not religious, they observed the
major Jewish holidays together, conducting services in those homes large
enough to accommodate ten or so families. Their cooperatively purchased
Torah was carried from home to home for religious services that they conducted themselves. After the services, the families shared a meal and
sometimes remained together overnight, sleeping in one of the outbuildings if there was no room in the house. The need for a central meeting
place was obvious to all.

HARRY SOKOL AND
FRIENDS, AROUND 1940.
SOKOL WAS ONE OF THE
EARLIEST SETTLERS IN
FARMINGDALE.
DESCRIBING THOSE EARLY
DAYS, HE TOLD THE
INTERVIEWER, "IN THE
BEGINNING, THERE WERE
SO FEW OF US, WE
HUDDLED TOGETHER
LIKE BABY CHICKS UNDER
A BROODER STOVE."

The abstraction of "community" which spread over many miles required a reference point, a place for the few scattered Jewish families who needed each other to meet for mutual support and warmth. The Jewish Community Center, built in 1929 by the donated labor of the farmers, became the center for the spiritual, social, cultural, and economic life of its members. It was a place where ideas and ideals flourished and socializing occurred regularly. Their simple small building was a synagogue, a social hall, a meeting place, and, primarily, a school for the children. For approximately half a century, the building served its purpose. When it closed, one woman, with tears in her eyes, summed it up: "Our center was small and unpretentious. But it had a heart and a soul, and it was a home."

Harry Sokol, who settled on a farm with his wife and parents in 1925 and who is one of the very earliest of the Farmingdale farmers, describes the socialization of the Jewish settlers in the community. "When there was about ten of us, we were getting together very often because there was nowhere else to go except one to the other. We met in homes. We met in Hamburger's and in my house." He talks about the decision to build a Jewish center.

We had to organize a school. We had five, six, seven kids. All of them were 100 percent Yiddish speaking. The National Council of Jewish Women sent us a Yiddish teacher from New York; Sore Tsuker was her name. She came to us, and she traveled around to the other communities too. She would spend a couple of hours a month with the kids. It started off every two weeks, but she didn't have enough time to come. She was teaching the kids Jewish folk songs and dances, but it was done in homes—whoever had a bigger, more comfortable home. And the teacher slept overnight in the farmer's home. But it was bothering us. How much can you do in some-body's home? So we started making plans for a building.

The local bank and the Jewish Agricultural Society loaned the farmers money for the building on a very liberal repayment schedule. According to Sokol, the bank president viewed the loan as an investment in the future. "He felt that a Jewish Center would attract more Jews. Because more non-Jews were not going to buy farms in Farmingdale. There was nothing to buy. It was poor land. But Jews will come, and there will be room for business, there will be room for real estate development. To the banker it was a paying proposition, and he gave us at that time one thousand dollars to start off. The Jewish Agricultural Society gave us three thousand dollars."

Having obtained the funds, the farmers had to decide on a suitable location; each farmer wanted it to be near his home and offered to donate a portion of his property for it. Finally, Peskin's offer was accepted, since he was the first farmer and ultimately responsible for helping most of the others settle.

The farmers pooled their talents to erect the building. Only one, Max Friedland—an experienced tool and die maker as well as a carpenter, elec-trician, plumber, and mason—was paid for his work. In 1929, the corner-stone was put into place. On January 4, 1930, the state of New Jersey, county of Monmouth, issued a certificate of incorporation to the West Farms Jewish Community Center. It was signed by eleven farmers. Mr. Hyman Grossman was designated the first president, and Mr. Harry Sokol was the first secretary.

Without plans or blueprints, the farmers built a structure of approx-imately forty by fifty feet. A memory of the Eastern European shtetl *shul* may have served as a model; the building with its scalloped roofline was reminiscent of a little Polish synagogue. Since funds were limited, the center was built on stilts, or pillars, above the sandy ground, allowing for the future digging of a basement. Like most of the farmers' homes, the building had no central heating, water, or indoor toilets. It did have elec-tricity and a potbellied stove which was vented through a window. Evidently, the farmers did not know much about venting stoves properly; many early farmers remember the black smoke that backed up into the room during a meeting.

Reuben Alfus described the center when it opened. "It had four walls and a roof—and that's all. No plumbing. A pot-bellied stove with a chimney through the window. In the basement was a dirt floor. That was our center."

Simple as it was, the farmers started meeting there every Saturday night. Harry Sokol sent out postcards that began with the Yiddish for "you are invited." The message ended with the words "unzer tsenter is varem un likhtik yeder shabos bay nakht." Translated literally, the message is, "Our center is warm and bright every Saturday night." But as Harry Sokol pointed out, *varem un likhtik* means more than simply "warm and bright." The words carry connotations of inner warmth and spiritual enlightenment.

To the Peskin children and the others, the "four walls and a roof" were like a palace, and the opening of the center was like a miracle. Sophia Peskin recalled her feeling: "Maybe it's not much now. By today's standards of temples and edifices, it may even look like a shack. But to us children then, it was like a fairy palace."

The entrance to the building was on the north side. Directly opposite, on the south side, was a raised stage for which the women had made a curtain and embroidered on it *JCC,* in large yellow letters. The stage was an integral part of the building, serving as a natural setting for the plays put on by the children and as a platform for the entertainers and lecturers from New York. Years later the stage was removed to make room for the expanding crowds during religious holidays. It was replaced by portable wooden boxes used only when the occasion demanded. It was a sore loss. Practical as the change may have been, portable boxes without a curtain are just that—plain wooden boxes.

Along the eastern wall was the *oren-kodesh.* It was a very simple affair: two wooden doors in front of a recess where the Torahs were housed, an eternal light suspended from the ceiling, and prayer books on shelves within the recessed area. On the western wall was a side exit door opening onto a rickety wooden staircase.

The furniture consisted of wooden benches made by the farmers. Tables for parties were made of boards laid across sawhorses and covered with white paper tablecloths. When laden with food made by the women, they looked like magnificent banquet tables.

"Mir zaynen geven gevaldig groyse oremeh layt, nor fun altz hoben mir gemakht a simkha [We were excruciatingly poor people, but we made a holiday out of everything]," said Reuben Alfus. "We were all poor; we were all in misery," said another farmer looking back, "but we all shared something, and it was beautiful."

On both a personal and a communal level, the farmers shared work, ideas, joys, sorrows, pleasures and piques, and the cost of running the center. When the Community Center in Farmingdale opened, the New York Stock Market had already crashed and the country was going through one of the worst depressions in its history. Money was extremely tight for everyone, especially for the new farmers of Farmingdale. Harry Sokol's optimistic message read that the center was warm and bright every Saturday night, but for six months the electric bill was not paid. Finally, when the electric company was about to shut off the service, the farmers scraped together the ten dollars they owed, and the lights stayed on.

Poor as the early settlers were, they did not dwell on their poverty or hardships. Rather they exuberantly celebrated on every possible occasion. A particularly joyful celebration took place when they were finally able to raise enough money to replace their wooden handmade benches with chairs. "What a beautiful party we had," said Helen Friedman. When central heating was installed years later, there was another party. And in 1946, when the basement was finished and furnished with running water, a kitchen, and two bathrooms, the party knew no bounds.

The community got together every Saturday night for meetings, parties, or cultural events. Families came with their small children, who fell asleep in their chairs or found a place under the wooden tables to sleep. The infants, wrapped in blankets, were placed on the stage, where they slept within sight of everyone. The farmers entertained each other by reading or reciting Yiddish stories and poetry; those who could, played instruments. They always sang their Yiddish songs, evocative of the old home which they left.

When the farmers exhausted their resources for self-entertainment, the Culture Committee arranged for lecturers and entertainers to come from New York. The whole community supported the programs. Sholem Asch, Peretz Hirshbein, Maurice Samuels, B. Z. Goldberg, Martha Schlamme, Ruth Rubin, Eli Mintz, Joseph Buloff, and hosts of others from the Yiddish cultural world of New York City brought their talents to the Jewish farmers of Farmingdale, Toms River, and Lakewood. In 1934, the famed Vilna Troupe put on a play in Lakewood, and car pools were organized so that the Farmingdale people could attend. Though living was rather isolated, there nevertheless were significant cultural ties to New York.

In 1938, Dr. Boris Shegloff, an immigrant physician-psychiatrist who needed to earn money until he could pass the American licensing examination, became the weekend Yiddish teacher for the children. He organized a series of popular lectures for an appreciative audience of adults, on subjects ranging from male menopause to the poetry of Peretz, Yehuda Halevi, and Baudelaire. Discussions followed the lectures, and the farmers' challenging and searching questions caused Shegloff to advise Louis Touretzky, a friend in the city: "Go see these farmers and the way they live. They are not at all what you think farmers are like. They are intellectuals and live an intellectual life."

Touretzky took Shegloff's advice, came as a guest to Hamburger's Evergreen Hotel, attended some meetings at the Jewish Community Center, and, as he told it, saw a group of farm families sitting *bay sheyne badekte tishn* (at tables spread beautifully [with food]). They were passionately discussing philosophical problems. Touretzky was so impressed that he sold a profitable fur-importing business in New York and settled in Farmingdale as a poultry farmer because the quality of life he observed appealed to him.

Soon after the Community Center was built, various organizations were formed in response to the varied needs of the settlers. Helen Friedman gave a chronological account of the organizations. "First was the Community Center itself. We needed a committee to run it. Then was the congregation. We bought land for a cemetery, which is very important for a community. We organized a school for the children and a poultry association for our business. But we also had a cultural life. We arranged lectures, shows. We had a women's club. We had so much in the community; it was marvelous, and we did good work. We had a great life in the community."

In spite of the professed secularism of the early settlers, their first co-operative purchase was a Torah; their first gathering was in commemoration of a religious holiday; and their top priority was to provide for the Jewish education of their children. Very soon came the need for a Jewish burial place. In 1935, within a few short years after the center was built, the members bought a parcel of land from the Freehold Workmen's Circle Cemetery so that they might have their own place.

Michael Hamburger kept a daily journal of his activities, and the journals from 1937 to 1948 which survived give the most accurate record available of the activities of the Jews of Farmingdale in the early years of the community. They chronicle a community of people very much aware of what was happening to one another—both the *simkhe*s (happy occasions; "We decided to have music at the Cohen's anniversary party") and the tragedies ("Today was the funeral of Mr. Lehrer"; or, "The Garfinkles had an accident. We need people to donate blood").

The journals show the lively interest of the farmers in ideas. "Philosophy class evening tonight. We are beginning to understand each other." (The philosophy class evolved from the Spinoza Society the farmers had earlier organized.) Or, "Dr. Shegloff lectured on psychoanalysis. Everyone enthused." And they reflect a community of poor Jewish farmers with a strong commitment to social justice who ended many of their meetings by collecting money for various causes: orphaned children, poor families, destitute rabbis ("We collected $11 for a needy rabbi"), non Jewish service organizations like the Red Cross, and Jewish institutions like their own Yiddish *shule.*

THE OLD JEWISH
COMMUNITY CENTER,
FARMINGDALE, ERECTED
IN 1929. THE CENTER
WAS BUILT BY THE
FARMERS THEMSELVES,
WITHOUT ARCHITECT'S
PLANS OR BLUEPRINTS.
BENJAMIN PESKIN
DONATED THE LAND, AND
THE PROJECT WAS
FUNDED BY THE JEWISH
AGRICULTURAL SOCIETY.

Hamburger's journals also show a community in transition. Settled initially by Yiddish-speaking Eastern Europeans, the community ultimately had to come to terms with increasing numbers of non-Yiddish-speaking Jews. The use of Yiddish presented a source of friction in the late 1930s for a growing membership which no longer was a homogeneous group of Eastern European immigrants. The language was attacked as being irrelevant and out of touch on all sides. But in January of 1938, the Ladies Club resolved, after a heated debate, to speak Yiddish; a month later, the center membership also voted to continue conducting meetings in Yiddish. Hamburger, who accompanied his wife to meetings of the Ladies Club, records that both meetings were full of dissension.

Although most of the American-born settlers understood Yiddish, many felt that the language stamped the character of the meetings and of the community as parochial—not part of the modern world. They either agitated against the use of Yiddish or withdrew from participation in the center.

In March 1944, the argument erupted again, and Hamburger records his feeling of futility. "Last night I was to the Ladies Meeting and Mrs. Alfus started a discussion about shall the ladies speak in Yiddish or English? I listened and admitted to myself that Yiddish is losing ground fast and I am beginning to realize that it's a pity the time and energy lost in trying to preserve it."

Even as the journals provide an ongoing history of community living, they also give a profile of a remarkable man and his family. In 1922, Michael and Tillie Hamburger settled in Farmingdale with their six-year-old son, Aaron, at the suggestion of the Jewish Agricultural Society. They were anxious to get out of the noxious city and raise their child in "good, clean air." Vegetarians, they were members of the Nature Society, whose titular head was Dr. Lieber.

The Hamburgers borrowed money from friends and relatives and bought a sixty-acre parcel of land containing an old house without indoor plumbing. They had no intention to farm, nor did they anticipate that they would open a hotel, a rooming house, and finally a "bungalow colony." They simply wanted to leave the city.

Hamburger, who had worked in a raincoat factory in New York, got a job in a similar factory in Red Bank, New Jersey, and commuted by train from Farmingdale, but he liked neither the job nor the chemicals to which he was exposed. A year later, he and his wife decided to open their large house to roomers. The following year they converted again to a vegetarian hotel called Hamburger's Evergreen Hotel, and attracted a clientele from their New York vegetarian circle.

From Passover in the spring through the Jewish holidays in the fall, they catered to guests. Working with a minimum staff, Tillie did all the cooking and cleaning while Michael repaired, enlarged, and beautified the place. But he was perpetually preoccupied with worry about how the family would survive the winter without an income. In 1937, Hamburger notes sardonically, "An old house without improvements cannot be converted to a fine hotel." The "hotel" became a rooming house, and the business was extended further to include a bungalow colony.

Hamburger obviously had a vested interest in promoting the area as a fine vacation spot. He became very active in the West Farms Lake Association and spent much time and energy trying to collect money for it. In 1939, Hamburger begins to worry about the impact of the nearby poultry farms on his business. He writes: "A new worry is bothering me now. The Greenbergs have begun to build and their chicken coop will stink up our place." In 1947, he is still concerned. "Garfinkle bought that strip of woods and he is clearing it and I'll have additional smell. No good." He concludes, "Since I am not a farmer in the right sense, then I don't know whether I'll remain long in the country."

In his journals, Hamburger notes the thoughts he had, the tasks he accomplished and had yet to do, the bills he must pay, and the status of his financial situation. The items reflect the personal hardships and concerns of a family working very hard at their business, always afraid that their debts will overwhelm them. They constantly needed to juggle money—taking from one pocket and putting into another—and, when things were really tight, borrowing from friends. "Borrowed from Harry $50 so I can pay to Weissberg his $70." And always repaying his debts with a sense of relief.

His entries are usually objective, written with restraint, and, for the most part, stated tersely. Occasionally, however, he confides his despair or elation to these private pages. One very touching entry concerns his wife's returning from the hospital. "This afternoon it started to rain, so we were sitting upstairs and talking. We were talking of the day she came back from the hospital. She was very excited, her hands were trembling when she was dressing to go home, and when she was home and upstairs in the bed, she was still flushed with the excitement of being home again. A little later she was crying, but it was out of joy. And every now and then she asked me, 'Am I really home?'" Another very brief statement only hints at the pain he felt at seeing his only child in the army. "It's much easier to see other men's sons go away to war."

There is an ongoing concern with health—his, his wife's, his family's, and that of the people in the community. It is one of the motifs in the books. He records community information such as "Jackie Grossman had 104° yesterday"; or, "I want to record here that Bernie Friedland had an accident and it's 6 weeks now since he is in bed with fractured bones in a few places."

Another theme in the books concerns community disputes. He records or hints at arguments that occur in and out of the center, often with his own sense of frustration at the contentiousness of the farmers.

A patient, rational, and moderate man, Hamburger was often called upon to serve on the Arbitration Committee.[1] So sensitive was the work of the committee, however, that formal records were not kept. Hamburger only hints at the work with an entry such as, "Helped to settle a dispute between HS and his father."

Concerns for his personal finances and his family's welfare and concerns for the community and its welfare parallel a concern about his family in

Eastern Europe. In 1937, when the community tendered him a fiftieth birthday party, he reflects on the nice things said about him and concludes that he does not deserve the praise. Thinking about his family in Europe, he regrets deeply that he cannot "spare a cent for them." But as the news from Europe becomes more and more ominous, Hamburger becomes involved in a continuing collection within the community for the Joint Distribution Committee and for the United Jewish Appeal. Never having a cash reserve in the bank, he, like many of the farmers, borrows money from the bank in order to contribute to the appeal or gives postdated checks.

In 1942, Hamburger is again working at a raincoat factory that has a government contract. But the work is very hard and taxes his health. At the same time, he is trying to make his rooming house and summer bungalow colony a paying proposition. In despair, he considers selling his place but is torn by the decision. "I hate to sell the place where I lived my most important conscious years of my life." He did not sell but doggedly persevered in his business until, shortly before he died, he realized a modest income and was able to pay off his debts.

Peskin was the pivotal figure in the formation of the Jewish Community Center, but Hamburger was certainly one of the central figures in it. He was intimately involved in the development of the center and in every phase of its intellectual, social, and cultural life. The nature of his business gave him more leisure time than the farmers had during the winter. His intense involvement in community life seemed to nurture and sustain him.

On December 19, 1939, Hamburger feels he must impose some limitation on his activities, which were taking so much of his time. He writes: "There are too many activities in our Community at present, which takes too much time away. I'll have to find a way to have a little more time for myself. I'll have to give up some of my activities at the Center. Just keep up the following work: (1) Once a month to the Workman Circle, (2) Twice a month Community Center meeting, (3) Once a month Verband." The schedule of meetings does not take into account the work Hamburger did for the organizations to which he limited himself or the many days he rode around collecting money for the center, the lake project, or the United Jewish Appeal. Nor does it consider his afternoon meetings or the frequent requests made to him to arbitrate disputes among the farmers.

The conflict between traditional Judaism and more modern philosophies was present in Michael Hamburger as it was in practically all the early settlers to Farmingdale. He professed to believe in the humanistic secular Judaism of Harry Waton, a lawyer-turned-philosopher. Yet Hamburger, although not a Zionist, helped to organize a Labor Zionist Verband in Farmingdale in 1938. He writes, almost by way of explanation, "I do it for Jewish traditional culture." And in 1946, when acute abdominal distress makes him fear that he is about to die, he philosophizes on the place of Jews in the world and, perhaps, the meaning of the Jewish community in Farmingdale. "We represent the idea of peace and brotherhood. But to the gentiles, we are a source of trouble, we destroy their equanimity. We must remain here as Jews, always a reminder to the Nations that they must become real Christians. They resent us and that's why they hate us."

When Hamburger decides firmly, in December 1941, that he will not run or be elected to any more offices, the executive board gave him the job of historian. Hamburger notes: "I'll have plenty of work on that. Anyway I'll take my time about it." If he wrote a formal history of the community, it is not extant. But his journals provide enough insight and information on community activities and history to earn for him the title of Distinguished Historian.

The Jewish community of farmers continued to grow, and the center had to be enlarged. In 1952, the charming front facade of the center, with its scalloped roof, was replaced by a modern square brick front that looked, in the words of one person, "like it was pasted on an old building." For the first time, some had a sense that the desire to conform to modern times was introducing something phony into the center, which had previously been simple but honest. In 1963, that feeling was reinforced for me in quite another way.

A professor of literature at Fairleigh Dickinson University was invited to speak at our center on some phase of American Jewish literature. The audience was lively and asked interesting questions. But while being driven to the bus, after the lecture, the professor expressed surprise at the life-style of the farmers and their Community Center. "After all," he said, "you are a middle-class group. I lecture in many Jewish centers, and they have swimming pools and gymnasiums and the kind of social halls you would be proud to go into. Your building looks so poor."

Hurt beyond words, I had to wait a few minutes to answer. "I am proud to go into our building," I said. But I was ashamed of a value system that drew its strength and pride from swimming pools and gymnasiums.

In the early fifties, the membership thinned considerably. The economics of farming had already forced many off their farms, and political wrangling and fighting within the community had intimidated, angered, or frightened others. It was a time when people were seeing Communists everywhere, especially among the New York radicals who settled in Farmingdale in the forties. The community became painfully polarized.

In fact, the split was symptomatic of a much deeper malaise. The economics of poultry farming was slowly signing the death warrant of the community of Jewish farmers. Young couples gave up farming and began preparing for other work. People went back to school to pick up additional training or resumed previous careers. Many continued living on their farms, but others had to sell to pay off debts. While younger people managed to go into other professions, many older people, who had looked forward to a pleasant retirement on the farm, had to accept Social Security or find new ways to live.

In 1970, the old center and its property, situated on a tract designated for a reservoir, was condemned and purchased by the state. In 1975, it was vacated. It stood for several years bereft of its innards until it was completely demolished. Not a trace remains of the "four walls and a roof," the "fairy palace," the meeting place of lonely immigrant farmers, the Yiddish school for their children, the center of the social life for young and old. Like a person who lived a good life, it deserves to be remembered for what it was.

9

Educating the Children

Yiddish Shule

Almost as soon as enough Jewish farmers settled to form a community, they made the Jewish education of their children an urgent priority. Although they were not religious, they were concerned about passing on a sense of Jewish identity. The teacher sent by the National Council of Jewish Women in 1929 could spend only limited time in each of the various Jewish communities she visited in central New Jersey.

About 1935, the Community Center affiliated with the Sholem Aleichem Folk Institute in New York to establish *Folk Shule Number Dray* (School No. 3) in Farmingdale. The first teacher was shared with Toms River, an older and larger Jewish community about twenty miles away. However, the shared arrangement was not satisfactory to Toms River, and Farmingdale soon was without a teacher. Harry Sokol substituted for three months, meeting with the children, reading stories, and singing to them until the institute sent Dr. Boris Shegloff to teach.

Like its predecessor, the Yiddish school of the National Council of Jewish Women, this school was also secular in character, and the language of instruction was Yiddish. Indeed, before the establishment of the State of Israel, no Hebrew found its way into the program. Texts were so edited that Hebrew words (which in standard Yiddish retain their Hebrew spelling) were spelled in Yiddish.[2]

The curriculum consisted of language arts (composition and reading),

Yiddish literature, Yiddish folk songs, and Jewish history. Twice a year, to celebrate the holidays of Hanukkah and Purim—historical holidays having to do with the fight against oppression—the children prepared an elaborate program that included dramatizations of Yiddish writers such as Sholem Aleichem or Peretz, recitations of poetry, and a program of songs. On the evening of the performance, the women prepared a home-cooked banquet. The programs were the highlight of the community's social life; people anticipated them for weeks and talked about them for months afterward.

The journals of Michael Hamburger have frequent references to the children, the *shule*, and the presentations. One entry in May 1937 reads: "The children of Farmingdale and Lakewood shule gave a concert and they acquitted themselves fine. The Farmingdale children made a hit with their clear Jewish talk." An entry in 1938 reports: "Perfectly successful party. The children excelled."

Dr. Shegloff was a remarkable teacher and is remembered as being a major influence on the lives of the children he taught, as well as a central figure in the intellectual lives of the farmers. Legend has it that in Vienna, before coming to America, he studied with Freud. Eventually, years after first arriving in Farmingdale, he headed the psychiatric department of a veterans' hospital.

For the children who attended the *shule* in 1935 and the years following, the weekend school gave them their only out-of-school socialization, a place where they could make friends. The Jewish children almost never played with their Gentile counterparts.

The students were divided into three levels of instruction—beginners, intermediate, and advanced. The classes were all held in the one large room of the center, one group at a time. Since the children walked or had to be driven to the center, all the children from one family arrived and left at the same time.

While one group of children was in class in one corner of the room, the other children amused themselves in another corner or, weather permitting, played games outdoors. Their exuberant energies and invented games were part of the background of Dr. Shegloff's class and competed with him for the attention of the students. Once, Shegloff hit upon a remarkable plan to control the noise: if the older students would be quiet and would prepare for their lessons, they would get a lecture on sex after the Yiddish recitations. After an amazed silence and embarrassed giggles, the older students became very quiet. And so, sex education in Yiddish was introduced into *Folk Shule Number Dray* in Farmingdale. It worked for some period of time but was not foolproof.

Antagonists of the children were the caretakers, an old Jewish couple named Gottesfeld who had moved to Farmingdale to be near their daughter and her family on a farm. Before they were hired, the women members of the center took turns cleaning the building. Upon assuming the responsibility, the Gottesfelds became zealous in their caretaking and considered themselves protectors of the building. Every day, and often twice a day, they walked the two miles from their home, pulling behind them a little homemade wagon piled with cleaning equipment and kindling for the stove. In spite of their having raised eleven children themselves, they had little patience for the antics of the young children congregated at the center two days a week. At first the old people merely complained to Dr. Shegloff, but then they angrily denounced the children who were making the building dirty. "Those wild animals," they would shout in Yiddish; "they leave their footprints all over, even on the ceiling." It was not unusual for an agitated Mr. Gottesfeld to burst in upon a class in session and berate a child in front of an exasperated teacher and amused students, who soon began to plot ways to upset the old man.

Another amusing game involved Shegloff's travel briefcase. He usually arrived from New York City on Saturday afternoon and was brought directly to the center for his classes and then spent the night at a farmer's home. On Sunday afternoon, he left directly from his classes back to New York. It became a game for the children to put gifts of various sorts into their teacher's briefcase to surprise him in New York. Once when an astonished Shegloff found a turtle which had wreaked havoc with his toothbrush, pajamas, and papers, he became an instant ally of the caretakers. The following Saturday, standing in front of the class with Gottesfeld at his side, the teacher yelled that Gottesfeld was right: he was not teaching children at all; he was teaching devils in his classes who really did walk upside down on the ceiling. And pointing angrily, he showed the children the footprints there—a mystery even to this day.

Yet, in spite of these occasional outbursts, the children loved their teacher and he, them. He had taken the teaching assignment initially out of his need to earn money, but he kept it long after he established a medical practice because of the children and his commitment to seeing them get a Yiddish education. He continued teaching until he moved from New York in 1942 to direct a hospital in Boston.

Shegloff took the Farmingdale children on weekend field trips to New York City, housing them in his own apartment or in those of Sholem Aleichem Folk Institute members. Believing that country children needed an exposure to the culture of the city, he took us to the Yiddish theater to see Maurice Schwartz perform and to the world's fair. He had us enter

Yiddish contests in competition with the New York children, and at least twice we presented our dramatic programs to New York audiences. After he left, he wrote frequent letters to the friends he had made in Farmingdale inquiring after each of the children he had come to love.

Shegloff's replacement was an equally gifted and sensitive man, Leon Chanukoff, a Yiddish novelist, literary critic, and artist. Like his predecessor, he too became devoted to the children, took them on excursions to New York, and entertained them in his own home. And he also left his mark on his students.

YIDDISH SHULE STUDENTS WITH THEIR TEACHER, DR. BORIS SHEGLOFF, OUTSIDE THE JEWISH COMMUNITY CENTER, 1938. THE AUTHOR IS TO THE RIGHT OF DR. SHEGLOFF IN THE BACK ROW.

The Yiddish school was completely self-sufficient financially. The teachers received direction from the New York office of the Sholem Aleichem Folk Institute, and the farmers received office help—the flyers announcing programs or meetings were mimeographed in New York and mailed from Farmingdale. The salaries and expenses of the teachers were borne by the farmers. In contrast to many of the city *shules*, Farmingdale neither asked for nor received any subsidies from the central office. Year after year, according to the institute records at the YIVO Archives, the executive board noted that Farmingdale was "a great success" and was "well established." The minutes of a December 17, 1942, meeting show Farmingdale as among twelve schools cited as having "a satisfactory number of children and materially very well organized."[3]

The only time the Farmingdale Yiddish school board asked the New York office for a subsidy was in 1952, when the farm economy was collapsing and the number of children interested in continuing a Yiddish education dwindled. The request was refused on the basis that only schools meeting a minimum of three days and taking part in all activities of the institute could receive financial aid or subsidies. Eventually, the Farmingdale farmers put on a drive for money to cover the year's deficit and raised the funds. When the school was officially disbanded in 1958 because of dwindling interest in Yiddish education as opposed to traditional Hebrew, a surplus in the treasury of $1,056.31 was turned over to the New York offices of the institute and was accepted, according to the minutes of February 6, 1958. By then the interest in the school had diminished; Yiddish lost in the battle with Hebrew.

Enough people argued that as the Yiddish language was growing obsolete, so were the efforts to continue the Yiddish *shule*. It not only failed to give non-Yiddish speakers mastery in the language, they claimed, but more seriously, it did not introduce the children to religion. Newer settlers in Farmingdale feared the children would grow up heathens without religion.

It was no longer possible in Farmingdale to go against the dominant trend in the larger Jewish community toward religious-oriented Hebrew schools. The Yiddish *shule*, which gave such pride to the earlier Jewish farmers and cultural treasures to their children, was without a home in the Farmingdale Jewish Community Center. After the creation of the State of Israel, a Hebrew school, more typical of the religious Hebrew schools in American small towns, was organized. Classes met at the center after school during the week and on Sunday mornings, permitting different age and class levels to meet at different times. Taught by wives of rabbinical students from nearby Lakewood, the school was almost entirely religious. Like other schools, it prepared the boys for Bar Mitzvah by teaching them to read Hebrew prayers and drilling the students on the meaning of religious holidays. The children rarely, if ever, presented programs for the parents or the community, who then became less involved with the school. In contrast to the warm memories of the former Yiddish school students, sentiments of those who attended Hebrew classes in Farmingdale were typically negative: "I disliked it very much. We had a series of dreadful teachers there, prejudiced, incompetent. I hated it."

American School

When the Peskins and Friedmans settled in the Farmingdale area, there were nine one- or two-room schools in the township.[4] The children were assigned to the school closest to their homes and either walked or were bused to school. For many native farmers' children, their education ended at the conclusion of the eighth grade. They were needed at home to work on their parents' farms. Nor did they start grade school until November, after the crops had been harvested. When the spring planting demanded it, they were in the fields rather than in their seats. Some youngsters never got beyond the sixth grade in school, and some never attained that level. "They were not so particular about your attending school. If you chose not to go, it was easier than it is today," said a native farmer who can trace his family roots in Farmingdale back several generations—his grandfather was born in the same house in which he was born.

Some schools housed all eight grades in one room. The West Farms school, for example, added a second room in 1926, and all eight grades were in one building. Mary Peskin was a student during its one-room days, and she described the building, which remained basically the same until it closed in 1939.[5]

> You walked into one of two doors, either the boys or the girls, and there was a closet or cloak room. You hung up your coat and lunch pail if you had one, and walked into the room. Each class consisted of a row of seats. When I was in the seventh grade, there were three of us in the class, and a couple in the eighth grade. We got better marks than the kids in the eighth grade, so we graduated into high school, and didn't go to the eighth grade at all. You were given work to do, and you did it at your seat while the teacher taught the other children. If you finished, you could listen or you could fool around. Usually, you'd listen; the teacher was strict. Besides, what you had missed from before, you could learn this time. I think it reinforced the learning.[6]

There was some benefit from having the same arithmetic, for example, repeated and reviewed for three years, as each class was introduced to the appropriate level while the others listened. But the endless repetitive exercises in addition, multiplication, and division bored the bright students. Nor were the slower learners advantaged by the system. The teacher had no time to spend with youngsters who could not grasp the math concepts or had reading difficulties. There were some twelve- and thirteen-year-old students in the fourth grade who could not read and were not motivated to do anything but think of mischievous tricks. But they rarely had an opportunity to carry them out. If the teachers learned anything in the normal schools (the teacher-training institutions) they attended, it was the necessity to impose rigorous discipline.

The teachers in those one- and two-room schools worked as hard as the farmers did. In addition to providing instruction, they swept the floors and fed coal and wood to the iron potbellied stove standing in the corner of the room. Boys brought in wood as necessary from the shed outside. A local farmer usually started the stove, but if he did not, the teacher had to build the fire herself when she arrived.

The school day started by warm-up exercises in the aisles when we first arrived in school. This was especially important if the stove had just been lit and the room was still cold. Exercises were followed by the Lord's Prayer and a Bible reading, usually by one of the students. The curriculum included gym, art, music, and all the traditional subjects, including history, civics, English, geography, and mathematics. The one teacher taught everything. At the end of the school day, she straightened out the room and put out the trash before leaving for her own home and her own family chores.

Every day a farmer brought a bucket of water to school, and the children drank from a common ladle. When the school acquired a ceramic cooler with a push-button affair on the bottom, students drank from a common cup.

STUDENTS OF THE WEST FARMS SCHOOL IN 1931. MARY PESKIN IS THIRD FROM LEFT IN THE SECOND ROW. ALSO PICTURED: JACK GROSSMAN (FIFTH FROM RIGHT, SECOND ROW) AND DOROTHY FRIEDLAND (FOURTH FROM LEFT, BACK ROW).

There were two recess periods, one in the morning and one in the afternoon, during which time the pupils put on their coats and hats and went outside to stand in line by either the boys' or the girls' two-seat outhouse. Into the outhouses they went, two by two. Under the circumstances, washing was impossible.

A local Parent Teacher Association chapter was organized in 1925, and one of its first purchases was a large kettle which circulated among the parent members a week at a time. Each was responsible for bringing it full of soup or hot cocoa to the school during that week and making sure each child had a cupful. The children ate the soup or drank the cocoa whether they wanted it or not. Some of the Jewish children, however, had difficulty with the soup; they were sure it was made with pork, which was never in their homes.[7] When the soup or cocoa was finished, the children wiped their cups with a handkerchief or a piece of paper and put them in their desks.

During the depression, the cup of soup was the only daily hot meal some children received. Jack Grossman, who attended the West Farms school in 1929, remembers children fainting from hunger in the winter and going to school without shoes in the summer. The communities around Farmingdale were far from affluent.

Every spring in the years 1922–30, all the school children in Howell Township, including their siblings and their parents, joined together on a large field in the town of Farmingdale for a May Day festival. The children prepared a calisthenics exhibition, decorated Maypoles, and did a Maypole dance in which they would wind streamers in a pattern around a pole. Each of the scattered schools in the township had its own pole to decorate in this way. According to Mary Peskin, each family brought a box lunch, and the families would eat together. "The May Day celebration provided one of the very few opportunities for the small number of Jewish families to interact socially wih the Christians," she said.

Another opportunity for social interchange between Christian and Jewish women was at Parent Teacher Association meetings. PTA meetings were held in the one- or two-room schools, after the children's schoolday ended. Among the Jewish women who belonged to the West Farms PTA were a few who had no children attending the school. Most of them could barely speak English. Nevertheless, they all took their turns with the soup kettle, wore their PTA pins proudly, and enjoyed the social outlet. Dressed in their hats and gloves, which they never wore to their own Jewish center meetings, they looked much like the Christian women going to church.

10

Organizing a Life

Because the community was new and did not have a social structure, the farmers were impelled to create one. In the city, their long work hours allowed for nothing but the daily struggle for subsistence. However, in their new rural homes, their participation and involvement with forming the institutions and organizations they needed to lead Jewish lives and the challenge to make it as entrepreneurs brought out capabilities in individuals which would have gone unnoticed in the city. The new immigrants found personal strengths they hardly knew they possessed. Before the Community Center was built, the settlers organized social, cultural, spiritual, and economic organizations. The Spinoza Society was one of the earliest groups formed in Farmingdale, before 1932.

As the community began to take shape, specific Jewish needs had priority, followed closely by economic needs. Eventually, forty or more discrete groups were organized, many meeting in the Community Center. Some, such as Jersey Jill, an egg-marketing cooperative, or the Allied War Relief, a wartime youth organization, were short-lived. Others lasted as long as the community and beyond: the Yiddish Emma Lazarus Reading Club, the Jewish Farmers Chorus, the Hazomir Chorus (the former was considered left-wing, the latter, Zionist), the Discussion Group.

Because a mutuality of interests drew people together, groups tended to be cohesive and enduring. For example, the Jewish Farmers Chorus, organized in 1952, met until 1978, when only a handful of its initial membership were still alive; the Discussion Group held meetings for more than thirty years. Although the community is gone, clusters of friends remain and consider themselves as extended families. People see each other socially and for holidays throughout the year and keep track of former members who have moved.

Meetings gave newcomers an opportunity to become integrated into the community. Almost everyone moving onto the farm came to the Community Center at least once and generally found a warm and accepting group.

George Brick, who moved to the area with his wife in 1947, said it was the first community they had experienced. "We never really belonged to any community in New York City. At the Community Center, everybody welcomed us, which was amazing because in the city you might know a few people in the same building, but you don't know anyone in the next. At the center, we met lots of young farmers and had so many functions to go to that we weren't lonely."

A few organizations are sketched below. No exhaustive history is intended, but enough are listed to give a flavor of the social life of the farmers.

Youth Organizations

The Yiddish *shule* provided instruction and socialization for the younger children in the early years. But the adolescents and young adults also had social needs. The Jewish Agricultural Society, trying to help Jewish farmers cope with them, sponsored a national organization called Rural Youth of America. A local chapter of the RYA was organized in Farmingdale in 1935, and it gave young people from dispersed areas an opportunity to meet.

Nonsectarian and interracial, the RYA clubs were in theory consistent with the ideal of a universal humanity which motivated most of the farmers. But in fact, only the Jewish youth attended the meetings. Mary Peskin Weisgold, who became the national secretary of the RYA for one year, remembers the group and their meetings. "We had older single men and younger ones too. It was a conglomeration of anyone who wanted to meet other young people. It was not especially set up for Jewish people, but it happened to be Jewish in Farmingdale."

In 1936, during the depression, the young people organized Friday night dances in the center, and a Works Progress Administration group of musicians played "for the proceeds of the hat." The dances went on for several years and became quite well known among young people in all the surrounding communities. One woman remembers them well. "The kids used to come from all over New Jersey, from Perth Amboy and Toms River. If we had to miss one of those Friday night dances at the Community Center, it was like a major crisis."

Conflict erupted over these dances, however, but not because they were held on the eve of the Sabbath. Friction resulted because there were blacks among the young people who came to dance. Some members, reacting to what they considered creeping Communism, objected to interracial dancing. Although they were not religious, they became passionate over the defense of the Sabbath and declared that it was disgraceful to hold dances then. The dances might have ended on their own in 1941, but the arguments and the discussions hastened their demise. For the young, it was a sore loss.

As one youth group graduated from adolescence to maturity, it was replaced by another youth group. The 1946 minutes of the West Farms Youth Group reflect the usual antics of young people and the more serious commitments and are indicative of a life-style among rural Jewish youth. The young members tried to help the center president collect outstanding dues because a wished-for youth lounge depended on it. They needed to know about Zionist ideology, to be involved with the social and economic issues of the time; above all, they wanted to establish contact with other young Jewish people in neighboring communities so that their social horizons could be enlarged. Following is a sample page from a book of minutes:

Minutes of May 18, 1946

The meeting was called to order on Sunday night, May 18, [*sic*] at 10:15 P.M. The minutes were read and accepted without correction.

The Dance Committee could not report as they had not met, but Gloria said she would go to Howell Township school to see if we could get it for our dance.

Cele reported that she had received a card from the Hightstown Club asking the club to attend their dance. Since the dance was the night of our meeting, the membership told Cele to write and explain this.

Jack read a letter which the Information Committee had drawn up and sent to Smith, Hawkes, and Auchincloss urging extension of OPA [Office of Price Administration]. He also read the reply he received from Auchincloss.

Gloria suggested that these letters be put on the Bulletin Board. Gert is going to look into the matter of a Bulletin Board.

Herb told the Club that Mr. Newdow is anxious to have a youth group and that if we help collect dues owed to the Community House, he would see that the cellar is fixed up. Since the Club was favorable to this idea, Herb said he will speak to Mr. Newdow further.

The Constitution was drawn up by the committee and read by Max and each part was approved individually.

Cele was instructed to have 200 cards printed up with our name as the West Farms Youth Group.

The meeting was adjourned at 11:30 P.M.

As more young people moved into the area with their parents and as many more reached adolescence, other groups were established within the center and outside of it. A Youth Group of the Farmers Union—also nonsectarian and attended only by the Jewish children—provided meaningful and creative experiences for many youngsters. Here they learned folk dancing, wrote and presented plays, had arts and crafts sessions, and met other young children. Although the Farmers Union group moved out of the center, the folk dancing and arts and crafts classes continued to be held there.

The Ladies Club

The National Council of Jewish Women played an important role in the early life of the community. After establishing a chapter for the Jewish farm women, the council helped organize meetings, established the first Yiddish school for the children, sent teachers who conducted the classes in various private homes, helped organize youth clubs, and sponsored lectures. The Ladies Club of the Farmingdale Jewish Community Center, which started soon after the center was formally organized, grew out of the work of the National Council.

The early Ladies Club was composed exclusively of the Eastern European women. It gave the women, many of whom lived in almost total isolation, an opportunity to socialize and interact with each other. Few had automobiles in 1937, but those who did had an unspoken obligation to pick up other people for a meeting.

An argument arose in the Ladies Club in the late forties and early fifties over the name of the organization. The name "ladies" became objectionable and undignified to some. After an extended argument, the name was changed to the Women's Club. A small victory, perhaps, but an affirmative action for liberation taken in the Jewish woods of New Jersey twenty years before the emergence of the modern women's movement.

As the American settlers began moving into the area, some of the younger women joined the club. Taking a leadership role, they evidently derived much satisfaction from their work, as a published talk by one indicates. In 1945 a transplanted New Yorker and former president of the then Ladies Club, Gladys Rosenshine, delivered a talk to a center meeting in which she spoke of the satisfaction and meaning to her of the Ladies Club. "In the time that I've been here, I've joined the now famous Ladies Club, and honestly speaking I look forward to the meetings with enthusiasm, because I am learning what the word unity really means. The women work, work all the time, helping every charitable organization that just knocks at their door. The pleasure I derive in knowing that I too am one of those workers is most gratifying."[8]

JEWISH MEMBERS OF
THE WEST FARMS PTA
OUTSIDE THE SCHOOL
WITH THE SUPERVISING
TEACHER, MRS. REICHEY
(STANDING, SECOND
FROM LEFT), 1936. ALSO
PICTURED: HILDA
GROSSMAN (FRONT ROW,
CENTER), TILLIE
HAMBURGER, AND HILDA
WISHNICK (STANDING,
FOURTH AND FIFTH
FROM LEFT). THE JEWISH
WOMEN OF
FARMINGDALE THOUGHT
THAT LOCAL CUSTOM
DEMANDED THAT THEY
DRESS UP FOR
MEETINGS.

Like the goal of so many other organizations meeting at the center, the focus of the Ladies or Women's Club was to raise money for charitable causes rather than for the center. During World War II, the women knitted hats, gloves, and scarves for Allied soldiers. They purchased khaki-colored wool, portioned it out, gave instructions to those who needed them, collected the finished products, and shipped them out. They also sent packages to Jewish boys in the armed services, and they continuously raised money for Jewish orphans. A 1947 letter of thanks came from Raymond Benson, a nephew of Mr. Peskin, for a package he received while stationed in Korea. "This letter is to thank you all for your thoughtfulness in sending me the package of food and cigarettes which arrived today. You deserve a compliment on your choice of items. Every part of the package was correctly chosen, from the contents to the padding—egg flats. I had to burst out laughing when I saw the flats. Thank you for the package and for a very new experience."

In 1944 the Ladies Club adopted a "daughter"—a seventeen-year-old refugee from Poland who had lost her entire family, her health, and a leg to the Nazis. Taking on the responsibility of helping her immigrate to Israel, the Farmingdale women obligated themselves to pay the expenses of her rehabilitation. The girl, Miriam Elimelech-Spiezer, thought of the women of Farmingdale as her aunts and mothers and grandmothers. Out of her need for family she carried on an extensive correspondence with them.

The association of the women of Farmingdale with Miriam is reported in a souvenir booklet which the Women's Club put out in 1955.

> During the dark days of the war, the club received an appeal from a young woman named Miriam, then in an Italian DP camp. She was in depression; she needed an artificial limb and had no way of obtaining it—she had no family left alive. The Club raised the hundreds of dollars needed for the limb to send to Miriam. A few years passed and suddenly news came from Miriam again; she was in Israel, married to a young man with the identical handicap she had, and they had a fine young son. But once more she needed aid; her artificial limb needed replacing; she needed food, clothing, etc. Once more the Club decided to help her—feeling towards her as an adopted daughter—and once more raised money for a leg—also sending many food and clothing packages—script—letters. Then a wonderful thing happened. Mrs. Manya Dubnik, of the Executive Board of the Club, took a trip to Israel—and went to visit Miriam. What a welcome the family gave her! The little boy, Hershel, joyfully adopted her as his "aunt from America" and all the members of the Club as his American aunts. Mrs. Dubnik came back with deeply moving accounts of her visit and pictures taken with Miriam, her husband, and little son. The women in the Club felt greatly rewarded for their hours of hard work.

In 1960, when I traveled to Israel for the first time, I was asked by the women in the club to deliver some things to Miriam. I was the second woman from Farmingdale to meet Miriam. The few remaining original members who had adopted Miriam put together money for gifts for her, her husband, and her son—then studying to be a Bar Mitzvah. I, a daughter of Farmingdale, delivered the simple gifts to another daughter of

Farmingdale. When I met Miriam in a hotel lobby in Tel Aviv, we both cried. She asked about all the women in the club—Mrs. Rachlis, Manya Dubnik, and Tillie Hamburger—and wondered why people were no longer writing. My minimal participation in the human relationship that had developed between this young orphaned woman and the distant farm women whom she considered her relatives made me think how little I had done for others. My husband felt it too, and he gave the Spiezers all the extra money we had with us, insisting above their protests that they take it. Grateful as the Spiezers were, it was the smallest of the contributions Farmingdale had made to Miriam's life.

In the same souvenir booklet, the Women's Club reports on an impressive list of projects undertaken for the benefit of others.

This Club, has, through the years, developed traditions of work, social and cultural activity, and community responsibility of such varied and high character as to make its members proud to participate in these works; and to deserve the fullest cooperation of the women in the community. It would be impossible to list all the Club's achievements, but we will mention some of the highlights. For the past two years the Club has maintained a boy in France in an orphanage under the auspices of the Commission Centrale de L'Enfance; at $300 per year—and is now sending him a watch to help him celebrate his Bar Mitzvah. $1200 was raised to purchase a room for five boys of Youth Aliyah, through Hadassah. A Nursery Unit of 10 beds was built through Pioneer Women, costing $1,000. Over 100 pairs of new children's shoes were sent to Israel—and many, many other projects of work for the children. Here at home support is given to all worthy projects; local hospitals, First Aid Squad, Cancer Fund, March of Dimes, Retarded Children, etc. In the past season the Club has affiliated with the American Jewish Congress—thus furnishing its members with fine programs of activity, education, and culture of this leading Jewish organization. Our season is always rounded out with pleasant social affairs; box socials, musical evenings, card parties, cake sales, etc., and all members are assured of opportunities for building ties of warm friendship with fellow members. We invite new members to come in and share the work and fun.

No mention is made in this report of work done or money raised on behalf of the center itself or of center activities. Yet, like women's auxiliaries or women's divisions elsewhere, the women of the center often were closely associated with the nuts and bolts of running the organization. They cooked, baked, and prepared magnificent spreads for every function, including center membership meetings, concerts and plays, and programs given by the children of the *shule*. They provided the *kiddish* (food shared by the members) after synagogue services; on occasion, they even catered Bar Mitzvahs. They sold tickets for the cultural series and staffed the entrance. If there was an illness in the community, it was the women who organized help for the family. They put out calls for blood donors if necessary, set up nursing schedules, took turns at the hospital for members who could not afford the private nurses they needed, cared for the children of the sick, and did many other helpful tasks.

The United Jewish Appeal and Other Charities

In their work on behalf of social causes, the Ladies/Women's Club was continuing what might be called a tradition of giving among the farmers. Although most farmers claimed not to be tied up in religious humbug, they never forgot the religious obligation of *tsdoka* and their responsibility toward less-fortunate Jews.

The Jewish farmers of Farmingdale gave an inordinate amount of money, which they often could not spare, to causes they considered worthwhile. As Helen Friedman remembers, "It was amazing. Everyone was poor; we didn't have a penny extra. The electric company was going to shut off the lights in the Community Center; the stove was smoking, so that sometimes you felt you would choke. But they always managed an appeal for orphans. We knew that the orphans were worse off than we were, so we had to give. What could we do?"

From an early orientation toward giving, it was only natural for the community immediately to mobilize into action when the dire news of the Holocaust began filtering in. In 1936, at the outbreak of the Spanish Civil War, some farmers, reacting to the threat of spreading fascism, joined the Abraham Lincoln Brigade and actually left their farms to fight for freedom in Spain. A few died there. Others raised money for all sorts of war relief and for the work of the Joint Distribution Committee and the United Jewish Appeal. Farmers who were barely meeting their farm debts borrowed money from the bank to contribute to the urgently needed appeal. As soon as they paid off one loan, they made another and donated the money. The volunteer farmer-collectors spent hours away from their farms, relentless in their work, in response to the desperate world situation.

UJA meetings generally drew a large crowd, and the community, as a whole, followed with interest the work of the fund-raising. The center walls proudly displayed the citations received from various agencies in recognition of the donations.

Today, however, priorities are different. One woman reflects the despair of many at the changing direction.

When it came to raising money for the UJA, Farmingdale was one of the leading places in the country. It raised the largest sums of money. It was part of the tradition and part of what was going on in Farmingdale. The new temple membership feels the strength of Israel depends on the American community, and therefore they have to spend their efforts in building up their own community to provide more facilities for their own members. They do not put the same priority on *tsdoka*. It's not the same.

The Discussion Group

The meetings at the Jewish Center did not satisfy all who came. Many, particularly the German Jews and the American born, created their own groups which met outside of the center. The Americans, who typically were voracious readers, vociferous talkers, intense searchers, curious, introspective, and aware of all that was occurring in the intellectual world, needed the kind of intellectual stimulation which they might have found in the professional life they rejected. Out of this need, they created a discussion group as a likely forum for an exchange of ideas—or, more accurately, a battleground for the confrontation of ideas.

The Discussion Group started, according to the testimony of enough to give it credence, when a number of people sitting down for a beer and sandwich after a meeting of the feed cooperative became involved in discussing an abstract question: Can a Jew be a nationalist and a Communist at the same time? The argument continued without resolution so late into the night that it was decided to debate in front of a larger group. The debaters, Boris Schwartz and Maurice Nappa, were not Americans but Europeans; the audience were Americans; the setting was Boris's farm, where everyone sat on chicken crates on the lawn; the time was one summer evening in 1944.

It was a loosely structured group to which no one paid dues. The meetings were held in different people's homes, and homemade refreshments were provided afterward. The members decided on a topic they wanted to learn about and then looked for speakers who could educate them. Usually they paid no speakers' fees, except for a minimal transportation fee of not more than fifteen dollars, which was collected by voluntary contributions.

When speakers were invited, they received the following note: "We are a group of farmers who have formed a discussion group to further our interests in the various aspects of our modern culture." The guest speakers read like a list from Who's Who: Irving Howe, John Berriman, Jackson Toby, Langston Hughes, John Higham, Paul Tillet, Bob Alexander, A. S. Neill, Mel Tumin, John Unterecker, Paul Fussell, to name just a few. The subjects covered the whole range of modern culture: motivational analysis, the political novel, modern interpretations of original sin, antiforeign movements, symbolist poets, Faulkner's South, why people dance, trends in British socialism. The sample list of speakers and topics offers sufficient evidence of the diversity of interests. In addition, famous musicians and dancers gave private concerts in different people's homes.

So ambitious were the members to get the best minds they could to address the group that a delegation of farmers once visited Albert Einstein in Princeton to tender him an invitation. Although he declined, Einstein was so intrigued when he heard who the petitioners were and what their mission was that he invited them into his home for a visit. As one person recalls the incident: "Einstein got all excited and said, 'Jewish farmers! Real farmers!' He wanted to know all about the farming community, and he wanted to know about the Discussion Group." Percy Siskowitz of Princeton, visiting Einstein at the time, witnessed this exchange and corroborates it as true.

The lecturers found themselves extraordinarily challenged by the group, whose members researched and prepared for the topics under discussion. The speakers often returned for repeat visits because of the value they themselves derived.

High on the list of group interests was psychology. At an informal discussion, one of the members introduced the radical ideas of Wilhelm Reich. Reich soon became a high priest to a number of these farmers, and Reich's Institute became the recipient of contributions that at another time or place might have gone to the UJA. So impressive was Reich's theory of the "orgone" to them that a number of the farmers ordered his Orgone Box and spent hours reclaiming lost energy sitting in the box.

As occurred in other groups meeting in the community, arguments raged within the Discussion Group as the Reichians battled those committed to other forms of psychotherapy. One group did not believe Reich went far enough and took up the cause of L. Ron Hubbard, the founder of the theory of "Dianetics," which subsequently became the basis for the religion of the Church of Scientology. Some of the farmers studied Dianetics and became practitioners themselves. Others in the Discussion Group fought for more traditional therapies and invited lecturers on Freud, Adler, and Horney.

Lectures on sex, male impotence, and female frigidity drew crowds to the meetings. "Over a hundred people would crowd into someone's living room; they were hanging from the chandeliers," said one man.

The interest in psychology did not originate with the Discussion Group, nor was it limited to the American-born, city-educated farmers, although they took it more seriously than the others. The 1935 journals of Michael Hamburger contain notes on lectures in the Jewish Community Center on male menopause and Freud's theories of psychoanalysis. Hamburger records that the farmers found the lectures stimulating and provocative.

The interest in psychological theory led some farmers to study psychotherapy seriously; eventually a few were licensed as practitioners. Others in the community, having become interested in behavior modification of various kinds, championed "mind control" as a way of generating the appropriate energy to stay emotionally and physically healthy.

It is hard to say whether the interest in psychology and the introspection it implies was stimulated by the farm experience. The lonely hours of working on nondemanding tasks, such as grading eggs, does in fact leave the mind free to think of other things. Perhaps individuals packing eggs spent the time in constructive introspection, considering what they were doing with their lives and where they were going. The radical decision to farm perhaps implied a degree of discontent or maladjustment to begin with. A relatively high percentage of farmers were in some form of personal therapy for themselves—but then therapy was very much in the forefront of modern medicine in the 1930s and 1940s, and many people looked toward it as a source of salvation, just as others might have looked toward political solutions or religion. However one accounts for it, the interest in psychology contributed to some of the intensity of the Farmingdale experience.

The Howell Nursery School

One of the major achievements of the American group of settlers was the establishment in 1944 of a cooperative nursery school, the first in the state. It was also the first nursery school which had a mental health clinic connected with it. Its tenth-anniversary journal opens with a greeting, a historical look at its progress, and an optimistic prediction for its future. At the time, the first enrollees were entering high school.

> From the first pioneering, knocking-on-doors days to the present, the nursery never had an easy economic road to travel; the time and work required of the parents consistently bore such high rewards for the children, that the doing has always been an enriching experience. Today, the value of the nursery is an established fact. . . . We say that its continuance is assured. In complete confidence we predict that by our twentieth anniversary, children of our first graduates will be enrolled.

The tone of the message in the twentieth-anniversary journal is not as optimistic. "The continuance of the school is not comfortably assured. It is dependent upon continued effort on the part of an interested community and devotion to the cooperative ideal on the part of the parents."

In fact, throughout its thirty-five-year history, the nursery school was a source of both continual financial worry as well as great pride. The school was housed in a building rented from the Farmingdale American Legion.

At the expiration of the lease, the nursery school board wanted to exercise its option to buy the building. When the American Legion tried to withdraw the option, the board of the nursery school went to court, won its case, and acquired the property. A community effort in the best sense, the school was financed by the sale of fifty $100 shares. Members and friends helped to build furniture, painted the building, and made the necessary repairs.

The school cooperative was developed simultaneously with FLF, the Farmingdale, Lakewood, Freehold feed cooperative. The same group was involved in the formation of both cooperatives; the men concentrated on the feed mill, while the women put all their efforts into the school. In 1944, the new American farmers were ideologically involved in group and community living and excited by the experiments in which they were participating. But as romantic as they were about their own lives, they felt the isolated life of the farm was a negative for children.

Enthusiastic and inspired both by their own vision and by the guidance received from the New York Bank Street College of Education, the members of the nursery school approached the larger non-Jewish community for support, but with no success. Vigorous efforts to attract non-Jewish and nonwhite students were futile. Scholarships offered through local ministers were not accepted. As a matter of fact, the importance and value of a nursery school education for children under five was approached with ridicule and hostility by the townspeople. The nursery school board never succeeded in breaking down the prejudices on the part of the neighbors. Morris Freedman, writing about the new Jewish farmers and the nursery school in Farmingdale, comments on the wall between Jew and Gentile.

All this enthusiasm for the nursery school . . . epitomizes one of the factors that keep Jew and Gentile apart. I think it may fairly be said that the Gentile farmers are not ready to understand this powerful—perhaps exaggerated—concern for the needs of the young. To non-Jews, it probably appears just as one more example of the newcomers' irritating compulsion to be "up to the minute"—and the resentment it arouses is probably not so much anti-Semitism as a generalized anti-intellectualism. The inability of the Jewish farmers to fit themselves to the established ways of the surrounding community makes it probable that the alienation of the two groups will continue for a long time.[9]

A full educational program for young parents at the nursery school provided them with speakers such as A. S. Neill from England's famed Summerhill School and well-known practicing child psychiatrists. A dance teacher from New York, employed for the children, gave evening lessons to the parents. Entertainers such as Tom Glazer, Pete Seeger, and the Weavers gave separate concerts for the children and their parents. A drama group was born out of the need for fund-raising activities for the benefit of the nursery school supporters. Dances, parties, banquets, outings, plays, and meetings, all directed toward supporting the school, provided social activities to the community.

In spite of an entirely Jewish class of children, the nursery school board of directors continued a pretense of being nonsectarian. Ironically, Christian holidays were observed. The children had a Christmas tree and an Easter egg hunt, and the school was open on the Jewish holidays. Eventually, the board provided the non-Jewish teachers with reading material about the Jewish holidays and requested the teachers to observe those holidays as well. But the Jewish holidays were not a substitute for what Freedman questionably calls the "traditional American symbols and customs" represented by the tree or the egg, nor did the larger community distinguish between the American Jewish farmers and the others. Freedman writes, "The members would like to consider themselves, at least on the broad social level, as typical integrated Americans with no distinguishing marks; yet their way of thinking and living does stamp them as different, and the fact is that they are rigorously set apart from any portion of the gentile community."[10]

For some of the American-born farmers, the totally nonparochial school became a substitute for the Jewish Community Center and played an important role in the lives of the children and their parents. Indeed, Freedman called it "a kind of temple dedicated to the children."

11

Making a Living

Many of the settlers in Farmingdale claimed that they moved to a farm in order to make a living. But their decision was far more complicated, and it is clear that the search for economic security was only a part of their motivation. Yet economics was implicit in the health and survival of the Jewish farm communities.

The new settlers arrived on the farm with a burden of debts and with little or no experience. They all knew they would be working hard with uncertain returns. It was not their intention to develop poultry farming into a major branch of U.S. agriculture, and indeed, many are unaware of their contribution in this regard. They settled on farms to make a living and to live a rural life. To do that, they had to be creative, to innovate, to devise ways of supplementing their income until their farm produce could be marketed.

Although the JAS played an integral role in the history of Farmingdale, it did not subsidize small factories in Farmingdale, as it had earlier in South Jersey. There already were several existing small ones in the central New Jersey area providing work opportunities for some of the farmers or their wives. But other settlers, remembering their factory experiences in New York City, looked for alternate ways to augment their earnings.

Supplementing the Income: Summer Boarders

Farmers chose different ways to supplement their income. Some farmers, like Friedman or Grossman or my own father, moved their wives and children onto the farm while they remained in the city, earning money at former occupations and spending one day a week with the family. Some retailed their own produce in neighboring towns or in the cities. Some, following the lead of the New York State colonies, rented out rooms in their own farmhouses to paying guests, a typical pattern for Jewish immigrant farmers in the Northeast. The farmers' city friends and relatives helped advertise the accommodations, spreading the news to coworkers and neighbors by word of mouth.

Many of the farmers who later settled in Farmingdale and other farm communities were among the immigrants who enjoyed low-cost vacations on farms in New Jersey, New York State, Connecticut, and other places in the Northeast. To them, farm life appeared more relaxed and rewarding than that of the city. In New York State, the farmers' summer enterprise was so successful that it turned into a major resort industry. But in New Jersey, it remained essentially a sideline.[11]

In Farmingdale, the summer boarders provided the incentive for an early cooperative effort on the part of the farmers. Called the West Farms Lake Association, it promised to benefit the whole community—bungalow operators, ordinary farmers, children, Christians, and Jews. The Lake, as the project was called, became one of the few integrated community efforts to which Jews and Gentiles both subscribed. The purpose was to create a community swimming place that would be supervised and safe. In addition, it was thought that a lake in West Farms would do much to beautify and upgrade the whole area. Certainly it would go far toward making Farmingdale an even more desirable place for summer vacations.

Up until 1936, people swam in a bend of the Manasquan River called "the swimming hole." To get there, one had to walk through a path in the woods along the river for about one-half mile until reaching a clearing. It was rather steep at the edge because marl, or white clay, had been dug from it. One farmer built a set of steps to make it easier and safer to get into the water. Since there was no place to change, some farmers built two small changing rooms. It was not clear to whom the property belonged, or if anyone received permission to make these improvements. No one questioned the right to swim or to change clothes.

The swimming hole also provided a place for summer people to take baths. With boarders and chickens drawing water from the same supply, however, the wells sometimes ran very low. Since the chickens always came first, there often was not enough water for luxuries such as baths.

On June 22, 1936, the cooperative West Farms Lake was incorporated by the state of New Jersey. The certificate of incorporation reads: "This corporation is formed to purchase, take over, and develop a certain tract of land in Howell Township, Monmouth County, on the West side of the road from Hamburger's Corner containing approximately eight acres more or less, with the intention of forming a lake or pond on said premises or on part thereof and to develop, maintain, preserve, and beautify the land abutting thereon."

Shares were sold to the community at large for ten dollars, each share permitting a family to use the facility. Those who rented out rooms had to buy enough shares to cover their boarders. Christians Emil Shippert, Paul Kleev, and Joseph Kovaleff were on the original certificate of incorporation. Tom Applegate, James Allaire, Edgar Murphy, and James Hall all bought shares. The journals from 1936 to 1942 of Michael Hamburger, whose sole source of income was from summer guests, give an indication of the continual preoccupation of the community in the organization.

Hamburger sold shares at every free hour he had because the lake could not be dug without some capital. A notation in his diary for January 31, 1937, has him attending a lake association meeting at 11:00 P.M. and then going to a party at the Snyders'. By March 9, Hamburger is discouraged by the neighbors' reluctance to give money, but he continues his efforts to sell with "Cohen, Tave, Shippert, or Wishnick, or with all of them."

As noncontroversial as the lake was, politically, the meetings of the lake association were, according to Hamburger, "very stormy. The members came with chips on their shoulders and there was plenty of excitements." Many of the problems concerned the inability to construct a working dam in the sandy soil.

What did these farmers know about the engineering problems involved in digging a lake or in providing ongoing maintenance? How did their former religious education provide them with the know-how to select an appropriate site and then study the water source, dam construction, and soil formations and composition? They remembered only the beautiful streams and lakes of their Eastern European countries, and they needed a body of water, no matter how small, in their new home. To compensate for nature's oversight in Farmingdale, they hired a supposed engineer who promised to give them a lake for the money they could raise. But trouble developed almost immediately, and Hamburger's journal of April 1937 notes that the engineer was "an anti-semite, according to his expressions."

Later, the difficulty was with the site. On May 1, the project looked bleak, and a revised estimate of six thousand dollars meant that more money had to be raised.

The slow progress of the lake became a sore point between Hamburger and his wife. While he devoted much of his energy to financing the venture, his wife had to cook and take care of ninety guests at their hotel. In his journal, the man confides that "the Lake will make the whole area more desirable and then I will sell my land, and get out of the hotel business."

The lake was finally opened in the summer of 1938. The property was fenced with chicken wire, steps were installed leading into the water, a refreshment stand was operating, and collections for added maintenance continued. Each shareholder was given wristbands with brass tags for himself and his family. But no one could keep track of those who were legitimate and those who simply lifted up the chicken wire and crept underneath.

The bottom was so soft that a swimmer entering the water would either sink to the knees or slip on the slimy bottom. Instead of bathing in the lake, one came out of the water with streaks of mud, difficult to wash off, and the summer boarders needed more water than ever to get clean. But for the children, it was every bit as glorious as the farmers envisioned it to be.

Periodically, however, the farmers would arrive and find no water. The ground around the dam had washed away, or tricksters had pulled the boards out of the dam. The repairs required money, and people were going in without paying. On July 31, 1940, Hamburger's frustration is recorded in his book. "No order at the Lake. People go in free. Something has to be done and I don't know what." Other troubles followed. "Can't stop the leak in the front; can't raise it in the back. . . . It's a lot of *tzores* [trouble]. . . . Boyce did not make it right and nobody to fix it." On December 13, 1942, Hamburger sells his interest in the lake property without comment about his feelings.

From the perspective of history, the project may have been totally futile, doomed to failure from the first. For years, it looked like a large puddle left over from the previous week's rainstorm—silent, empty, depressed.[12] But from a different point of view, the West Farms Lake Association was another dream that, for a while at least, animated the lives of the Jewish farmers who envisioned recreational and aesthetic possibilities. And for years, a few local people would gather there in the summertime, with blankets and babies, exchange news with each other, and watch their children play in the shallow water and the mud.

Most farmers in Farmingdale gave up their summer boarder business during World War II, when the farm operation had become suddenly more profitable. But a few bungalow colonies remained in the area and continued catering to summer people until the early 1960s. New roads, more bus routes, and comfortable cars made the journey from New York to central New Jersey seem shorter, and the men commuted to bungalow colonies like Bergerville and Hamburger's Summer Colony.

The exodus of Jews from New York to suburbia marked the end of the summer bungalow business around Farmingdale. Like the farms, they have disappeared; all is suburban housing now.

Farming, the Depression, and the Jewish Agricultural Society

Although small numbers of Jews settled in Farmingdale before the Great Depression, many more came during and after. The Jewish Agricultural Society reports that between 1930 and 1935 its offices were flooded with Jewish immigrants wanting to get out of the city and on farms where at least they could be certain of having something to eat.

Because farmers in Farmingdale and elsewhere were finding it very hard to get adequate financing, the JAS decided to direct its energies toward helping those already on farms weather the financial crisis. It gave loans on the flimsiest of security. For example, the Kassenoff family in neighboring Toms River received a chattel mortgage on the strength of "one Jersey cow called 'Daisy' weight 800 pounds, five years old; one Guernsey cow called 'Becky' weight 1000 pounds. This chattel mortgage shall include the off-spring of the above mentioned stock, or any stock replacing the existing stock now on the premises or mortgaged herein."[13]

During these very difficult times, the federal government curtailed its financing to poultry farmers. Gabriel Davidson, managing director of the JAS in 1932, in making his report to the society, refers to the prejudice which put the Jews at a particular disadvantage.

There is another factor that must be reckoned with, namely the prejudice grounded on the belief that a stranger, coming from the city, possessing no agricultural background, and especially the urbanized Jew, cannot make his way on the farm. Federal loans are made through local Farm Loan Associations composed almost wholly of staid native farmers who have fixed points of view and who are skeptical about the possibility of success of anyone not born and reared on a farm. This attitude works to the particular disadvantage of Jewish farmers, who have no farm record by which they can be judged. . . . The same factors which work to the disadvantage of Jewish farmers in the matter of Federal Land Bank loans also work to their disadvantage in the case of loans through other channels. [14]

Most of the farmers in Farmingdale managed to hang on to their farms in the depression era and to pay their bills. But so sensitive were they to the feelings of the larger community that when one of their number walked out on his farm and away from his bills in 1933, the rest, hard-pressed though they were, taxed themselves and as a community absorbed the outstanding bills of the defunct farmer. According to Jack Grossman,

> One farmer moved out in the middle of the night, the only farmer who ever moved out without paying his bills. They had a special meeting in the Community House because he owed money to the feed mills and all around and it was going to be a calamity to every other Jew if this bill wasn't paid. They assessed all the members and it cost my father $200 or $300, which was a fortune. But they got the money together and paid off his feed bill and hardware bill, whatever he owed. The Community paid it so that they wouldn't take it out on the rest of the Jews. That was only one family that moved away like that without paying their bills. Even during the depression.

In 1935, the Jewish Agricultural Society helped to establish a credit union in Farmingdale to enable the farmers to get short-term money—a problem for many. Upon the purchase of shares, the farmers were entitled to borrow money on very minimal interest, 1 percent on the unpaid balance. For each five-dollar share purchased, the farmer could borrow twenty-five dollars on his own signature. Bertha Jones, who had been a bookkeeper in New York before becoming a farmer, voluntarily took care of the books for three years without pay, until 1938, when she was given between fifty and one hundred dollars per year. By her testimony, "The farmers repaid the loans, one or two dollars per week. If they didn't pay on time, they were fined, and the fine went into a reserve account."

The Credit Union became a regular feature of the Saturday night meetings and gatherings at the center. Mrs. Jones arrived two hours early, and the farmers who had business to transact did it during that time. Later when meetings were no longer regularly held at the Community Center, the farmers transacted their business at the bookkeeper's home. In the early 1950s, the Credit Union was dissolved.

Poultry and Eggs: The Major Crop

Although the Jewish farmer nationwide could be found in every branch of farming, the Jews of Farmingdale and other New Jersey communities were primarily in poultry and eggs. Inexperienced as they were, they made eggs the leading farm commodity produced in New Jersey, contrary to the pronouncements of Rutgers economists who, as late as 1958, still insisted that "education, training, and experience are essential prerequisites for success in meeting today's problems in the breeding, feeding, housing, and marketing of poultry."[15]

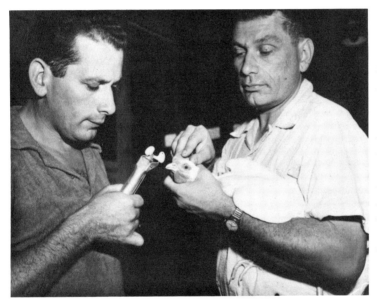

"SPECKING" THE BIRDS: LOUIS AND MILTON HARWOOD, AROUND 1950. THE HARWOOD BROTHERS WERE AMERICAN-BORN SETTLERS. THEY INVENTED THE "SPECS" AND MARKETED THEM AS A WAY TO PREVENT CHICKENS FROM PECKING ONE ANOTHER TO DEATH.

Between the years of 1940 and 1955, the output of poultry and eggs in New Jersey increased 231 percent compared to that of other farm products. According to a bulletin by the U.S. Department of Agriculture, this increase in output was encouraged by wartime requirements and accompanying high prices and was sustained when poultrymen adopted new developments in nutrition, breeding, disease control, and other innovations in poultry farming. In 1956, poultry farming was the top agricultural enterprise in the state, and 37 percent of the state's farm cash income was accounted for by poultry. Over 15 million laying chickens produced more than 2.5 billion eggs, making New Jersey the fifth-ranking state in America in egg production. Monmouth County, in which Farmingdale was located, led all counties nationwide in the number of laying birds. Three other New Jersey counties—Ocean, Cumberland, and Atlantic—ranked among the top ten in the nation in the number of chickens.

Nearly all of New Jersey's eggs were produced on family-sized farms, varying in size between one and ten thouand layers. A minimum size of flock for efficient, economical production was three to five thousand layers.[16] The Rutgers economists concluded that "poultry farming in the Garden State is Big Business." But the economics were getting more and more difficult. The investment of real estate, livestock, equipment, and feed amounted to about twelve dollars per layer, while the profit, in a good year, was about two dollars per bird. It required considerable juggling by the farmers of long-term and short-term loans just to make a living.

Cooperatives

Although the early settlers were largely ignorant of farming, they had learned about American capitalism in New York's sweatshops. Their previous experience made them sensitive to the vulnerability of the individual worker, and their active participation in creating unions taught them the importance of cooperative and united efforts to correct deplorable conditions for both the worker and the small tradesperson. Organizing cooperatives to protect their economic interests on the farm was a natural outgrowth of their city experience.

In 1927, before the Community Center was actually built, the farmers formed a cooperative known as the Farmingdale Poultry and Egg Producers Association, Inc. A certificate of incorporation was issued on November 19, 1927, which enumerates the objectives of the corporation.

1. To engage in any activity in connection with the marketing, selling, and buying of vegetables, eggs, poultry, feed, and other products and of articles, products and incubators directly or indirectly used in connection with the egg, poultry, or vegetable business, all of which is to be done not for pecuniary profits but for the mutual convenience of the members of the corporation.

2. To handle, buy, sell, and ship machinery, incubators, and other products in connection with the egg, poultry, and vegetable business and to hire, sell, or supply to its members the said machinery, equipment, supplies, poultry, eggs, vegetables, and other products of every kind and description and to do the things necessary in connection with the advancing of any one or more of the above enumerated objectives.

The location of the principal offices in the state of New Jersey is given as "the home of Louis Cohen, at Farmingdale, New Jersey, and the name of the agent therein and in charge thereof and upon whom process against the corporation may be served is Louis Cohen." Cohen was the first secretary of the corporation.

Twelve farmers signed the document as trustees: Benjamin Peskin, Louis Tave, Michael Hamburger, Louis Cohen, Harry Sokol, Jacob Kleiner, Philip Soloff, Michael Shapiro, Max Friedland, Alter Rifkin, Meyer Fine, and Jacob Cheskin. It must have taken a few more months to work out the details of the organization. On December 1, 1927, the certificate was filed at the Monmouth County Clerk's Office; on July 2, 1928, Harry Sokol was issued Certificate No. 7. It reads: "This is to certify that Harry Sokol of Farmingdale, New Jersey, having paid his fee of Five Dollars, is a member in good standing in the Farmingdale Poultry and Egg Producers Association in accordance with the by-laws thereof. Louis Cohen, Secretary." On it is affixed the corporate seal.

When Israel Friedman returned to Farmingdale in 1936, he immediately organized a small cooperative to buy vaccine and poultry equipment. His previous organizational experience in America included work on behalf of a laundry union in New York City and participation with the Workmen's Circle to organize Yiddish *shule*s. He extended his cooperative expertise to the farm and, in so doing, found both the intellectual challenge he needed and the opportunity to provide an economic benefit to the farmers. Friedman claims that his efforts on behalf of community organizations were a crucial stimulation to his life. At ninety years of age, he commented on his farm years. "My work for the community gave me life so that I could endure everything else. I was thinking all the time I did the miserable farm work. And I thought: If working on the farm has to kill me, my mind can work on something else—on an idea. It was that work that gave me the strength to live until now." Ideas and ideology were never far removed from the efforts made by the farmers, whether they concerned the building of a Community Center or the creation of a Jewish farmers cooperative such as the Farmingdale Poultry and Egg Producers Association.

Primarily, the cooperative was formed to give the farmers some control and economic benefits in their buying of farm supplies and marketing of their products. It was also a self-education group in that the meetings were designed to help the members deal with the poultry problems they encountered and to keep abreast of the latest in farm technology. Speakers came from Rutgers and from the Jewish Agricultural Society to address the farmers on farm-related problems and topics.

But farming concerns did not constitute the total interests of the Jews, and the meetings provided an opportunity to exchange information about all that was happening in the world outside of Farmingdale. Thus, every meeting of the Poultry and Egg Producers Association also had an item on its agenda called "Good and Welfare" that dealt with the well-being of the world Jewish community. While the farmers could reach some agreement on the control of lice in the chicken coops or the most economical way of purchasing feed, the broader problems of the Jews in the world elicited as many opinions as there were people.

The ensuing discussions identified opposing ideologies which began to polarize the community. Two groups emerged whose boundaries were never very clear—the right and the left. Ultimately, the farmers had two of almost every organization they created: two reading circles, two farmers' choruses, two egg-marketing cooperatives, two feed cooperatives, and two fund-raising drives for the benefit of beleaguered Jews.

Abraham Dobin, an agent of the JAS who had much contact with the early settlers, felt that the later tensions and divisiveness in Farmingdale began with the economic organizations—the cooperatives. There were serious ideological differences in how their functions were defined and perceived. Louis Harwood, who settled in Farmingdale with his parents after graduating from City College in 1933, remembers the meetings of the Poultry and Egg Association.

> The meetings were basically devoted to the business of poultry problems. But you had to have a "good and welfare" program where you discussed more important things. Whatever opinions people had, they were very vigorous about them. A great many people thought they had the truth firmly nailed down, and they became furious at other people who didn't believe it. When you'd come to a meeting, you'd get furious arguments. There were a lot of opinions on various subjects: Should you buy feed together? Should you market eggs together? In the Poultry and Egg Association, there were arguments that went on until two, three, four in the morning over business problems, poultry problems. There were political arguments going on side by side. For example, they would take up at a Jewish poultry meeting in the Community Center the question of how to control lice in the coops. And then it would come to the general "good and welfare," and they would discuss the problem of the Spanish Civil War. Solving the problem of the lice, that was easy. But solving the Spanish Civil War! That was a lot more complicated. There were some furious arguments. Eloquence—you never heard such eloquence in your life. Half Yiddish, half English, depending on how you could express yourself more beautifully.

As the number of Jewish farmers increased and the arguments intensified, the Poultry and Egg Association was no longer adequate to meet the varying demands and needs of its members. New organizations had to be created. The early Jewish farmers, who knew very little about farming and even less about the complexities of marketing or about formulas for mixing feed, nevertheless organized separate cooperatives for marketing eggs, buying feed, and for breeding and hatching chicks. The American-born, university-trained settlers became involved in these activities and made a real contribution to them.

Many of the economic-based organizations, but not all, met at the Jewish Community Center. Although their memberships were not limited to either Jewish or Farmingdale farmers, they ended up being almost totally Jewish.

LEO NAPPA COLLECTING EGGS, AROUND 1950.

With the growth of the Jewish farm movement in New Jersey, farmers from dispersed areas often combined their efforts in economic and social organizations. The Federated Egg Producers Cooperative (FEPCO) was one egg-marketing cooperative whose main office and headquarters were in Toms River but whose board of directors consisted of farmers from Farmingdale, Lakewood, and Toms River.

When FEPCO became identified by some people as a left-wing cooperative, another marketing cooperative, Farmco, with a more conservative political outlook, was created. Later, when the poultry business was very bad, a third cooperative, Jersey Jill, was born. It ostensibly shunned politics altogether and concentrated solely on efficient business and marketing practices. Nevertheless, it was short-lived.

The conflict between the radical socialist ideology of many of the farmers and sound economic practices was nowhere more apparent than in the cooperatives, where it was hoped that a coalescence between politics and profits could be accomplished. In the first issue of *The Mixer*, newsletter of the FLF, the lead article was a statement of purpose.

> In order for a cooperative to succeed it is not only necessary to build large . . . mills . . . but also to have an ideal that will follow on equal footing with the material things we build.
>
> We editors . . . feel we speak for the majority . . . when we say we should like to associate ourselves with the democratic ideals of our great United States. The ideals of Thomas Jefferson, Thomas Paine, Abraham Lincoln, and Franklin D. Roosevelt will constantly be embodied in our every thought. . . .
>
> Basically our objective is to build a stronger, more progressive cooperative movement in our community. [17]

At the FLF, discussions and arguments over political issues augmented pragmatic considerations having to do with the practical running of an organization on sound business principles, causing furious battles. Amour Morgan, who settled with her husband on a farm near family and friends, talks about the conflicts. She feels that the Jewish farmers were good intellectuals, but not very good businessmen.

> If there were meetings about how to conduct farm business or farm life, the whole question of profit came up. And the question of exploiting help. These were good Jewish intellectuals. They were all very bright guys who were very strong-willed in their ideas. I don't think any of them were good businessmen. My uncle was never a huge success. My father was not a success. None of these guys were. My father had a little candy store, and then he had a little laundry store. He was a big intellectual. My uncle was a painter—a house painter. They could sit and discuss and argue for hours. They were the Jewish intelligentsia from Russia. These are not business people. You have to be much more pragmatic to run a business.

Nathan Deutchman pointed out the same conflict. "There were those— I hate to call them economic determinists—but they believed that the cooperative was formed for a given reason and that given reason only. Of course, there were others who believed that the cooperative was formed for more than one reason. Some people believed that the meaning of the cooperative is to change your thoughts and priorities of how to live, that there are other aspects to the cooperative besides the economic."

Although the founders of the cooperatives viewed them as having an obligation to educate their members in cooperative ideals, it was precisely that which got them into trouble. Amour Morgan explains:

> Cooperatives have a prime function too, since they are economic organizations. Their prime function is economics, and the only way you are able to gather in more and more people is if you are a viable organization. That is to say, an organization that does for its members more than they could do for themselves or through private sources. And in this case, unfortunately, I don't think the FLF succeeded, nor did FEPCO succeed. I don't think they had enough qualified leadership to bring them into that direction. They were good leaders, but limited. They did not understand business too well, and the people they hired were not too much better. And the policies they practiced did not end up doing the things that they should have done.

The Central Jersey Farmers' Cooperative Association, organized in 1930 with the help of the Jewish Agricultural Society, became one of the major co-ops in New Jersey. Before the FLF, most Farmingdale farmers belonged to it and regularly attended its meetings. As described by Leon Bibel, a former farmer and an artist who lives in North Brunswick, "The Central Jersey Co-op was a rallying point for the farmers. . . . One had to belong, really, to know what was happening in the industry." It outlasted almost all the other cooperatives in the state, but in the mid 1970s, it too closed its doors, a victim of the disintegrating farm economy in the state.

Charles O'Reilly, who started working for the Central Jersey Farmers' Cooperative in 1936 and was its managing director when it closed in 1974, has nothing but respect for what the farmers accomplished through their cooperatives. "The motivation at the beginning was simply to be able to pool needs of all the farmers and have them buy feed and supplies at the best possible prices." But O'Reilly also cites as another motivation "a stand-offish attitude by the existing community toward the Jewish farmer. . . . The people experienced a coldness or a lack of warmth on the part of the community towards them. So it was a logical move for them to band together and try to help themselves as best they could."

The Central Jersey Farmers' Co-op was more efficiently run than many others, and politics did not play the same role in its business decisions as in the FLF, for example. But it too closed when the nature of farming changed. O'Reilly accounts for the decline of the industry as an evolutionary development. "The nature of the industry changed. It became not a family enterprise anymore, but it moved into an automated integrated type of operation. . . . The size of investment required was no longer the few dollars that ordinary people could rake together to try life in the country."

More efficiently run cooperatives certainly could not have prevented the death of the poultry industry in New Jersey. But the political activity of the farmers caught the attention of the U S Department of Agriculture and the FBI, which began surveillance of Jews in Farmingdale.

In the years following the Korean War, price supports for eggs were dropped but were maintained for grain, putting the small farmers into a very tight economic squeeze. On top of this, more efficient methods of transportation of cheaper eggs from the Midwest (where the feed was grown) increased the competition for eastern markets. The New Jersey poultry industry, composed almost entirely of small Jewish family farms, collapsed. Without a powerful lobby representing them, the farmers could not adequately fight all the forces of government and private industry. [18]

In fact, the American economy appears to have no room for the small family operations of yesteryear. The small shopkeeper, the small tradesman, and the small farmer are all outmoded, and a whole way of life has passed.

12

Coping with Problems

Within the Community

The early days when the few Jews planned together for their needs were the halcyon days in the life of the community. But even then the unique character of Farmingdale could already be discerned. If arguments and contention are characteristic of Jews, these became the hallmarks of the Jewish farmers, who appeared to have an insatiable appetite for discussion. Perhaps it was a carryover in America of the old *pilpul*, the disputation of Talmudic scholars over interpretations of biblical laws and injunctions. Certainly, the form of the *pilpul* remained in the passionate debates about ideology, social justice, or even such seemingly noncontroversial subjects as farming techniques. Heated discussions increasingly became a concomitant to the total living experience of the farmers. They accompanied meetings, social functions, and cooperative sharing of work.

While farming gave the Jews an opportunity to work for their ideal worlds, Farmingdale also gave them a ready group of other Jews prepared to meet the intellectual challenges which their opposing ideologies inspired. Strong opinions were continually confronting other strong opinions. The result was arguments, differences, insults, shouts, finger-pointing. All were part of the ambience of the meetings held at the Jewish Community Center. Israel Friedman found the arguments enormously stimulating and vitalizing.

The main thing in life is the brain. How was it in Farmingdale? In the way of the body, the work was hard. But in the way of the brain, it was one of the best times of my life, because over there we had a group of people that, even when we were talking about Communists, I was happy that we have such a group of people. It gave me a stimulus that I should go around thinking. Even while I did my work. In New York, I didn't have a chance to develop my mind because I worked from seven in the morning till eleven at night, and I had no chance. On the farm in the wintertime, I had plenty of time, and even in the summertime, I could take an hour or two and go talk with people. I could talk with people who understood how to argue, and we could still be friends. They understood ideas. Over there I lived because I used my brain.

Friedman, who disavowed any parochial connections with religion, nevertheless puts the heated political discussions and arguments into a philosophical and religious framework.

The whole Talmud is argument, discussion. You say like this, and the others say like that; and we fight—you know, we argue. Once someone asked God: "How can You stand that all the time? They are arguing about the Torah. They fight, they argue." And God answered: "Don't you understand? They are not arguing for themselves, for *koved* [personal honor], for pride; they are not talking for money. They are arguing for Me. These men think that I like it like this, that's what they think I mean. So why should I be angry? They argue for Me." People have the right to have their ideas. The community is for everybody. We came to the community, and we argued for our beliefs. Every faction wanted to have its opinion imposed on the whole community, so then it started—the trouble. We couldn't stand it the way they did things, and they couldn't stand it the way we did things. And we had a group, and they had a group. And we were arguing and fighting, and everybody wanted to rule the community and make it better.

The Community Center, which represented structure and order to the tiny Jewish community, became a place for working out grievances, a type of court of last resort to which the Jews looked for justice. From the very beginning, there were differences of opinion, but they were handled within the community. After all, immigrant Jews, uncertain in their relationship to the larger non-Jewish community, not very fluent in English, insecure on their farms, would hardly take arguments they had to a civil court of law. The process would have been too frightening, bewildering, expensive, and humiliating. "Jews didn't want to air their dirty linen in public, suing other Jews. We didn't have to show this to the world," said Deborah Snyder Kern.

Instead, the farmers established their own procedures for settling arguments. Their model was the *bet-din*, a rabbinic court composed of rabbis and governed by the Torah. A committee, variously referred to by those interviewed as the Arbitration Committee or a *bet-din*, heard the grievances and gave advice which the farmers had previously agreed they would follow. Deborah Kern's parents had frequently served as moderators on the Arbitration Committee. She shared her memories of how it operated. "Each disputant would pick someone to speak for him. It would either be a man or a couple. And both would pick a neutral party. They would have as many sessions as they needed to bring out all the conflicting issues. The work of the committee was very secret, and the people took their jobs very, very seriously. They didn't give details to anyone. I know my parents didn't. They didn't gossip about what went on."

I remember a dispute my father had with our next-door neighbor which the Arbitration Committee was called upon to adjudicate. Our chicken range bordered on our neighbor's farm. In the corner of our property was a beautiful full-grown oak whose branches shaded the neighbor's lawn. Our chickens roosted on the tree and sometimes flew off onto the neighbor's property, mingling with their chickens. The problem arose when my father wanted to get his chickens back, and it was difficult to decide whose chickens were whose. It became so unpleasant that the committee had to be called upon to settle the argument, and my father finally chopped the tree down. I do not know whether this was the solution proposed. Maybe it was. Once the tree was removed, there would be no further problem with our chickens going over to the neighbor's farm. But it broke my heart to see that beautiful tree being destroyed.

The rulings of the objective and nonpartisan Arbitration Committee were binding on the disputants, until one or the other of the principals decided that the committee's ruling was not appropriate. However, this was the exception rather than the rule.

Family problems and perceived injustices occurring within the community were brought to the committee. Michael Hamburger, president of the center for many years, notes in his journal of 1939: "Grossman came around to tell me that Nappa is charging too much for the land to the refugees. We will have to investigate."

Few disputes were easily disposed of, as repeated references in Hamburger's journals make clear. In one 1937 reference, Hamburger confides to his journal his regret at being unable to control an argument. "I am a little sorry for my words last night at the meeting. But I couldn't restrain myself." The dynamics of the meetings themselves can only be guessed at by such entries as "Mrs. Kramer was insulted by Weisfeld's remarks at the last Vervaltung meeting." Surely it must have been something more than a lukewarm insult to have warranted inclusion in the journal. Or, "At night, very stormy meeting. Peskin made unsupported accusation against administration and the meeting ends in an uproar." Again, "At night, Council meeting at which we only quarreled." At one point, Hamburger sees only two possible solutions for the center arguments: "The officials should resign or the few faithful should consolidate and let the others go." He gives no reason for the arguments but notes efforts to effect some harmony. "A Caucus tries to bring peace to West Farms. Their condition is to oust Cohen, which can only bring more enmities."

The ordinarily patient and philosophical Hamburger is upset by the constant fighting he was unable to control. "Tonight's meeting was a stormy one due to Nappa's address. Somehow they cannot hear each other. I cannot find a solution." And he is preoccupied by the need for peace in the community. "Am trying to find a way to bring peace among our members, but I can't. I'll call a meeting of just a few to discuss ways and means."

Although there is a rare note in the journals that indicates minimum, if not totally satisfactory, peace ("Meetings last nite quiet, but Snyder is wounded in his pride"), personal differences and confrontations continue to find their way into the meetings of the center and into Hamburger's journals. "Center meeting. S. Rifkin attacked verbally Weisfeld without reason"; and "At Center meeting we had a bomb shell by Nappa. I appointed a committee of five to investigate."

In 1940, an International Workers Order branch was established in the center, and the arguments grew even more heated. On March 23, Hamburger records "a very stormy meeting on account of the new IWO just organized."

The political polarization began to affect the very crucial work of collecting for the United Jewish Appeal. An uneasy compromise was worked out with the IWO to the effect that if the members cooperated in the collection and contributed money, the organization could then designate Jewish organizations to receive a percentage of the total collected. The compromise did not last long before it erupted into more bitter confrontations and accusations. The IWO members were accused of inflating Stalin's coffers. On May 5, Hamburger notes: "Exciting meeting last night. Peskin raised again the issue of the IWO but Boyarin and Friedman counteracted. In the meanwhile, we had quite a lively discussion." Eventually, the IWO moved its meetings from the center, but the members kept their individual membership in the center, where they continued to be vocal and outspoken advocates of their causes and antagonists of those opposed to them.

The contentiousness of the farmers which the journals reveal so clearly

MICHAEL HAMBURGER AT THE CENTER, AROUND 1940. HAMBURGER'S JOURNAL ENTRY OF DECEMBER 16–17, 1941, READS: "WAR WAR WAR[.] AND THE SAME DEPRESSING FEELING THAT I HAD DURING THE LAST WAR HAS GOTTEN HOLD OF ME AGAIN ONLY THIS TIME IT'S WORSE BECAUSE KAISERISM WASN'T AS GHASTLY AS HITLERISM."

as part of the history of the center life was present in most of the organizations which the farmers subsequently formed and gave their meetings a particular flavor. Most of the members were socially minded freethinkers; all were interested in Jewish life, but they had varying interpretations about its responsibilities and meaning.

Among those who came from Eastern Europe in the first two decades of the century were many who had a strong emotional investment in the dream of the Russian revolution and a missionary zeal in their efforts to bring the dream to others. Their enthusiasm, however, often met obstinate resistance from disenchanted believers or from those with other ideas. The resulting confrontations between different points of view ended in disastrous arguments, painful accusations, and, eventually, a fragmentation of the community.

Before the Cold War and the McCarthy period of the 1950s, the needs of world Jewry kept their differences in check. As the news of the Holocaust filtered in, the urgent situation of families in Eastern Europe united the Farmingdale Jews, and a continuing appeal for money brought in large donations. The United Jewish Appeal repeatedly cited the Farmingdale Jewish community as having raised more money in proportion to its size and per capita income than any other community. But politics kept intruding on the social lives of the Jewish farmers.

The divisiveness reached its height in 1953, coincident with the decline of the farm economy. Overproduction of eggs, the recession following the Korean War, and the withdrawal of government price supports caused a severe trauma to the industry from which it never recovered. In addition, the Cold War between America and Russia had escalated significantly.

Tensions and political differences increased. So intransigent did some people become in their positions that it was no longer possible to effect any kind of compromise. The early shouting, finger-pointing, and name-calling gave way to increasingly uglier accusations. Although there was never a real conservative right-wing sentiment among the farmers, the Jews of the community identified each other as being on the right or the left. It was rumored that some Jews informed federal authorities about the suspected subversive activity of their neighbors.

Early in 1953, the right-left issue burst out afresh, occasioned by the so-called Doctor's Plot in the Soviet Union. Stalin accused Jewish doctors of trying to poison Soviet leaders, and Jewish intellectuals, of fomenting dissent. The ultimate fates of the accused remain uncertain, for they were never heard from again. The outcry among world Jewry found its expression in Farmingdale, and a group proposed to the center board that the Farmingdale Jewish Community join organizations around the world in a resolution condemning the action. Another group, feeling that the Soviet Union was being unjustly accused of anti-Semitism by those interested in seeing the Cold War continue, succeeded in blocking the resolution. The memory of that time is still very bitter to some, who accuse the left of dragging to the Community Center all sorts of people to vote against the resolution, "bringing them in even from the graves," said Harry Sokol, "people who had never before been seen in the Community Center." Nor is the memory any less painful for those who were on the other side. Nathan Deutchman candidly admits that he was wrong to oppose the resolution. "I believed that anti-Semitism had died in the Soviet Union. It's easy to say now in retrospect that I made an error, because the Soviet Union did not put an end to anti-Semitism. In fact, you can say that it is greater in the Soviet Union than in any other country in the world. But at that time, I did not see it this way."

Louis Bially, identifying himself as still being left-of-center and working for his ideal world of peace and brotherhood, admitted that he, like so many others, was wrong.

> The "Doctor's Plot" was a big fight in the community. The left said it was not true, there was no plot, the accused were guilty. They believed that Stalin was a god. We were all fooled. He was not only not a god, he was a murderer. He killed so many—Jews and non-Jews. And he killed the best twelve Jewish writers that we had, [including] David Bergelson, Peretz Markish, Itzik Phefer. At the Community Center, when the topic was brought up, there was a big storm. According to my thinking now, the right was correct. But then I was fooled like the others. There was a sharp division. It was terrible. Before, we worked together; then, we became enemies. People didn't say good morning to each other.

A MEETING AT THE
CENTER, 1952.

In 1953, Joseph McCarthy started an investigation into what he called subversive activities at the U.S. Army base of Fort Monmouth, ten miles from Farmingdale. The local press reported on witnesses called to testify. Among those with obvious Jewish names were some identified as farmers. Although a few Jewish farmers in Farmingdale did supplement their incomes by taking jobs at Fort Monmouth, it was never clear why particular individuals were summoned by the investigators. The manager of the FLF cooperative, who had never had any connection either with the army or with Fort Monmouth, was also summoned to appear. More than one hundred people were dismissed from their jobs as a result of the investigations, ninety-five of whom were Jewish, and among these were some Farmingdale farmers. It took years of litigation before those dismissed won reinstatement with retroactive pay.

The tensions of that period were reflected in the Jewish community. Older farmers, frustrated by increasingly harder times and facing the grim prospect of actually losing their farms, began to blame left-wingers in the center for the plight of the poultry farmer. Some younger people, threatened by a loss of jobs because of past radical associations, turned on their neighbors. A deep split developed that was as painful as it was ugly. Friends of long standing no longer spoke to each other.

Some farmers wrote to the local press and to the New York Yiddish press about what they considered to be Communist influences in the area. The press headlined the story with sensational banners such as the one in the Yiddish *Forward*: "How Communists Take Over a Jewish Community of Farmers." The Federated Egg Producers Cooperative sued the *Forward* for printing libelous material. Harry Green, a New Jersey civil rights lawyer, was prepared to take the case to the highest court, but the newspaper made a financial settlement.

At the center, a group fought for the expulsion of supposed Communists. When that effort failed, half the membership broke away and tried to form another Jewish Community Center. The letter that went out to gain support stressed "good citizenship" and "the American way of life" as the virtues the new Jewish center would promote.

> Through the pages of history we find that man has always banded together to protect himself against those elements which threatened him and his family, whether spiritually or physically. Local events of recent months have shown that history is still repeating itself and that now more than ever there is an urgent need for a focal point of strength. This, in a rural area, is its Community Center. We feel that a Jewish Center would promote good citizenship and a full understanding of the American way of life. [19]

The Jewish Community Center of Farmingdale was deeply divided. Yet it persevered in its efforts to provide for the needs of its now-declining membership. The United Jewish Appeal and the Culture Committee continued to appeal to the broadest base of people. An intensified effort was made to unite the community by providing leadership and facilities for a variety of youth activities. The newest farmers, the Holocaust survivors from Eastern Europe, completely aloof from the political arguments in the center, instituted regular Saturday morning services which were conducted without a rabbi. The board continued to function, but it took a long time for the schism to mend; the community was never quite the same.

As the split did not occur overnight, so did it not completely disappear. Some of the older settlers of different political opinions lived near one another in neighboring Lakewood, but did not talk to each other.

The topic of politics in the Jewish Community Center of Farmingdale is still a sensitive and painful one, and people shy away from discussing it. Most of the people interviewed, regardless of their political orientation then or now, claim that the period was so long ago that they no longer remember it, although they have no such difficulty in the interviews remembering earlier times. More than half of the sample of 120 farmers claimed that they were never involved in politics in any way and were never interested in politics. Twenty specifically said they did not want to talk about it. During the interview some people asked to have the tape recorder turned off when it came to discussing the political divisions in Farmingdale. They then proceeded to instruct the interviewer in the wisdom of ignoring this part of the history of the community. "There is enough to talk about without bringing up an issue that is liable to be painful to some," said one man. "Why drag over old coals?" asked another. Yet, surprisingly, almost 25 percent of the total admitted to having been visited by agents of the FBI.

What was there about the character of the Farmingdale community or the people or the nature of their societal living that made such a bitter split occur? Joseph Zelnick sees an economic answer to the question. "These were people who were willing to go out on a limb on certain issues and were even more strengthened by the fact that, as farmers, they didn't have to worry about job security to do it." When asked why the FBI was so interested in the community, he responds: "They were interested because we were what you might call premature civil rights advocates. We were involved in the important issues of the day—what we deemed to be important in terms of civil and human rights. Those issues were called Communistic."

The arguments and the fights within the center and the reputation that it acquired in the surrounding areas alienated some people who had been members. Louis Harwood commented: "My reaction was to walk away from it. I didn't like it at all. Once or twice, I tried to participate, but verbal brickbats were flying so furiously through the air that I got scared. I decided that I wanted to lead a more peaceful life. So when these battles went on, I learned to stay out of them."

The reputation of Farmingdale discouraged others from settling in the community. One family of Holocaust survivors wanted to buy a farm in Farmingdale but settled instead near Freehold because, by their testimony, "when we were looking for a farm, the real estate agent told us we'd better not look in Farmingdale. It was too pink."

Yet, in spite of Farmingdale's reputation, in spite of the fights and the bitterness which they engendered, in spite of the financial reversals some experienced as they witnessed the fruits of their hard work disappear like last year's snow—in spite of all, almost everyone interviewed expressed, in one way or another, the same sentiment as Joe and Jesse Zelnick.

We really did love those days and would have been happy to continue them. We loved the people, the whole farm group. They were such unique people in terms of their commitment to social justice and their willingness to get involved in all kinds of things—community affairs, national affairs. Their willingness to contribute their efforts and their money. There was a vibrancy I had never seen before and haven't seen since. They were willing to remove themselves from their immediate lives and get involved in issues which had international, not only national, implications, because they thought it was important to do so. They were people with a working-class background committed to social justice, people whose horizons were much broader than just their farms.

The commitment to social justice remained with the older farmers after they left their farms. But the vibrancy which was part of an honest, if misguided, trust in a Utopian society where Jews could take their equal place in a common humanity was replaced in some people by deep disappointment.

For the old believers who came to America full of hope and who carried their enthusiasm to their small farms and to the community they helped create, the loss was acute. When it became clear to those on the political left that the dream they believed in so passionately was in fact a disguised nightmare, they were almost totally bereft. Not able to go back anymore to a former religious structure that had sustained their parents and grandparents, losing hope for the better way they envisaged, they were lonely, sometimes bitter, often very sad.

One such man was Joseph Galstuck. Like Friedman and Bially, Galstuck also came to the farm because he was looking for a "better and a quieter life." As if to extend the likeness, he too had been trained as a rabbi at a yeshiva. His family in Europe had a number of rabbinical scholars who had published Yiddish and Hebrew commentaries on the Bible. At the yeshiva, the young scholar, in common with Friedman and Bially, became enlightened and thereby encountered another world. Inspired by the ideals of the Russian Revolution, he broke with his home and religion, which he saw as frozen in tradition, and came to America. Here, he started working as a milliner and was active in the Milliner's Union. An intellectual with poetic sensibilities, Galstuck began translating American and

English authors into Yiddish. His translations of F. Scott Fitzgerald, Mark Train, and D. H. Lawrence were published in the *Milliner's Journal*.

However, much as Galstuck enjoyed an active life with New York's literati and cognoscenti, New York itself was not a congenial place, and in 1942, he settled on a farm in Farmingdale, where he immediately became very active in its social and cultural life. In Farmingdale, he continued to believe in and work for the ideology he brought with him to America— the ideal of social justice as symbolized by the Russian Revolution. But in time, questions began intruding themselves, he said, until "slowly, slowly, one day I awoke and no longer believed."

He was interviewed in 1974. Of his former ideology, he simply said: "I was wrong. I was very badly mistaken. I was blinded by a dream I wanted, I needed, to believe." The change in his beliefs alienated him from his former friends. He spent much time alone with his wife. Together, they helped the older poor people in the low-income housing where they lived make medicaid or other insurance claims. For diversion, he read continuously.

He said he learned how to read when he was young, in the yeshiva. It was the only thing which sustained him at that point in life. "Without reading, my days would be intolerable," he said. Asked what he was reading, he said he decided to read the King James Version of the Old Testament, since he had not read it before. He was not at all interested in the New Testament. He then began, spontaneously, comparing the King James Version with the original Hebrew.

"The English is nothing," he said with some passion. "The Hebrew is so beautiful, the poetry so meaningful and rich and melodic." Holding up the King James, he said emphatically, "This is pale—nothing in comparison."

I had not known, or had forgotten, that he could read and understand biblical Hebrew. "But Mr. Galstuck," I asked, bewildered, "if you can read the Hebrew and it's so much more beautiful, why are you reading the English translation? Why don't you read the Hebrew?"

It took him a few moments to answer, and the answer seemed mixed with pain and regret. "I'm not religious—I don't believe in religion. It's too far away—too long ago."

To read the sacred Hebrew words as an intellectual curiosity, a diversion, was impossible for him. Denying that he was doing it, he had yet gone back to the beginning. He had wandered through the Diaspora, had taken on and discarded different ideologies and a different language, and searched at the end, as at the beginning, for the source of beauty in life. He had found it briefly on the farm. After he died, his wife summed up his life. "Joe was born poor; he died poor. In between, he always tried to be honest." She gave me her husband's Yiddish typewriter because "Joe would want you to have it."

Louis Bially, talking about his later ideology and his disappointments, came to the realization that much of his political energy was spent ineffectually. He was philosophical. "A lot of people realized, and I was one of them, that we won't solve any world problems in Farmingdale, even if we agitate for this way or another way. It is a world of big powers. Every country seeks to exert its influence, nor do they consult us. So maybe we shouldn't reckon what they are doing. Some came to their sense. Others are, until today, mired in the same mud."

The Farmingdale people were described as "people whose horizons were much broader than just their farms." At the same time, their memories were longer, their roots deeper, their hopes stronger. At the heart of the fights in the Community Center was perhaps the frustration of a people who knew they could never reach their extended horizons. Yet, in retrospect, there is something very beautiful, even if sad, in the Jewish farmers of Farmingdale believing so strongly in their ideologies and the effect of their own passionate beliefs that they were convinced, absolutely convinced, that the arguments and discussions in their Jewish Community Center would really affect what happens in Washington, Moscow, or Jerusalem.

Within the Larger Community

Although the Jewish farmers had problems and serious arguments with each other, their contentions were a family affair. But their problems with the outside community were something else. From the earliest days, the settlers had to cope with or accommodate themselves to the insensitivity and hostility of some of their Christian neighbors.

When the new Community Center was almost completed in 1929, a cross was burned opposite the building. In 1942, at a time when the Jews of Farmingdale were preoccupied with the fate of their families in Eastern Europe, swastikas were smeared over the front of the center building, and a picture of a Jew hanging from a gallows was painted in black.

To the farmers, such an incident was a grim reminder that America did not necessarily protect them from sharing the fate of their relatives in Europe. The Jewish community drew together in an even tighter circle. The children, identifying with the life-threatening situations in Europe, were petrified.

I remember very vividly the day of the swastika incident. We were going to the center for our Yiddish school class. Although I usually walked, my father drove me. From the road, we saw a group of people standing in a small circle and talking. We knew it was serious, and both of us thought it was an accident and someone was hurt. When we pulled up and got out of the car, we saw those swastikas. I remember how my bowels constricted, I got so scared. My father put his arm around me, and we joined the circle. The people were trying to decide what to do about it. I think they were afraid to call the police. They covered the swastikas and the gallows with some cement mixture. For years after that, those blotches stood out from the rest of the wall like reminders of our differences—telling us and the world that we were Jews.

Aside from the cross burning and the defacement of the Jewish Community Center, no actual attacks were made on the persons or the property of the Jews, although the Jews were mimicked, laughed at, and called traitors to the United States. Over and over, native Americans advised Jews to go back to where they came from.

Yet, the Eastern European settlers who were interviewed, with few exceptions, seemed oblivious to the manifestations of anti-Semitism. Their children, however, who were raised on the farms and attended the local schools, remember all too well their discomfort and their pain. In the rural schools they attended, they were subjected to the taunts of the other children and to accusations that Jews were Christ killers. They were made to feel alienated on two accounts: (1) they were the children of immigrants, and (2) most of them had started school in New York City and had brought their advanced learning and different speech rhythms with them.

Bilingual, some trilingual, they often spoke to each other in Yiddish. The teacher sent for parents and warned that the children would not be American if they did not speak English exclusively. Harry Sokol remembers telling the teacher: "Don't worry. Soon they'll speak English as well as anyone else."

When Jewish children sat next to Christian children at the two- or three-seat desks, the Christians moved far from them, accusing the Jews of having cooties. Jack Grossman reports that this behavior ironically spared the Jews the embarrassment and annoyance of lice contamination. When the county nurse came to examine the children's hair, not one of the Jewish children had lice, whereas, by his account, "plenty of the others did."

Mary Peskin Weisgold tells of a very anti-Semitic teacher who openly called one of the children a dirty Jew. The child went home in tears and came back with her father, who, in no uncertain terms, told the teacher he would not stand for that kind of talk. He went before the school board and lodged a formal complaint which resulted in the teacher's being relieved of her duties immediately—which does say something for the courage of both the Jewish farmer and the local school board.

Sophia Peskin never forgot how a group of boys threatened her with a knife on her way home from school because her people killed Christ. Others report how, as young boys, they were dragged into the woods and made to expose themselves. Many of the people interviewed who rode the school buses or walked the country roads with their Christian schoolmates report continuous fights. They remember, but their parents do not.

Why the parents refused to see or hear this prejudice can only be guessed. Perhaps if they thought about it too much, they would have been forced to move back to the Jewish ghetto environment of New York City. For many, that was totally unthinkable.

Although there are no more Jewish farmers to speak of, the anti-Jewish feeling in Howell Township persists to the present day, and it is far from innocent. In 1973, when the old center property was sold and a new center was built in another part of the township, eight-foot-high swastikas were painted on the walls of the building as soon as they were put into place. In 1976, our bicentennial year, the new Solomon Shachter Hebrew Day School in Howell Township, just completed and ready to open for the fall term, was burned to the ground in a fire of undetermined origin. In 1977, the dormitory of the new Talmud Torah High School was destroyed by fire. In 1980, a series of anti-Semitic letters to the editor, casting aspersions on the character of the Jews in Howell Township, was published in the local press. In 1982, the first night of Hanukkah was observed by the surrounding community by the painting of fresh swastikas on the temple walls. The Jews living in the area know that they can expect periodically to see more of this kind of behavior. They shrug and say, "It's their problem, not ours." But it is painful nonetheless.

Alongside the anti-Semitism there existed a deep suspicion of Jews as radicals whose loyalty to America was very suspect. For years, the FBI had an active interest in Farmingdale. Exactly when the FBI began its surveillance is not clear, but a 1943 report characterizes the Jewish community as a "Communist commune." The report reads:

Just outside of Farmingdale, New Jersey, which is the center of one of the largest egg producing counties in the U.S.A., is located what is known as West Farms Community.[20] This is strictly a Communist commune with approximately 155 families living in the area and are producing poultry and eggs. They have a cooperative known as the FLF Co-op. This set-up has a community house, the Communists are active holding meetings, etc. Some of the farm members work at times at the Freehold, N.J. Cooperative. For many months the Farms Security Administration maintained an office at Freehold, N.J. The FSA is in daily touch with the West Farms Project.[21]

Another citation in the files reports the new farmers as Jewish refugees or "members of the Jewish faith who had formerly been employed in either the metropolitan area of northern New Jersey or in New York City." One FBI informant advised the authorities: "These new farmers, who actually make up a majority as far as population is concerned in several of the townships in Monmouth County, have been deeply resented by some of . . . the 'old-timers' or farm career men. . . . Most of the old-time farmers have either accused the newcomers as being Bronx farmers or running to the farms since 1940 to either evade the draft themselves or to buy farms for their sons. . . . Another blanket rumor is that all of these newcomers were Communists."

Before 1953, the FBI was very circumspect in its work. But in the years following, in the wake of the Army-McCarthy hearings at nearby Fort Monmouth and the climate of witch-hunting in the country as a whole, it became a more overt and ominous presence.

The FBI agents were constant visitors to the community, questioning frightened and confused farmers about their loyalty, examining the mail from the local feed mill, even going so far as to have weekly surveillance of a farmer's house from the living room of a neighboring Christian. According to these Christians, agents of the FBI, the state police and detectives from an agency gathered at their home every week to watch and record the arrivals at their Jewish neighbor's home, a farmer-musician who had choral rehearsals at his home one evening a week.

People began to speculate about who in the community was informing on them. One Jewish woman recalls a visit she had from the FBI.

> I had just dropped the kids off at the nursery school. I brought them inside, and I was coming out. As I opened the gate leading out of the school yard to go to my car, two gentlemen walked up to me. They wanted to know what I could tell them about the people involved in the Farmer's Union, about their politics, and their thinking. . . . I said I had no information for them. I was flabbergasted. I told them, "I just can't imagine what you're leading up to; I don't know why you would be interested in what I know. I have nothing to tell you." I was petrified. I couldn't stop shaking the whole time I was driving home.

While some Jews considered the radicals to be dangerous and in need of being controlled, many in the non-Jewish world considered all Jews suspect and the Jewish farmer a person disloyal to the basic institutions of the country, conspiring to overthrow the government. The government's withdrawal of price supports for eggs—but not for grain—seemed to come almost in response to this idea.

Poultry farmers, the majority of whom were Jewish, were caught in an economic squeeze and were helpless. They fought, but without effect. They sent committees and delegations to the Department of Agriculture to present their grievances and to propose solutions that would save their farms.[22] Governor Meyner and Secretary of Agriculture Philip Alampi of New Jersey were among those who interceded on their behalf. A non-Jew from Rumson sent a telegram to his friend Representative Auchincloss, asking that the congressman receive a delegation of farmers. In his telegram, the man felt impelled to assure Auchincloss that the Jewish farmers were loyal Americans. "These men are 100 percent Americans and are representative citizens of one of New Jersey's outstanding industries. Therefore, I urge you to give them your invaluable counsel, advice, and help, because the people behind the egg industry are in desperate straits."[23]

Nothing helped. In addition to the political pressures the poultry industry and the Jewish farmer suffered, there were also the pressures that accompanied the rapidly advancing technology. Refrigerated trucks and trains brought cheaper eggs from the Midwest to the eastern markets. Differently designed chicken coops housed hundreds of thousands of chickens in cages under one roof. Like other small family farmers across America, the Jewish farmer could not compete against the giant conglomerates which had begun to buy up small farms and incorporate them into vertically integrated agribusinesses. Poultry farming in New Jersey and in the country had drastically changed.

I cannot now account fully for the decline of poultry farming in New Jersey or rationalize the injustice of the charges directed against the Jewish farmers of Farmingdale. It is sufficient to say that the charges evolved from a stereotypical way of considering Jews which, in turn, produced other stereotypes.

Just as the anti-Semitism persists in Howell, so does the suspicion toward Jews and the stereotypes which give rise to both. In Farmingdale the stereotype has gone full circle. Non-Jewish farmers today repeat the old saws: "Jews are not really farmers—they are businessmen. Besides, poultry farming is not farming at all." Other stereotypes are also being voiced: "The Jews came to the farm to keep their sons from going into the service. As soon as the war was over, they left." They will not listen to the fact that the percentage of Jewish farmers in the army was at least as high as that of the non-Jewish farmers in Farmingdale.

Some people today deny that Jewish farmers made any significant impact on Howell Township or on U.S. agriculture generally. "Claims that they did are greatly exaggerated," they say. Finally, lowering their voices and asking for the tape recorder to be turned off, some Christian people interviewed shared their final perception. "The real truth is that the Jews who came here were Communists. Some of them were working for Russia."

Part 4
Growing Up in Farmingdale

13

Going Back for the Record

As housing developments rapidly replaced farms in the vicinity of Farmingdale, young families with large mortgages moved into the area, and a new group of people joined the Jewish Community Center. They were attracted by the low membership fees and the congeniality of the center, where they could observe Jewish holidays and meet other Jewish people. Even while the old settlers and their families were selling out and leaving, the membership of the Community Center grew.

In 1970, when the center property was condemned by the state to make way for the Manasquan River Reservoir, its membership consisted almost entirely of suburban families whose wage earners commuted to New York or northern New Jersey. The money realized from the sale of the Community Center was used to buy land and to build a more modern temple located closer to new housing developments.

In 1974, the last Yom Kippur services were conducted at the center, and in the summer of 1975 the Torahs were moved in a ritual procession from the old building to the newly completed temple. I and many of my former neighbors were there on both of those occasions. Wanting to preserve a record of this rural synagogue of farmers in the backwoods of New Jersey where I had come of age, I asked a few old-timers if I could videotape the last Yom Kippur service. Although I had grown up in the community and was well known, I did not know what reaction I would get from my request. After all, Yom Kippur is a very holy day, and observant Jews do not even turn on their electric lights.

Walter Tenenbaum, the farmer-*khazen* (cantor), told me that a newspaper photographer had asked if he could take pictures during Rosh Hashanah and was flatly refused. Walter was indignant. "He should take pictures in our synagogue during our High Holiday service to sell his newspaper? No! Absolutely not! But you, Gittele.[1] What you are doing is something else. You are working for Jewish history." He agreed to the taping and requested that it be as unobtrusive as possible. "Please, I don't want to see a microphone in my face while I am *davening*."

On the evening before Yom Kippur, before Kol Nidre, I arrived from Princeton (where I now live) with a one-person television crew, a camera, and a monitor which was set up in an adjoining cloakroom. With me were my coworker, Linda Oppenheim, and my thirteen-year-old son, Benjamin. Another son, Richard, who still lives in Farmingdale across from the site of the old center, was there to help us set up.

All day, in anticipation of my return, I kept thinking about previous Yom Kippurs in Farmingdale. My earliest memories are associated with my father, Benjamin Wishnick, who never went to the synagogue, and my grandmother, whom I accompanied to services when she lived with us.

My father was an iconoclast, or, if not that, at least an unbeliever. When he came from Europe to America, he threw it all away—synagogue, prayers, beliefs. An uncle once told me that my father's rebellion was a result of his having been made to feel deeply ashamed in the synagogue of Skalat, Galicia (then part of Poland, now the Ukraine), his European home, because he could not read Hebrew, and so religion came to represent oppression and tyranny. My father's mother had died when he was eight, and his schooling stopped; he was needed to help look after his younger siblings. Nor was his father very learned in the Scriptures either. He was a poor *balagula* (wagon driver) who tried hard to provide for his four motherless children. Periodically, the community got together to buy feed for my grandfather's horse, because if the horse took sick, then the community would have to buy food for the family. My uncle said that the synagogue *hokhems* (wise men) would make a person who could not read Hebrew feel lower than the heel on a shoe and that my father suffered terribly from this humiliation. Perhaps. On the other hand, my uncle, who could read Hebrew and was considered the family philosopher, had discarded the old beliefs before he came to America. He never missed an opportunity to rail against religion and its adherents. His explanation did not seem adequate, but it did make me wonder about my father. I painfully regret the lost opportunity to ask him about his life before he came to America.

I never seemed to find the right moment to ask him questions. I'm not even sure that questions I have now occurred to me as a child. When I finally awoke to the realization that I needed to know more about him, he was already dying. I was sitting next to his hospital bed when he was brought down from one of the last of his numerous surgeries. I awoke him from his drugged, anesthetized sleep and urgently asked, "Pa, Pa. How was it when you were a boy?"

He had difficulty focusing, and then his eyes cleared briefly, and he looked directly at me. To this day, I am haunted by his response. "Now? Now you ask me? Now it's too late."

I also wonder about other things. For example, how did he feel when I, at age ten or twelve, became his tutor in helping him prepare for his citizenship test. Although he could read English, the test material was difficult. I read him the Declaration of Independence and the Constitution, explaining in Yiddish and English what I understood. I am sure he was not resentful; I can still see his smile during our sessions together, as if he enjoyed some secret joke. But did he remember those earlier times when, as a young man in Skalat, he was ashamed of his lack of education?

I remember going to the synagogue with my father in New York, before we settled on the farm. Maybe he wanted to please my grandmother, who lived with us and whom he adored, or perhaps he celebrated in the traditional way, with a congregation, the birth of a child. At any rate, he never, to my knowledge, went to the synagogue in Farmingdale. As a matter of fact, his religious rebellion there took a strange turn.

Our farm was very close to the Community Center-turned-synagogue, and people walking to *shul* had to pass our house. Every year on Yom Kippur, as the first Jews passed by, my father stripped to the waist, took a hammer in hand, and climbed onto the chicken-house roof—the tin portion—to repair it. I can still see his brown sinewy body outlined against the clear blue sky of early autumn. Perhaps that was his way of praying. I like to think that those prayers, if that is what they were, were totally acceptable. Years later, I related my memory to a Hasidic seatmate during a return flight from an academic conference. He smiled gently at me and said, "Ah, dos pintele yid blaybt."[2]

As a child, I was not equipped to reason in this way. On Yom Kippur, my father's presence on the roof made me cringe in mortification. I wanted to walk with him to the synagogue, as my friends walked with their fathers. Although I went with my grandmother, I would have preferred it if my father were there too.

My grandmother, a large black scarf covering her head and half her face, sat quietly in a corner of the synagogue, on a rough wooden handmade bench. She could not read, but she must have known the service by heart, because she was able to recite something at all the appropriate times. The fact that there was no rabbi did not trouble her in the least. I do not remember her talking to anyone during the services. She paid close attention to what was going on; often, she would sit and cry. Her scarf hid her face, but I knew she was crying by the way her body moved. But she always stopped to talk to me when I came to her.

One year, I was playing outdoors with the other children, climbing up and down the cement steps leading to the building and jumping down, three or four steps at a time, while the services were going on inside. I missed my footing and rolled down the flight of steps, hitting the back of my head. When I got up, I was covered with blood spurting from under my hair. I became so frightened that I started to scream hysterically. Everyone ran out of the synagogue. I remember being enveloped by a *talis* and my grandmother looking at me, worried beyond words, tears in her eyes and on her face. People were saying, "Es, vet ganz zayn, es vet shoyn ganz zayn" (It'll be alright). Then my grandmother and I walked home together, she holding on tightly to my hand. I still carry a lump on the back of my head as a souvenir.

Those memories came flooding back to me while I prepared to return to Farmingdale, now an adult, and no longer a participant in the community. When we arrived at the small boxlike building, we began setting up the cables and machines, hiding microphones under tables so that they would not be noticed and offend anyone. The synagogue was a plain room, without decoration. Green linoleum tiles covered the floor; nondescript drapes hung at the sides of the windows; an eternal light was in front of the ark where the Torahs were housed. A small bookcase on one wall held the prayer books; next to it was a box containing a whole jumble of *taleysim* (prayer shawls).

Working in these familiar surroundings, introducing or imposing modern technology on old rituals, I felt both excited and apprehensive. I found the room clean, dignified, expectant—not at all primitive, as some people claimed. I was happy to be there and to be part of the record I was going to preserve.

We finished the work of setting up as Kol Nidre was about to start. As people came into the room, they were obviously puzzled by the camera, standing in a corner. In the cloakroom, Linda, Benjamin, and I watched the opening of services on the monitor, and we felt very much a part of them. However, we were uncertain about how much we should record and were concerned about whether people felt uncomfortable with the camera there. It was very hot and close in the cloakroom; needing air, I went out.

Outside, I saw my old neighbor Yakob sitting with his brother-in-law

Mottel. I had known Mottel's family since they first came to America and before they moved to Farmingdale. They had survived the Holocaust by hiding for four years in the Polish woods near their town of Skalat, where my father was born. Yakob was from Warsaw; he is a graduate of Auschwitz, Birkenau, Dachau, and Maidanek, and the only survivor out of a family of seven children. When he saw me, he gave me his hand and a wan smile. "Gittel, good to see you. Happy New Year." But his head seemed to be bobbing around in circles.

"Mottel! What's wrong with Yakob?" I knew something was wrong.

"I no feel good," Yakob whispered just as his wife, Khayke, came out of the synagogue. She grabbed my arm.

"Please call Dr. Haut right away. Call Dr. Haut. 5521."

Khayke started to scream in the direction of her husband. "Yakob! Yakob! Vos iz?" As I rushed to the phone, she ran for some water.

I called the doctor, who said he would send an ambulance immediately. When I returned from the phone, at least ten people surrounded the poor man, whose head was now making larger and larger circles. People pulled open his shirt, six different hands began massaging his chest—some sideways, some up and down. Khayke stood there spilling water over her husband, begging him to speak to her. "Yakob, zog epes, zog epes" (say something). She was hysterical. People were running out of the synagogue; someone found a tablecloth and spread it out on the ground. Three men helped Yakob stretch out; his wife wanted to lie down beside him, but she was urged away. Tenenbaum ran out as the ambulance arrived and motioned the people to come back into the synagogue. Khayke grabbed my arm.

"Gittel, please come to the hospital with me."

She was crying hysterically again. I went into the back of the ambulance with Yakob and an attendant while Khayke was coaxed into the cab, next to the driver. As soon as the attendant put an oxygen mask on Yakob's face, the color returned, so that when Khayke looked back and anxiously asked me if her husband was talking, I could tell her that he was looking better.

I held my neighbor's hand during the trip to the hospital. No one spoke. I remembered my videotaping and the efforts I had made to get a historic record of the Farmingdale synagogue. In spite of myself, I had to smile. I hoped there was no connection between my work, the violation of the holiday, and Yakob's seizure. I also hoped the taping was proceeding without me. I shrugged and thought about priorities—one is always responsible to them. If the videotaping was not done, well then, so be it. It was *bashert* (destined, so ordained).

At the hospital, the attendants jumped out of the ambulance, thrust a small oxygen tank in my arms, and told me to run alongside the stretcher. Yakob on the stretcher was attached to the tank. I ran with the attendants into the emergency room, Khayke running ahead, opening doors. Here, in the nonsectarian world of the hospital, peopled with starched white coats, Khayke was much subdued.

An Indian doctor in attendance looked at Yakob and spoke in a poor but understandable English. I became the interpreter in both directions. The doctor touched Yakob's shirt and said, "You sweat much." Yakob answered, "S'hot." I said, "He said he was hot." Again, the doctor had the shirt in his hand, "You sweat much." But Khayke's wits had returned. "No, no, I spilled a little water on him." Yakob repeated, "S'hot."

Their two children, Barry and Sarah, arrived with Khayke's brother, Mottel. Barry was wearing his yarmulke and looked paler than Yakob. A religiously observant boy, it was the first time he had ever ridden in a car on Yom Kippur. They were all asked to wait in the waiting room. The telephone rang a number of times, and I heard a male nurse or orderly answer, "Yes, he's here. No, we don't know yet." Eventually, I heard an impatient, "Look, we're busy. We have nothing to tell you yet." Little did he know how persistent the callers would be.

By the time the cardiograph was wheeled alongside the stretcher, Yakob seemed much better and almost appeared to be enjoying himself. A black orderly started to attach electrodes to Yakob's legs and arms. Rolling up the left sleeve, the orderly briefly looked at the number tattooed on Yakob's forearm. To him, it was a curious kind of tattoo; he put the electrode squarely over the number.

When the cardiogram showed no abnormality and the doctor concluded that Yakob had suffered an attack of indigestion, Yakob remembered that he had eaten his meal quickly so as not to be late for Kol Nidre. Everyone was now smiling and laughing. The children came in and kissed and hugged their father, who was still attached to the machine and could not sit up. As he waited patiently to be disconnected, he remembered the videotaping. "Gittel," he asked, "you think I am on the picture?"

When I returned to the center, the services were over, and everyone but our little crew was gone. The taping had continued.

At the synagogue the next day, many curious people wondered when they could see the tapes and asked if I would leave a copy for the center records. People seemed pleased that a record of their service was being made. But one man, leaning on his cane and leaving the synagogue for a break, returned my greeting with the words, "It's Yom Kippur." I felt ashamed to have violated his sense of a holy day.

As the service resumed, I got behind the camera, panned the room, and zoomed in on faces, trying to follow the service from this strange vantage point. But I did not like doing it. It put too much distance between me, the service, and especially the people, to whom I wanted to talk. Several years had passed since I had seen many of them, and much had happened in the intervening time.

The auction of *aliyas* began for the honor of being called up to bless the reading of the Torah. I remembered that Benjamin had just become a Bar Mitzvah and I wanted him to have *shlishi* (the third honor). Someone else also wanted it, and we bid against each other while the rest of the congregation watched with interest. I jumped the bidding from twenty-five dollars to *tsvey mol khay* (twice *khay*, or "life," which is the Hebrew equivalent of eighteen). My competitor finally realized I meant business; Benjamin had *shlishi*. He ran to the car for his *talis* and returned proud and ready to take his part in the service. As he said the blessings, many heads nodded in approval, but I was lost in thought.

Memories merged. My father, a hammer in his raised fist, ready to start banging on the tin section of the chicken-house roof as the first Jews passed our farm on the way to Yom Kippur services; the president of the center, his hand raised over the reading table, ready to slap it down as each auction was completed. Benjamin, my father, rejecting the old beliefs; Benjamin, my son, trying them on like his *talis*, meeting them new. And I—outside of them both, finding meaning in making historical connections—connected through my separateness.

On July 20, 1975, we returned to the old building with a different television crew. We came to record the formal closing of the Jewish Community Center. The Torah scrolls were being moved to their new home, the recently finished Temple Ahavat Achim, which would serve a completely different congregation..

One month earlier, I had been at the old center for a Sabbath morning service during which my first granddaughter received her Hebrew name. My son wanted his child to be named in the synagogue he had attended as a boy and where he grew up to manhood. It was a small gathering; barely a minyan was present. My father-in-law, the baby's great-grandfather, the only great-grandparent there, recited the *musaf* service with much feeling and emotion. It was the last time I heard Ike Dubrovsky pray. He, too, had been one of the Farmingdale farmers.

After the Sabbath service, while people talked and enjoyed the *kiddish* my son had provided, the telephone rang. A member of the new congregation wanted to know when the next Las Vegas night was going to be held. I, who had violated Yom Kippur in this place a few months before, reminded the caller that it was the Sabbath and suggested he find a more appropriate time to call.

A month later, the old farmers gathered there for the final time. Among those who came to say good-bye to the building, the place that was always more than a building and more than a place to the farmers who built it, were Benjamin Peskin's two daughters, Sophia Dubrovsky and Mary Weisgold, and their husbands. Sophia and Mary said they absolutely had to come; they had no choice—"Like you must go to funeral," Mary said. Sophia looked around at the building and said, "It has changed. It has changed a great deal." Someone asked how she felt, and she burst out crying. Joseph Tenenbaum, born and raised in Farmingdale and in his second year of medical residency in New York, had left his busy schedule to be at the symbolic ritual. When asked why he came, he said that the community had been an important influence on his life and he simply had to be there. Many of the early settlers were there, too, with canes or walkers. The center was as clean and neat and simple as ever. In the corner was the box of prayer shawls, in the same jumble as they had been on Yom Kippur, and the prayer books were in their case, as if waiting.

VACATING THE OLD JEWISH COMMUNITY CENTER, JULY 1975. THE TORAH SCROLLS WERE MOVED TO A NEW TEMPLE FOUR MILES AWAY. THE BRICK FACADE WAS ADDED WHEN THE CENTER WAS "UPDATED" IN THE 1950S.

A *khupa* (wedding canopy) was set up at the foot of the stairs, the stairs on which I had played and fallen long ago. Down the road, two men waited in a horse-drawn carriage to receive the scrolls and take them the four miles to their new home. Tenenbaum led the group in singing as the scrolls descended and were carried under the *khupa* to the carriage. The horse was jittery and reared, which somehow seemed to accentuate the awesomeness of the occasion.

I stood at the side, photographing the scene. Through the lens of the camera, I saw the carriage drive off down the road and a man bend down and pick up a horseshoe. So that was why the horse had shied; she had thrown a shoe. I turned to the center, still looking through the lens. No one had remembered to close the windows. The building stood there, looking for all the world like a forgotten child. I started to take a picture but lost heart, and putting the camera down, I joined the procession moving away from the old toward the new.

I could not help thinking back to the time when our belongings were packed into a truck parked in front of a building on Fifth Street in New York City while I said good-bye to childhood friends. I was sitting on mattresses in the back of the truck and looked out the window as the driver pulled away from our old home to take us to a new one in Farmingdale.

14

Settling into a New Life

My parents were both born in Galicia, then part of the Austro-Hungarian Empire and now part of the Soviet Union: my father in Skalat, my mother in Toste. They did not know each other before their arrival in New York in the same year, 1922. Their journeys to the New World were quite different. My mother, having received a ticket from her older sister living in New York, came directly to her sister's home. My father, joining a group headed for Argentina, where he never intended to remain, worked his way across the ocean. After six months in Buenos Aires, he signed on as a stoker on a steamship headed for New York.

In New York, he lived with his only relative in America, a married cousin who had a large and growing family. Having had some experience making brandy in Skalat, my father convinced his cousin that there might be a good living in making and selling brandy and whiskey. When their homemade still exploded together with their profits, he and his cousin decided that my father needed another trade. Without much effort, he learned the hand-laundry business and soon had his own laundry on the lower East Side. Somehow, he was introduced to my mother, who was then working "by dresses." In a short time, she had worked her way up from seamstress to pattern maker to dress designer. They married, and within two years my brother Herbert and I were born. We lived in two rooms behind the hand laundry.

ROSE KATZ WISHNICK,
THE AUTHOR'S MOTHER,
IN NEW YORK, AROUND
1921.

In 1928, my parents bought a farm in Whitesville, New Jersey, near Toms River, where there was a small community of Jewish farmers. They went into this venture with my father's landsman, Morris Deutchman, and two thousand dollars borrowed from the Jewish Agricultural Society. Either the farm or the partnership was bad, because a year later they sold the farm and paid off the loan, and the partners went their separate ways. Morris Deutchman settled on another farm in Vineland; my family moved back to the lower East Side, where my father opened another hand laundry. Again we lived in two rooms in the back.

We had come back to the city in time for my sister Priscilla to be born. We were still living in the same two rooms behind the laundry when my younger brother Arnold was born two years later. By then my grandmother lived with us.

I spent much of the day in the hot, steamy laundry, where my father and mother seemed to be ironing forever. A burner from a small stove was on at all times to heat the irons, and several were on the stove at once. When we were very little, we helped my mother or my grandmother put the edges of curtains on the nails of the curtain stretchers. Little fingers were good for this job, I remember my father saying. The only language I heard was Yiddish. The customers, the friends who came, and the family all spoke Yiddish.

My older brother and I played in the large laundry bins. Once my mother and I came into the store and found my father in his underwear huddled up in a bin, his face and hands tied. At first I thought he was playing a game, but when my mother started to scream, I knew it was not funny. My father had been robbed of his cash and his clothes.

Schoolchildren wore uniforms when I started school in New York City. Boys wore white shirts and ties, and girls wore white middy blouses, red ties, and navy blue skirts. Perhaps because we were in the laundry business and had to be walking advertisements, our clothes were starched stiff and literally sparkled. My mother insisted that I walk to school with the collar of my middy blouse standing stiff like a white casing around my head; she did not want it wrinkled by my sweater. Outside the classroom, she removed my sweater and put the collar down.

In the morning, my mother picked up bags of dirty laundry from the teachers, and in the afternoon carried back clean, neatly wrapped packages. Her business transactions which attended our going and coming to school embarrassed me a great deal.

I started kindergarten before I was five years old. Shortly afterward, we moved to a four-room apartment, our very first. Although it seemed enormous after the laundry, the only place we could play was on the sidewalks.

Once I ran across the street in pursuit of a cat I wanted to pet. I did not see my two-year-old sister run after me. Suddenly, I heard a screech of brakes and saw a big commotion around my sister, who was lying in front of a car. Someone carried her screaming into a drugstore and laid her on top of the counter while the druggist examined her. She was not really hurt, but my mother was beside herself.

Another time, my baby brother Arnold crawled out of the apartment onto the fire escape and parked himself near the open steps. A crowd gathered below with arms outstretched, ready to catch the baby, who seemed about to fall. My mother and I, coming down the street with laundry, saw the scene. She dashed into the apartment, crawled out onto the fire escape, and slowly put her hand out and pulled Arnold back into the apartment.

I think she decided then and there that New York City was not a place where she could safely raise her children. She insisted on moving back to a farm, but my father resisted the idea. I still remember the intensity of the argument my parents had about moving to a farm again. My father yelled, "We tried that already. I am just beginning to build up a business!" My mother yelled back, "Stay with your business!" My grandmother just sat in the corner and covered her face with her hands.

For the second time, the Jewish Agricultural Society played a role in our lives. When my mother appeared in their office with her determined plea that she needed to live on a farm, the agent sent her to Farmingdale, a small new Jewish community with much potential, and closer to New York City than Whitesville was. The agent arranged to have Mr. Peskin meet her at the railroad station on her arrival. Leaving my father in the city, she traveled alone to central New Jersey to shop for a farm. She remained two nights with the Peskins and returned to New York with a receipt for a down payment. Evidently, she convinced my father that she was serious, and they must have reached some sort of agreement. The compromise they worked out was that he would remain in New York, working in the laundry, while she would move to the farm with us four children and would raise baby chicks. When the chicks became chickens and layed eggs—the cash crop—my father would join us. Shortly afterward, she and the children, ranging in age from one to seven, moved to Farmingdale. It was the fall of 1932. I was six and one-half years old.

Because of my mother's previous experience on a New Jersey farm, she knew what to expect. But this time, instead of two families living together, she would be alone with her children. The only person she knew in Farmingdale was Mr. Peskin, whom she had met for the first time when he picked her up at the railroad station. For all she knew, the Peskins would be the only people with whom she could talk. She barely knew English.

The moving van carrying our whole family and all our possessions arrived at our farm on a late afternoon. My brother and I ran into the house, which was huge compared to our apartment—and dark, empty, intimidating, and cold.

In the morning, we had our first visitor, a man by the name of Mr. Cherkiss who was white-haired, handsome, and soft spoken. He came by to say hello and to tell my mother about the Community Center, which was down the road. Cherkiss, neatly dressed in city clothes, did not look like a farmer to me. He looked like what I would now call a country squire. Indeed, he was not a farmer. I always wondered about him, where he came from, where he went to. He had no family, as far as I know.[3]

After helping my mother set up the house, my father returned to New York City, and we were on our own for six months. My father visited weekends, always bringing something—a box full of pencils, some pads of paper, a puzzle which we could not put together. We had no other toys at home, but the farm was a ten-acre sandbox, and the trees were made for climbing. We spent hours playing in the sand and trees.

There was always an uneasy feeling when my father came for his short visits. He seemed to be inappropriately dressed; he was either very busy, or he would sit around. I remember one morning when he and my mother had a very intense discussion which turned into a real row. My father pulled out a pack of farm bills from his pocket, tore them up, and threw the pieces on the floor. Angrily, he said he was leaving and wanted none of the farm. He only wanted to be able to see his son now and then—as if he had only one child. Storming out of the house, he started to walk in the direction of the railroad station. My mother, in her slip, ran down the road after him. Things seemed very wrong. Somehow, my parents must have worked out their differences, because my father sold his business, settled on the farm, and lived there until he died, becoming part and parcel of the land, responding to all its vibrations.

I do not remember exactly when my father finally joined the family. It must have been within six months because I have a letter written by my mother to her family in the city, and it indicates clearly that my father is with us. The language of the letter is Yiddish, but it is Yiddish written in the Roman alphabet rather than the Hebrew, and at first glance appears to be German. It is sprinkled with new English words that had found their way into her vocabulary. The letter is undated and reads, in my translation:

Dear Mother and Everybody:

I can write you that we are all in the best health. We wish to hear the same from you. Mother, you write that you would come here Sunday. It seems as if you fool me every time. We waited for you, and I called the station two times to find out if you arrived. I wanted to send Hulick for you. Mother, you must be afraid of a snowstorm. There can be no other reason. Mother dear, I can write you that on the 14th of March we are getting in another 800 baby chicks. The chicks we have are fine. We have already separated them and are keeping the cockerels in the garage.

I hope you and Helen [my mother's sister] can understand what I am writing. If you cannot understand some words, try to piece it together. Helen, write me if you and Frieda are coming for Passover. Do you want us to send eggs? Helen, this is just for you. If Mother does not want to come, I will not take out the Passover dishes, because I have so much work that I cannot seem to get finished. But please don't tell Mother.

Please write me, Helen, to tell me when the new month of Nisan will come out. I want to light a memorial candle for Father. I forgot to ask the *shoykhet* [ritual slaughterer].

Did you have a deep snowfall in New York? Because here we only had snow once.

I have nothing else to write. Benny [my father], the children, and I all send our best wishes and regards. Please answer. Rose.

Write me how Renee [a niece] is. Is she better? Is Frieda taking her to the doctor? Write me everything, I beg you. I would write more, but my Priscilla is crying, and I have to go to her. Good night.

Another undated letter contains more news of the farm.

Dear Sister Helen and Family:

I can write that everything is in order out here among us. We hope to hear the same from you. Helen, I thought that this Saturday, I would go to New York, but Herbert does not want to go. He says there is nothing to do in New York. He says, "It is too dirty there." I don't know if I spelled his words right. So I remain again at home, now. Please write me when you are coming here. And if Sidney is working, and how is Frieda and Charley and the children, because I have nothing else to write. We all send you our regards. A special regards and a separate one to Mother and Leonard. Please answer.

Clearly, my mother was busy but lonely for her family in New York. However, by the time the second letter was written, she appears to have adjusted to her new life.

Before my father joined us on the farm, he lived by himself in the laundry, having given up the apartment when the family moved. We never discussed the time he spent there, but years and years later, after I was married, with children of my own, he visited me. Taking an old crumpled piece of paper out of his wallet, he said: "I've kept this a long time. Maybe you'd like to have it now." It was a letter we children had written to him when he lived alone in New York, before coming to the farm. "Herbert wrote this page, you wrote that one, and your Mother helped Arnold and Priscilla," he explained. I could not discuss the letter with him or ask him about that period in his life. Both of us were tongue-tied by the surge of emotions. He had carried the memory and the letter with him all those years. Handing me the letter, written on a piece of school composition paper, he left. Page 1 is headed "Farmingdale" and starts:

Herbert Wischnik

Dear Father I can let you know that we are all feeling fine hopeing to hear from you the same. Dear father since you are away from use we are feeling very lonsome with out you we hope the day you are comeing out to stay with use for life.

On the other side is my note.

Father let me know how all my frends are in new york. I am not very
lonsome for them. How is Reeni Howard Shela. How is Lenad how Helen
how is Sidney how is Fany. Good Buy.

And in very shaky script: "Arnold sends his regards. Papa Priscilla wants a
regard too."

Meeting People

Winter passed and spring came. I met Mary, a woman boarder who had
rented a room at a Jewish farmer's home because she was sick from factory
work in the city. Mary organized four or five girls my age into a girls' club
and took us on walks in the woods. There she showed me things I had
never seen. Where in the city can one find a jack-in-the-pulpit or a lady's
slipper? At night, these same woods, with their heavy darkness, were
frightening, but during the daytime, I found a world of magic, especially
when the sun shone through the trees. Then it was as if I were the first
person in an unexplored world.

The woods we most often visited belonged to Boris, or Benjamin,
Bierstein. I am not exactly sure of his name—he was always called simply
Bierstein. We met him a few days after we arrived in Farmingdale. He
stopped by to say hello and to tell us he was a neighbor. Thereafter he
became a constant visitor.

Bierstein was not like the other farmers, or like many other people I
knew. He owned six acres of woods on a hill just opposite the Community
Center. There he lived in a small cabin with no plumbing or electricity,
sharing his cabin with Sadie Schwartz, to whom he was not married—
certainly a radical life-style for 1932. They were subsequently the subject
of many whispered conversations between me and my friends. Bierstein
also had exotic and strange animals on his farm which he kept for his
own interest rather than for food or profit. Shiny bantam hens, speckled
pheasants, goats and kids, rabbits, and once, even, a suckling pig. It was
definitely not a Jewish farm.

Bierstein enjoyed showing off his stock of exotica, and during my childhood and later, when I had children of my own, I often visited to see the
beautiful birds and animals. He sometimes scattered pennies around and
covered them with sand so that children could play at finding treasures.
He enjoyed company, and he was proud of his little farm. He kept it and

his woods immaculately clean and was always busy raking his leaves into neat piles. As he got older, his raking became more eccentric, and young boys in the neighborhood rode their bikes or their horses through his freshly raked piles, scattering the leaves before the wind had a chance. But that was much later.

When I was a child, Bierstein, while not exactly my Socrates, constantly provoked me into lively arguments and discussions and forced me to think clearly about the logic of my answers. He was a tall man, straight as a ramrod, with a strong ruddy face and a brush of gray hair. With leather puttees buckled over his trousers and up to his knees (my father also wore puttees; he either copied from Bierstein or vice versa), he looked like a Russian Bolshevik. When he appeared at our place, usually early in the morning or in the later afternoon, he carried his paper, the Yiddish *Freiheit* or the English *Daily Worker*, and a long thin switch or willow branch to chase flies away. He liked to talk, using an article from the paper as a starting place, and would gradually become more intense and passionate. My father, who also liked to talk, used to spend a lot of time with him, but eventually he had to get on to his o''er work—my father had a conventional flock of chickens, two cows that needed attention, and four children to feed. I was left with Bierstein. I soon learned the fun of challenging his assumptions and playing the devil's advocate just to see how he would get out of the argument.

I knew nothing about politics then; all I knew was what I learned from my city relatives: that the workers were exploited and that strikes were somehow valiant, glorious, and justified battles. Within that context, there was yet plenty of room for discussion and argumentation. One loud and passionate discussion that went on for a long time occurred when daylight saving time was instituted. Bierstein declared it was a capitalist plot to deprive the workers of their favorite hour of morning sleep. I argued that the longer summer day gave the worker more time to enjoy the sun, but neither convinced the other. These discussions with Bierstein spilled over into my school program.

We had something called Current Events, for which everyone had to prepare a short talk on a topic found in a newspaper or heard on the radio. Invariably I brought in items related to my current discussion with Bierstein and a clipping from either the *Daily Worker* or the English column of the *Freiheit*. These were the only papers I saw or knew about. It took years and years for me to understand why the teacher gasped and the students snickered at my reports.

Bierstein took us to our first Community Center meeting. My father was living in New York then, and my mother, eager for the social opportunity, took us all with her. She carried Arnold (only one and a half years old), held on to Priscilla (three and a half years old), and instructed my older brother, Herbert, and me to hold on to her. Bierstein led the way. It was very dark. In contrast to the street in New York City, the sandy road was like a desolate world, the expanse of field or woods unbroken by buildings. I was very frightened and hung on to my mother's coat for dear life. I thought that if I let go, I would be lost forever. When the lights of the center appeared over the rise in the road, they were like beacons pointing the way at last to a warm safe place. It seemed as if we had wandered for miles and hours, when in fact we lived only about three city blocks from the Community Center. I never got over my fear of dark country roads and never walked alone at night, not even after close to forty years of living in Farmingdale.

I do not remember much about that meeting, except that I stayed close to my mother, who greeted people in familiar Yiddish. After that, we went to the center every Saturday night. My mother, who had a beautiful voice and loved to sing, was always asked for a song, in which the others joined. There was one song which my older brother and I dramatized while she sang; it seemed to be a hit, because we did it often enough.

At the center someone or other was always being honored. During the course of the evening, a man would stand up, fill a glass with wine, extend the wineglass in the direction of the honored person, and begin, "Lomir ale, in eynim, in eynim, khaver Peskin makabl ponim zeyn" (Let us, one and all, honor our friend Peskin). Everyone lifted a wineglass and joined in the singing. I usually fell asleep sitting on a chair at these socials, and the walk home seemed even longer and darker than the walk over.

At Home and in Town

I think there is nothing like the first remembered spring or summer on a farm. I remember having a dog named Fritz and walking barefoot on the sandy roads, where cars rarely appeared. What did come down those less-traveled roads were merchants' vehicles bringing goods and services to the farmers.

Most of our shopping was done from bus, car, or truck shops which came into the driveway just outside our door. A green grocer came twice a week in a converted schoolbus to sell sparkling fresh vegetables, fruits, and things like herring, lox, and Greek olives. A baker from Freehold, the closest large town and eight miles away, brought fresh bread every morning. Eventually, the baker's wife, who delivered the bread, became a customer for cracked eggs. I think the eggs were bartered for the bread. The baker's wife often came into the house after her rounds in the morning for a cup of hot coffee and one of the rolls she had just delivered. I now appreciate the luxury we had of going to our mailbox at seven in the morning and taking out a bag of rolls, bread, and breakfast buns, sometimes still warm. A fish man also came to the house with his truck, converted from an old car, in which he had ice and fish. I have an image of a warm spring day and the fish man demonstrating to my mother how fresh the fish were. He pressed a fish, and a stream of water spouted in the air. They both laughed. A dry-goods man, Levinson, came from Toms River. His was also a handmade truck, converted from a car. The back of the car had been cut away, and a wooden box constructed to make a miniature store. I do not know how old I was when, one day, I looked past the bright colors of the socks, aprons, and fabrics and saw two people, a man and his wife, worn out with work, carefully tying and untying bundles of underwear or towels and talking quietly to each other. In the winter their hands seemed purple with cold. The woman had two fingers missing from one of her hands. They spoke no English at all, at least not to us. We conversed only in Yiddish. They had a young child who sometimes came with them; he would lie on bundles of towels in the truck, sucking on a bottle of tea. I remember wondering how it was possible for people who looked so old to have a baby.

Not all goods and services came to the house, however. Farmingdale, the town center, was two miles from our farm, and we walked there when we needed haircuts or when my father and mother had to go to the bank. Main Street seemed like a busy place to me. The only other city I had known was New York, but I did not compare them.

On the corner of Main Street and Asbury Avenue, the primary road leading out of town and to Asbury Park, there was a general store that sold everything. Hats were pinned on a line across one corner. Shoes hung on another line. Flour and sugar were sold from barrels in the front of the store; nails were in a bin; penny candy, ribbons, and a myriad of other things were in glass cases and jars on the counter. In the middle of Main Street was a bakery with big brick-wall ovens. The bread smelled delicious but never tasted as good as our morning rye bread. My father occasionally gave me a few pennies to buy a gingerbread cookie, and the owner of the bakery often gave me another one as a gift. Farmingdale also had two doctors, a non-Kosher butcher shop in which we never shopped, a pharmacy, and a small grocery store. None of the shops was owned by Jews when we moved to the farm, although some years later there was a Jewish grocer and druggist. The atmosphere of the town was friendly, but cool and distant. It was not my environment, and even as a child I felt a stranger.

I always walked to town with my father. Once in a while, I would hear people mimic his speech or make jokes in an affected Yiddish accent. My father did not pay the slightest attention; maybe he did not even hear the remarks. But I did not know whether to laugh (which I did not really feel much like doing) or to cry.

The railroad station was also in Farmingdale, and it was from there that we left for New York on occasional visits. However, my mother traveled to the city regularly, carrying with her eggs from our farm. I recall watching my mother and father walking down the sandy road toward the station two miles away, carrying a case of thirty dozen eggs between them. Before they were out of sight, I saw them change hands several times. It is not a happy memory. Even then, I knew that a case of eggs is heavy—it weighs about sixty pounds—and I wished they had a truck or a horse and wagon so they could be spared the burden. My uncle met my mother at Liberty Street in Jersey City, helped her carry the eggs to the ferry and then to the train, and eventually to the Bronx, where he lived. She sold the eggs to people in his apartment building and then came home with the money and the empty case.

My Mother's Death

Two years after we moved onto the farm, my mother died. I was almost nine years old. I do not really remember when she became ill, and I have only vague memories of her confinement at home. I remember going to New York with her to see a doctor. At the time, we had an egg dealer who picked up our eggs. Early one spring morning, my mother and I went into the truck with the eggs and rode to New York with them. I made the trip sitting with a helper on a carton of eggs in the back of the van while my mother sat in the cab with the driver. We took the train back home, and my mother was very quiet and sad on our return journey.

She was in bed at home for some months. Our friends the Hamburgers, both of whom were serious nutritionists, arranged for Dr. Lieber, the head of the naturalist movement in New York, to come to Farmingdale and examine her. I remember him standing by the window looking out while my mother was on the bed turned in the direction of the doctor's back. He left the house shaking his head.

My mother resisted going to the hospital. Both she and my grandmother were deathly afraid of them because in Toste, where they were born, when a person went to the hospital, he or she was never seen again. Because of her fear, my mother had delivered all her babies at home.

The few families in the community rallied together, almost by instinct, and considered it a personal responsibility to offer help and support. A committee took turns taking care of the children and providing nursing assistance to my mother. Pauline Sokol described the scene to me years later. "She was so sick, so sick. She couldn't eat anything. I made her some loose cereal and fed it to her like to a baby. Her face was gray. Your sister, a thin little girl with big eyes, just stood by the bed and wouldn't go away. I took the baby, Arnold, home with me. He was only two years old. In my house, he cried and cried till my heart was breaking."

Eventually, my mother had to be taken to the hospital, and the Hamburgers drove her there. She knew that she was going to die and asked each of us in turn to take care of each other and of my father.

When she needed blood, a call went out to the community. Sophia Peskin, eighteen years old, was the donor. Those who had cars took turns driving my father to the hospital, and many neighbors helped on the farm.

Details are not clear, but in some ways it was an exciting time. There was always lots of company around; my grandmother was with us, taking care of the house and cooking delicious things for us. Although I must have known at some level that my mother was very ill, I lived with the expectation that she would get well and come home.

The night of her death, I was sleeping with my grandmother in my mother's bed. I remember waking and seeing many people in the bedroom, and my grandmother sitting on a chair crying and swaying, as if about to faint. Her crying in front of company embarrassed me, and as I peeked out from under the covers, I smiled at the guests as if to apologize for my grandmother. I did not understand all the commotion. No one told me my mother had just died.

The next morning, the relatives from New York were there. I was playing with my cousins outdoors on that cold December day when one of them asked if I was going to the funeral. It was the first direct word that I had. I could no longer pretend not to understand, and I ran into the house, screaming at my father, "Where is Momma? Where is Momma?" He started to cry, picked me up, and then we both sat down and cried.

When it was time for the funeral, my father told me I had to stay in the house and help take care of Priscilla and Arnold, but I disobeyed him. I had heard that the funeral would be held at the Community Center. When everyone left, I broke away and ran alone down the road to the center. I went into Bierstein's woods, opposite the building, and sitting on the crest of the hill, I watched the long black car parked in front of the center.

There was no sun, no flowers, no leaves, All was bare desolation. I then must have gone to the door of the center because Harry Sokol, remembering the time some forty-five years later, told me he saw me outside. "You were standing outside wearing a jacket too small for you, peeking through a crack in the door and shivering as if you would never stop." He went out, picked me up, and carried me in. I do not remember it. I retain an image of a coffin draped in a black tapestry with a Jewish star on it. Someone brought me home; I was not taken to the cemetery. I waited with a cousin, my sister, and my baby brother. Of the children, only my older brother, Herbert, went to the cemetery.

My grandmother had covered all the mirrors in the house with white sheets. I did not understand why and was frightened by the thought that ghosts were being sealed in the mirrors.

We had much company during the whole week following the funeral. In addition to the relatives from New York, others from the community came to visit. Among them were the two teachers from our school. Not knowing that flowers are out of place in a Jewish house of mourning, they arrived with a big bunch of yellow chrysanthemums. I remember my grandmother opening the door for them—she, not speaking any English; they, not knowing any Yiddish. My grandmother looked at the two women standing there, uncomfortably holding on to their flowers, and she did not speak. Nor could they say much either. I was sitting on the kitchen floor, playing a game with Arnold. I looked up at the scene and felt both deeply ashamed and strangely intimidated by Christian teachers in our home and by my grandmother, holding on to the door, looking at them. She did not ask them to come in or take the flowers from their outstretched hands or go out. She just stood there looking at them. I was acutely and painfully embarrassed. Finally a cousin who could speak a little English appeared, came to the door, and, taking the flowers from the teachers, thanked them for coming. They did not come into the house at all. The next morning, I found the yellow chrysanthemums on the trash pile outside. They had seemed so pretty to me; I wanted them for my room, but I was afraid to get too close to them. For a long time, I did not understand why the flowers were thrown away.

I had a very hard time accepting my mother's death, although the day I returned to school, everything seemed just as it had been before. But when I came home, I instinctively called out, "Momma, I'm home." There was no answer, and I remembered there would never be one. I looked out the window and thought I saw my mother standing near a tree. I ran out toward the tree and searched among all the trees, until, exhausted, I flung my arms around one trunk and cried as if there were no end to my tears. My father came and took me back into the house.

I did not see my mother's grave until a headstone was erected some nine months after she died. After that it became a yearly ritual to visit the grave with my grandmother. Every year, it seemed as if that was the most dismal day of the year. Invariably it rained. My grandmother held on to all four of us as we walked slowly and quietly to the grave. Half of her seemed to disappear in the black shawl that was tied under her chin. It was a long walk uphill on a loose gravel and pebble path until we got to the grave. When we reached it, my grandmother, quiet until that point, put our hands on the gravestone, and then the quiet gave way to her melancholy wailing and keening.

In Yiddish, she spoke to my mother. "Mayn sheyne blum, mayn kind, mayn Reyzye. Loyf un bet oys far de kinder gezint. Bet az Beni zol zayn gezint un kenen akhtik gebn oyf di kinder. Er zol zayn a gutr tate. Oy di mame, oy di kinder. Mayn sheyne blum." (My beautiful flower, my child, my Rose. Run and plead for the children to be healthy. Plead for Benny to be well so that he can take care of the children and be a good father. Oh, your mother, oh, your children. My beautiful flower.)

My sister and younger brother always cried—it was so terrifying—while my grandmother hugged the headstone as if it were the warm body of my mother. Then, after about an hour, or so it seemed, we all picked up pebbles and put them on top of the stone or in the corner of the grave. As we left my grandmother pointed to the adjoining plot and every year would say: "Ikh vil du lign, lebn mayn tokhter. Ikh vil dos shtikl erd." (I want to lie here, near my daughter. I would like to have this piece of earth.)

My mother is buried in the Workmen's Circle Cemetery in Freehold. Her death was the first such tragedy in the community, which, in 1934, had not yet anticipated that it would need a burial place. After that, it became an urgent priority of the community members to buy a parcel of land from the Workmen's Circle and have a Farmingdale section in the Freehold Cemetery. My father is now in that Farmingdale section, separated by several acres from my mother. And while my grandmother did not exactly have her wish, she is two graves away from her daughter.

15

Life with All Kinds
of People

Hilda and Other Women

My grandmother lived with us between my mother's death and my father's remarriage. Old for her time (she was in her late sixties), she managed the house and children, catered to all our personal idiosyncrasies, and provided us with her love and warmth, which we needed, and her wisdom and values, which we absorbed. My father helped her with the household tasks and with taking care of the babies, Arnold and Priscilla. He also took charge of the dirty laundry. It never seemed odd to see him ironing clothes because I had seen him doing that in his laundry shop.

While role expectations for men and women was a concept I thought about only later in my life, I experienced, early on, men and women doing interchangeable tasks. After all, my mother had moved on the farm alone with four children, prepared chicken coops, and raised a stock. She took care of chicks and children simultaneously and in her spare time made our clothes. I remember how she once made me a wool suit out of my grandmother's bathrobe. She worked constantly at whatever had to be done. My impressions of women were based on the models of my mother and grandmother, augmented by Hilda and the other farm women I knew.

My father married Hilda London fourteen months after my mother died. It was a marriage of convenience for both of them, arranged by my father's landsman living in Brooklyn. Hilda was thirty years old, never married, living with a younger married sister and her family in a four-room Brooklyn apartment. My father needed someone to look after the children and help on the farm; Hilda needed to be married and live somewhere else.

I think he went to New York once to meet her, and she came to Farmingdale once to meet us. But she made no impression on me; I did not know who she was. Then, one day, my grandmother cooked and baked every specialty we loved—blintzes, borscht, kreplakh, varenikes (or piroshki), cookies, and fruitcake—called the four of us together, and said simply that she must move back to New York. She left out the front door as soon as Hilda came in the back door. She did not stay to greet our new stepmother; it was too painful for her to see her daughter's place taken by a stranger. I later learned that my grandmother walked to the home of Max and Esther Klein, neighbors who lived down the road, and waited until she could get to the train for New York.

My father did not take time off his farm routine for Hilda, his bride, on the day she arrived. He sent Herbert, then eleven years old, to the train station two miles away to meet someone Herbert did not know, and to help carry her things while they walked back to the farm. My father did not inform us he had remarried. As far as I could understand, Hilda simply appeared and my grandmother disappeared. There seemed to be no rhyme or reason to anything.

A second major rift in my life within a short period of time, my grandmother's departure was even worse for me than my mother's death. Hilda never filled the void. She was not pretty or sensitive or creative like my mother, or soft and wise and kind like my grandmother. Nor did she know how to cook. My grandmother had been a caterer in Europe and could pull magic foods out of the simplest of staples. When we could not eat what Hilda prepared, she became angry and surly. Once when she berated me soundly for not eating her pea soup, I burst out crying. She tried then to reach me, "Don't cry. I'm going to be your mother. I'll be good to you. I won't hit you."

I was not convinced. For weeks after she arrived, I would come home from school, throw myself on the bed, and cry. I was now in double mourning, for both my mother and my grandmother. My father tried to console me, telling me that everything would be all right. But he could not convince me either. Hilda stopped being sympathetic and became impatient. "Crying again," she would snap. "Look what a mess you are making of the bed."

I stopped crying but developed migraine headaches which sometimes lasted for days. The only way I could control the pain was to lie or sit perfectly still. My headaches and my quietness were much more acceptable to both my father and Hilda. Although I outgrew the migraines, I learned the wrong lesson. Stoically bearing sorrow is not the best road to happiness.

Hilda wanted us to call her Mother and spent considerable time trying to get us to do so. But we never did. I could not accept her as my mother, and since my father never told me directly that he had remarried, I invented the myth that Hilda was our housekeeper. I told my friends that we had a maid, and even felt a new status. Who else among them had a servant?

In fact, in many ways, Hilda was treated like hired help. For the first time, I noticed that she and my father had separate and distinct jobs. She did all the housework; packed the eggs; cleaned the freshly killed chickens, including those my father sold to summer boarders; processed the milk from our two cows, making it into cream, cheese, and butter; and prepared the rooms and bungalows for the summer people. My father no longer helped in any of these tasks. He did all the outdoor work on the farm—the carpentry, masonry, plumbing, and electrical work. He fed, watered, and bedded the chickens, collected the eggs and the money from them, and, after he purchased a car, drove around making deals of various kinds. Once a week he drove my stepmother to Freehold or Lakewood for supplemental grocery shopping. Every week he gave her a spending allowance which she called her *paydeh,* as if she received a salary.

I watched my stepmother turn from a well-dressed city woman to a farm wife. When she first came, she changed into a good dress every evening in preparation for her walk. I do not know where she walked. She considered Saturdays a day off, dressed in an even better dress and coat, and walked up and down the road several times. There were not many places she could go unless she walked to a neighbor who, likely as not, was too busy to talk or visit during the day. Or she might have walked to Farmingdale. Once or twice, I accompanied her. Although she continued walking in the evening during her whole life in Farmingdale, she soon stopped changing her dress. Soon after that she did not differentiate between Saturday and the rest of the week, with one exception. The house always received a thorough cleaning on Friday mornings, and she baked hallah and prepared traditional Sabbath foods. This was our only connection with observance. For the most part, the days blended into each other in an unbroken and monotonous chain of work.

When I was about eleven, my job was to grade the eggs with my stepmother when I came home from school. We worked in the basement, grading each egg separately on a small hand scale, brushing the dirty ones by hand with a sandpaper brush. Hilda sat on a low box in front of an upturned crate which held the scale. We both pushed a case of graded eggs away; periodically my father would appear and stack the crates one on top of another, labeling them with his co-op number so that they could be identified and he would get paid. From sitting thus for years, bent over the hand egg scale, my stepmother's shoulders got so round that she appeared to have a hump. One of the last modern machines to come onto our farm was an automatic egg-grader. It was then possible to stand and put dozens of eggs on the scale at the same time. But it was too late for Hilda's back to straighten out.

As soon as I came home from school, I had to change my clothes and go down into the basement. Each time I saw a floor full of baskets of eggs, my heart sank; I knew I could not go upstairs until they were all graded and packed. I hated the job; it was repetitious and boring beyond belief. My sister and I would sometimes liven things up for ourselves by throwing the eggs to each other as if they were balls to catch. But actually, I learned a kind of discipline which has been invaluable, helping me through graduate schools and through many tedious tasks. To this day, when I have work to do that is tedious and boring, I always remember those eggs. I know there is an end to boring jobs, and I keep telling myself, as I did when I was a child, "When the eggs are done, I can come up from the basement."

My brother claims he received a broad-based education on the farm which enabled him to go into the construction business. He helped my father build the chicken coops, lay the water pipes, hook up the electricity, do the masonry, and repair the roofs. When he started building for others, he already knew a great deal. And he too had acquired the necessary discipline to see a job through.

I must say, however, that my brothers' chores did not seem as monotonous as mine and my sister's. The boys moved around the chicken coops and did a variety of tasks, from feeding the chickens, to collecting eggs, to opening or closing the nests. When my father expanded the farm operations to include a hatchery, my brothers worked there, setting trays, monitoring the temperature, turning the eggs, and checking for the infertile ones to be removed.

My father recycled everything, even the infertile eggs. He reasoned that they could be cooked and fed to the chickens, who needed protein. My sister and I were given the added chore of boiling and peeling those rotten, putrid eggs, which had already spent ten days or so in the incubator. It was a job that often made me retch.

Certain arduous seasonal tasks—taking the chickens out on the range, vaccinating them, or raking the hay from the fields—were very hard, and as many hands as could be mustered were pressed into service. Neighbors were called upon and also helped. We worked around the clock until the job was done. And we, in turn, also had to help the neighbors.

All the farm women and girls I knew packed eggs and did other chores on the farm. Some of the women worked right alongside their husbands, cleaning out chicken coops, preparing the outdoor ranges for the chickens, doing the same heavy manual work as the men. These were the women who peopled my world. I looked at them, at their work-worn hands and faces, their rough clothing, indistinguishable from the men's, and I resolved never to live on a farm or have anything to do with a farm when I grew up.

A RARE MOMENT OF RELAXATION: BENJAMIN WISHNICK AND HILDA LONDON WISHNICK, THE AUTHOR'S FATHER AND STEPMOTHER, IN FARMINGDALE, AROUND 1955.

Farm Helpers

My father's work on the farm grew in proportion to the increasing size of his flocks. To save money, he bought the ingredients to feed chickens in bulk and mixed the mash himself. He emptied the sacks on the floor of the feed room and blended everything together with a hoe, raising up a cloud of dust in which it was impossible to breathe. The mash and corn were put into bins, and one of our games was to jump into the bins and cover ourselves with mash or get lost in the corn. If there were rats in the bins, we did not notice them.

My father's energy was not inexhaustible. It soon became clear to him that he needed help, and he eventually hired helpers. The first two farmhands I remember were local Christians: Levi, an old man, and Bill, a teenager. They became part of the landscape of our farm.

Levi Marriner was an old-time native farmer whose roots extended far back. He helped farmers in odd jobs: digging, painting, planting, or putting in fences. A tall thin man with a ruddy face and a set of false teeth too large for his gums, he would appear every spring in faded denim coveralls and a large straw hat and spade out a garden. We walked alongside him in the rows of freshly turned earth while he patiently explained what he was doing and why.

Bill was a local boy who must have needed room and board as well as a chance to earn a little money. I had difficulty understanding why he did not live at home. I knew little about economics, the depression, or adolescent rebellion. I only knew that the worker's bed in our basement hardly seemed like a good place to sleep. The boy must have been sixteen or seventeen. When he had nothing else to do, he went down to his basement room, stretched out on his bed in his working clothes, shoes and all, and drank beer or smoked. My father had helped him buy a bicycle, and one day he rode off on the bicycle and did not return.

My father needed more dependable help, and he turned to the Jewish Agricultural Society. The JAS had an agricultural training school and during the war extended its operations to train young refugees arriving in America for farm work. Two farm workers were sent to us by the JAS; after the first left, the second arrived. Each lived with us for an extended period of time and became like family.

Charlie Wolf was a young single man who had somehow managed to leave Lithuania before the Nazis closed all avenues of escape. He actually had family living in Farmingdale—the Tenenbaums. Charlie was an earnest, gentle, and playful young man who was very attentive and kind to all of us. We thought of him as a big brother and followed him around everywhere.

He needed the period on the farm as a way of becoming integrated into American life. He also needed to learn English, and I remember telling him what I was studying at school. When the WPA set up a language school in the community, Charlie attended with nine farm women, my stepmother among them. He said it never bothered him; he enjoyed learning with the women. When he felt it was time to leave us, we had another tearful parting.

Charlie's departure was soon followed by Sigfried's arrival. Sigfried Hertzberg was a refugee from Germany and had farm experience there. For the seven or eight years he lived with us, he shared a small upstairs bedroom with my brother Herbert, across the hall from the bedroom Priscilla and I shared. A lonely, eccentric middle-aged man, he looked constantly bewildered, as if trying to understand the traumatic events of his recent past. He spoke German, not Yiddish, and certainly not English. Although he tried to teach us little German songs, we could not easily communicate with him, as we could with Charlie, who spoke Yiddish to us. Even as a child, I understood how hard Sigfried worked. After lunch and supper, he stretched out on his bed in all his working clothes. Like the teenage boy, he did not take off his shoes. He just lay there, smoking smelly cigars, which I hated. My father helped him buy a bicycle also, and a few times a week he pedaled to the town of Farmingdale, where German speakers gathered in a tavern. Siggy would return late at night, singing German songs, and stumbling up the stairs to his bed. On the Jewish holidays, he prayed in the synagogue at the Community Center; aside from that, I do not think he had any other social outlets.

Eventually, my father helped him buy a motorcycle, and he could go further afield. I believe he visited German families living near Lakewood.

The labor of the workers was supplemented by our child labor. Before running water was installed in the chicken coops, we pumped water from the outdoor shallow well into huge buckets to be carried to the coops. My father's carrying buckets of water on a contraption he built, a wooden harness of sorts for his shoulders, remains in my memory as a bittersweet image. I remember pumping pail after pail of water for him. When the pails were filled, he squatted, balancing the boards, and slipped them under the upright handles. When he got up, four heavy pails of water were suspended from the boards on his shoulders.

Although he never talked about his life in Skalat, where he was born and grew up, I knew that his skill in carrying the water was practiced and developed in another time, in another place. The whole farmyard scene—the Yiddish which we always spoke, the distance, psychological and actual, from the Christian town and neighbors, the workers—I recognized as strangely familiar and from another world.

Neighbors from That Other World

Rural life on the outskirts of a small town such as Farmingdale shared elements of life in Galicia, where both my parents were born: the natural landscape; the diversity of tasks to be done; the close-knit Jewish community whose members all had a similar history, spoke the same language, and established the networks of self-help systems they had known in Europe. Familiar also were the Christian neighbors who were as remote and distant as they had been in my parents' early years.

It is not that we did not interact with the Christian community. We did. But emotionally, we kept each other at arm's length. I regret now the imposed distance. Not until I left Farmingdale did I feel comfortable socializing in Christian homes. As a child, I rarely played with Christian children and went into the homes of the 4-H members only for meetings.

Our closest neighbor was Charlie Hulick, an old Christian farmer. After my mother's funeral, and every day during the mourning period, he came and fed the chickens, stopping first into the house to leave a green mason jar of cold fresh cream or some butter or cheese. I think of him often, of his kindness and his simplicity.

His home was directly opposite ours. As a matter of fact, our property had once been part of his family's farm. I remember him as being a very sweet, always old man. Although none of us, except perhaps my father, had ever been into his house, his farm was familiar to me, my brothers, and sister. He had a well with spring water on his place, and whenever we visited, he drew a bucket of cold sparkling spring water for us.

Charlie represented another world to me. Local history had it that his wood-shingled saltbox house had originated before the Revolutionary War. I knew he was a real American, in contrast to me or my father. His roots were in that soil, on that spot, and they went back a long, long time. His grandparents, his great-grandparents, and those before, had planted the same fields he planted, walked the same road, and gone to the same church. I never knew a grandfather or the paths my father walked when he was my age. Charlie continued a tradition in a direct, observable, and understandable way, whereas our family seemed to have no tradition whatsoever in America except for the traditions of certain foods—hallah on Friday, matzos on Passover. Even what little religious observance there once had been was thrown away—was called irrelevant, superfluous, and out of touch with real life.

But Charlie was different. He was part and parcel of the landscape. Years later, even after I had been in Farmingdale a long time, after I married and established a home of my own on a farm, I sometimes had the urge to run out onto our fields and lie on the ground and hug it close to me, to be a part of it in the way Charlie was and I could never be.

Charlie was a native farmer who knew what he had to do every day. I think he had little if any formal education, although he must have attended, at least for a time, whatever local school there was. I unexpectedly gained some insight about him from a vignette shared with me by one of the people I interviewed. Dorothy Friedland Hamburger grew up in Farmingdale and knew Charlie before I did. She told me about how her father had purchased their piano from the Hulicks.

It seems Charlie's mother played the piano, and it was her prize possession, just as a car later became Charlie's. When she died, the piano remained in the front room for years, in magnificent but silent splendor. Charlie and his father were happy to sell it when Max Friedland, who wanted his daughter to have music lessons, approached them. The Hulicks had actually been worried about keeping it in good shape.

Dorothy and her father went into the Hulick home and found the house in terrible repair. The holes in the floors were so large one could see the basement underneath. Farm tools and implements were piled up all over the parlor, competing for space with vegetables in different stages of desiccation and decay. In one corner of the room—pristine, pure, and polished—stood the upright Steinway, kept in tune all those years by the farmer son and husband, neither of whom played.

In some ways, Charlie was a bridge between an old world and a modern one. In 1932, he plowed his fields with an old horse, drawing a primitive contraption. But he also had a brand new shiny Ford in a barn converted to a garage.

He kept the car in something like slipcovers. It was a remarkable occasion when he took it out for a drive, and the four of us children lined up on our lawn to watch him. Sometimes he invited us along; these were memorable excursions. He never went faster than about ten miles an hour. The two miles to Farmingdale took almost fifteen minutes. For us, that was just fine.

Everything connected with the car was enacted in a ritualistic way—from Charlie's removing the slipcovers to his backing out of the barn slowly, halting alongside of his house, then slowly and carefully maneuvering onto the road. When he would stop for us, we climbed onto the running board and into the car, seating ourselves in the cool dark interior with the same quality of deliberate ceremony. I remember how quiet and full of awe I was in the leathery back seat. It was like sitting in a church pew. The wheels generated a cloud of red dust in the sand road, which was really a wagon path. For all the world, Charlie's car was like Elijah's chariot ascending in a red cloud. And Charlie himself was a transformed Elijah on a heavenly mission taking little Jewish children as witness to a miracle.

On our return, we were deposited on our doorstep, and the chariot slowly swung into his driveway and halted again beside Charlie's house. There it received a careful examination and a rubdown. Every speck of dust was coaxed out of the corners, and then, very slowly, the car was eased into the barn-garage and returned to its slipcovers.

Years later, my mother's cousin—the only remaining member of a large family completely wiped out in a typhus epidemic—who had come to America with his aunt, my grandmother, achieved the pinnacle of success in this land of golden opportunity with the purchase of a car. Living in the Bronx, working in a slipper factory, and then becoming part owner of the same factory, Moshe was able to buy for himself in 1936 a new, shiny, maroon Pontiac. The car became the same sacred icon to the immigrant Jewish boy from Toste, Galicia, now New York businessman, as it was to the native Christian farmer from Farmingdale.

For Moshe and the family of cousins he transported, every journey was also a heavenly voyage, and every return necessitated the same careful, scrupulous attention that Charlie paid to his car. When the Pontiac arrived from New York to Farmingdale, it was parked in a shady place, not too close to the trees—the wind might brush the branches against the body and scratch it, or the birds might deposit something. And not in the hot sun—the paint might crack or peel. The Pontiac was polished and rubbed down and, like Charlie's chariot, put under slipcovers.

In time, financial reverses, unscrupulous partners, and business failures forced my mother's cousin from Toste to say good-bye to his Pontiac and to his New York business. I think the former was much the harder parting. Fortunately, I did not see the leave-taking, but I did meet him at the bus station after that, when he came to visit us in Farmingdale. It was sad to see him get off the bus, not so much because he lost his pretty toy, but more because the whole American dream which his car symbolized had evaporated.

Ages and ages after Charlie took us for a ride in his proud Ford, he was defrauded of his property by other native Farmingdale people. A lonely old man with no relatives, still scratching out a living from his fields, or living because he still was scratching, he signed his farm over to townspeople he thought he knew, in return for their promise that he could have life rights to his home and his property. They assured him they would give him money for subsistence and would care for him when he needed it. After he signed the legal papers, they forced him off the farm. People from the local church, old-time farmers, took Charlie in.

The last time I saw him was the summer of 1961. He was planting a garden for the people with whom he was living, and I was riding by on a bicycle. I got off my bike, went over to him, and reminded him of who I was. A smile lit up his face like sunshine, and then he asked sadly, "How's Ben? I heard he was poorly." My father had then been dead four years. When I told him this, he said, "Ah, but I'm sorry. Ben, he was a nice man. Well, I won't be a bother to people for too much longer." And he turned back to his hoeing and his cabbage plants. I could only say, "Good-bye, Charlie. Good-bye." But he did not hear me or see me anymore.

I see him yet, an old man in a very battered straw hat, permanently bent into his hoe and into his garden rows, rubbing the earth between his fingers.

My memories of Charlie Hulick are in sharp contrast to those of another Christian neighbor whose property backed onto ours. While I roamed freely on Charlie's farm, I did not go onto the other neighbor's property which I passed every day on my way to school. But my dog did. He usually followed me, returning home by himself as soon as I went into the building. On our morning walk, the dog regularly cut across the neighbor's yard and garden, irritating the man no end. Once the farmer came out of his house, yelling at the dog and threatening that if the dog came on his property one more time, he would shoot him. But the dog was untrainable, especially without a leash. Sure enough, the next day when we passed the neighbor's farm, the dog was ahead of me and on the forbidden ground. I ran into the garden after him and scooped the dog up into my arms at the same time that the angry farmer came out of his house with the muzzle of a gun extended in our direction. I stood facing the gun, the dog caught up and clutched to my breast, tears running down my face. I pleaded: "Please, please, don't shoot my dog! Please!"

It did not occur to me to run away. Nor did it occur to me that if the dog was shot, I would be too. The Christian farmer stood there menacingly for a while, poised with his gun as if he was trying to decide whether or not to shoot. Finally, lowering the gun and muttering something about keeping that darned critter off his property, the neighbor sort of slunk into his house. The dog never went into the garden again.

City Friends, Country Boarders

My friends and I did not discuss our feelings about the farm or our frustrations about growing into the women we saw in our small provincial community. Either we did not have the sophistication and imagination to do so, or we could not articulate our yearnings even to ourselves. I could not allow myself to bring into full consciousness my claustrophobic sense of a small constricting world closing in on me. All these feelings were made even more acute by contacts with city relatives and summer boarders who sharpened the differences I already felt.

From the age of twelve or thirteen, I traveled to New York alone to visit relatives in the Bronx or Brooklyn. These winter visits to the city, important as they were to me, intensified my feelings of loneliness when I returned. To me, the city was dynamic. It had life, adventure, and possibilities for romance undreamed of in Farmingdale. I had to visit New York, but I knew all the time that it was not my world either.

But in the summertime, New York came to our farm. After my father remarried, he decided to rent out rooms to city people. Whether he needed to extend his income (which was a likely possibility), or my stepmother's family and friends came to visit so often that he decided he might as well charge rent, or he was looking for added excitement in his life, or for all of the above, he became a summer landlord.[4]

Our first customers rented rooms in our small farmhouse. All of the extra furniture, including the beds, were piled into one room, where we all slept in the summer while the boarders had the other rooms. The cramped sleeping arrangements were not as annoying to me as spending the day with guests always underfoot.

Every morning, a baby would wake me up with some infernal screaming or continual banging on a highchair, and I would start the day by cursing under my breath. It was even worse that the baby's mother was typically only amused.

The boarders had kitchen privileges, sharing our one icebox and one stove. It was a terrible loss of privacy. When they cooked, I felt very hungry; by the time we could eat, I had lost my appetite. They suspected me and my siblings of eating their fruit, which made me angry and uncomfortable. To make matters worse, I had no place to put my own things. After my mother died, my father had given me her wristwatch, which became my most treasured possession. I kept it in a little covered ceramic bowl in the kitchen cupboard. When it disappeared, I knew exactly which of the guests had taken it, but I could prove nothing.

My father, on the other hand, enjoyed the interactions with the summer people. Our summer life-style also must have gotten to him, however, because he eventually prepared different accommodations for the summer people. He innovated by building a convertible brooder house which was used in the winter to brood baby chicks and in the summer to house boarders. By installing removable partitions in the brooder house, he could transform the building into six small summer apartments for the boarders.

The boarders purchased whatever food we had to sell on the farm. They bought freshly killed chickens—killed by my father and dressed by my stepmother. They also bought whole milk fresh from our cows, freshly churned butter, cheese, and cream, and vegetables from our garden. My father may also have purchased bushels of vegetables from other farmers and resold them to the summer boarders. I am sure the added income was welcome.

But for my father, it was not only a business proposition—it was a theatrical experience. He loved the excitement and the attention of the women whose husbands were away during the week. He never took their complaints seriously but maintained good-humored relationships with them, and he was a good listener. The women challenged his imagination. His chickens never talked back to him, but then they did not get into the absurd situations that people did, creating complications which needed to be handled with great delicacy and tact. My father was both a natural impressario and an objective observer of the comedy. At times he assumed the role of matchmaker and became a participant in the action. He brought together the most unlikely of couples, seating them on a bench under a tree to talk, and sat himself on a nearby bench to watch and listen.

Each of the two-room summer apartments had a large screened-in porch and an adjoining toilet shared by two apartments, but the farm acreage extended the living space. Outdoors, my father built showers with solar-heated water, which he said was a special treat for summer people, and a solarium consisting of four walls on a patch of open field. City women need the sun, he would say. The women retired to the solarium every afternoon for a sunbath, taking with them a cot or a blanket. Sometimes they complained about the briars that scratched them, to which my father responded that those scratches were especially healthy. They were, after all, from blackberry bushes. A washtub for doing laundry was tucked in a corner behind the bungalows. Swings for the children, outdoor wooden tables and benches, and some wooden lawn chairs, all made by my father, completed the outdoor amusement area. On most warm evenings, every-one—guests, children, and my family—sat outdoors. The adults usually spoke in Yiddish, always returning to the subject of "the old home" that they had left in Europe, and sharing stories, jokes, and songs. At such times, it never occurred to me that the city was a better place to be.

The summer children were allowed to help with the farm chores, which they enjoyed doing, especially the haying. Our fields were cut in the summer for the hay, which needed to be raked. Our only tools were old-fashioned hay rakes; we did the job by hand, pitching the hay up on the flatbed truck and then stacking it around a pole by the pitchfork-full for the cows to eat in the winter. Raking and pitching the hay up onto a truck in a hot sun is a backbreaking task, but it had to be done. If the hay was rained on after it was cut, it would rot and then not be good for the cows. For the summer kids it was a great novelty, but they could leave the work anytime they wanted to. For us who belonged on the farm, it was a different story.

When the summer boarders arrived in their bungalows, life became much more tolerable, and I actually looked forward to their coming every summer. They brought city excitement, sophistication, and young people. Some friendships turned into marriage, and others continued for years, inspiring vacation visits both ways. But at the same time, the summer contacts also heightened my awareness of separate worlds and intensified my feelings of deprivation because I lived on a farm.

During a winter visit to one of my summer friends living in Brooklyn, however, I was cured of some of my illusions and gained, instead, a new appreciation for my home. My summer friend Arleen always seemed so sophisticated: her clothes looked glamorous, her hair was in the latest style, she knew how to talk to boys, and she seemed to be studying everything in school. After just one year of high school French, she seemed to speak the language fluently. In her Brooklyn high school, she had a choice of courses which we never dreamed of in Freehold High. She knew the importance of the "Hit Parade" and all the currents hits. I felt like a real hick next to her.

When I visited her in New York, I found that her whole family of five lived in four small rooms in a fourth-floor walk-up. Her brother slept in the living room. There was not an inch to spare in the apartment, and clothes hung behind every door. The street was the only place in which there was space to move, but after a while the street lost its novelty. We just stood around or walked a little bit. We did not go anywhere. And if you forgot your gloves, four flights up is a lot of walking. She still seemed smarter than my farm friends, but I lost some of my awe of her city sophistication.

The summer friends I made enriched my life, but the urban contact made me that much more different.

16

Schools

Jewish, American, and Beyond

Yiddish School

The only socializing we did during the school year was in school, and we went to school every day: to our two-room schoolhouse for five days a week, and then to Yiddish *shule* on Saturday afternoons and Sunday mornings. Since we never played with Christians, the *shule* gave us an opportunity to meet with other Jewish youngsters. It was our most important social activity, but it was more than just a social experience. We did learn.

I and some of my friends continued going to Yiddish *shule* until we were about sixteen. Entirely a secular school, the curriculum consisted of language, literature, history, and folk culture. Religion was hardly mentioned, except for holidays which celebrated historical events, such as the fight for freedom at Passover, Purim, and Hanukkah. Although we spoke only English among ourselves, we were all bilingual; Yiddish was the language of instruction. We learned no Hebrew, no rituals, and no prayers. I do not remember anyone who attended that school preparing for a Bar Mitzvah.

The dramatic and choral programs that we presented two or three times a year were the high points of our growing up. We put on adaptations of stories by Peretz and Sholem Aleichem, sang melodies to the lyrics of Abram Reisen or Mani Leib, recited poems, built scenery, and were imaginative in our use of props. The whole community came to these presentations and talked about them for weeks and even years afterward.[5]

New Arrivals

In the Community Center there was a constant preoccupation with the events in Europe and about people named Franco and Hitler. In my Yiddish history class we studied the Spanish Inquisition and heard stories about how Jews were tortured in the fifteenth century. Someone reported that Hitler was using old tortures in modern Germany. My friends and I talked about ways in which we could train ourselves to withstand torture in the event we were seized and imprisoned. I used to think about it a great deal at night before I fell asleep. One summer night, I was awakened by loud passionate talk coming from our kitchen. My father was telling New York relatives visiting us about a Farmingdale contingent of the Abraham Lincoln Brigade and about young men going to Spain to stop the fascists. I was convinced that my father intended to join them and that he would be caught by the people of the Inquisition. I began to cry so hysterically that my uncle came into my room to find out what was wrong. He assured me that my father would not go to war, but I continued to worry for a very long time.

I knew that the new arrivals in Farmingdale were German Jews, but I did not know they were refugees. I found it strange that they did not speak Yiddish; to me, Yiddish was synonymous with being Jewish. Nor did their children attend the Yiddish *shule*, which met on weekends.

I saw them only during the High Holy Days of Rosh Hashanah and Yom Kippur, when the Community Center became a synagogue. They greeted people cordially and politely, sat quietly during the service, shook hands with those near them when they left, wished people a good year, and retired until the following Rosh Hashanah. The only community activity in which they participated, as far as I could determine, was the United Jewish Appeal. But even in the brief encounters we had, I could see they were different from the others.

Everything about these newcomers said "culture" and "education." They always looked neat and clean; their clothes fit them well and looked expensive. Our closest German neighbors, the Gutmans, kept their farm in immaculate condition. The outbuildings looked as if they were freshly painted every year; flowers and shrubbery were neatly trimmed. There was not the same wild profusion of bushes on their ground as on ours. For all that one could see or smell, there were no chickens, even though we knew the Gutmans were farmers. Their two sons did not seem to have farm chores to do after school, unlike the rest of us. They had to study their school lessons and practice their violins. The fact that, at a young age, they were preparing for college and a future professional life made them different from the other Jewish children I knew.

From Monday to Friday we attended the West Farms school. I am not sure how many students were in it; my guess is there were no more than fifty distributed among the seven classes (kindergarten through sixth grade) in two rooms. My early memories about school are fragmentary. The two-room schoolhouse without water, electricity, or central heat was quite different from the large brick structure that was my school in New York City. Because I knew how to read, I was put into the second grade rather than in the first with my age group. Since the language of my home was Yiddish, my speech rhythms and accents were different from that of the other children, who laughed whenever I opened my mouth. However, there were some children in the classroom, housing kindergarten through third grade, who knew no English at all. I remember Davey, a very young child, going up to the teacher, pulling at her dress, urgently saying, "Ikh darf geyn pishn" (I need to go pee). The teacher could not understand him and asked the class in general if anyone knew what he said. A few of us giggled, too embarrassed to translate, while Davey became more and more distressed and pulled even harder on the teacher's dress, trying to make her understand. Finally, he just peed on the floor, and I looked away ashamed.

The toilets were outdoors, and I did not like using them at all. Once, after school, when they were being painted by the teacher's husband, I had to use the toilet and could not wait. I asked him not to look, did what I had to, and he continued painting. The next day, the teacher lectured me about using the toilet while a man was working there. I was mortified from head to foot.

Once I came home from school and told my mother that everyone had to say prayers. My mother wanted to know exactly what the prayer was, and although I did not know it was the Lord's Prayer, I told her that we had to put our hands together on the desk, bow our heads, and say out loud, "Our Father, who art in heaven, hallowed be thy name." My mother told me not to say it, and she went to school with me and my brother to speak to the teacher. I was sorry I had said anything, especially since I enjoyed the ritual; I continued to say the prayer but did not report it to my parents.

Discipline in the classroom was ironclad: firm and very strict. Some of the punishments for the infraction of rules may have been cruel and excessive, but they were effective. I remember once, at the beginning of the school year, when books were distributed. The teacher counted the number of children in a row, put that many books on the first desk, and instructed us to take one and pass the rest behind us. When the pile came to my seat, I took a book and, instead of passing them in the normal way, balanced the pile on my head for the person behind me to take. I thought it was funny, and so did the person behind me. But the teacher did not. She made me stand in front of the room balancing books on my head while everyone laughed. I can still relive the humiliation and embarrassment I felt. One child stood in front of the room, on another occasion, with his mouth taped, an object lesson for all of us that unnecessary talking was forbidden. My brother had to sit on display in the waste basket because he had thrown paper from his desk into it. I suppose the rigid discipline was necessary. How else could the teacher have juggled her complex schedule and gotten through the year? But it did make the atmosphere rather cheerless.

Our library consisted of a table in an alcove on which books were spread. The Monmouth County Bookmobile brought books to us each month. There were never enough to go around, and so we read the same stories over and over again.

The school was about a mile from our home, and we walked in all sorts of weather, carrying our lunch and thermos bottle. I remember sitting in the classroom one spring day when there was a rattling and scratching at the door. When the teacher opened it, my baby brother, three years old, marched in, stark naked except for a pair of shoes. A very surprised teacher gasped, "To whom does he belong?" My older brother, one year ahead of me in school, got up, took Arnold by the hand, and walked him home. It is an amusing memory, but I still can recall the shame I experienced. It was for more than just a naked little boy; somehow it seemed to say something about our way of life.

In school we studied Christian holidays as if they were as national as the Fourth of July. But they provided a break from the boredom of the school routine. During the Christmas season, we made red and green paper chains which were hung from corner to corner and draped over the top of the blackboards. I enjoyed singing the Christmas carols and making gifts to exchange with other children and for our parents. I always made a gift for my grandmother, which I sent to her in New York. At Easter time we made paper baskets into which the teacher put candy bunnies and jelly beans.

But even as I enjoyed the fun, I always felt uneasy about the references to Jews in the talk about holidays, particularly during the Easter holiday. At some point, I learned that Jews were the Christ killers, but I had very little understanding of exactly who or what Christ was. The whole idea of virgin birth and Holy Ghost were foreign to me, and I could not comprehend it at all. I did not know why I should feel guilty about killing

Christ, but I did. At home, if Christ was mentioned, it was only in a derogatory context, and then accompanied by spitting three times: "Pfoo, pfoo, pfoo."

We did not celebrate any holidays at home—not Jewish ones, and certainly not Christian ones either. "We are not stupid religious Jews," my father said. Yet, during Passover, we had to take matzos to school in our lunchboxes, and food like hard-boiled eggs and tomatoes. It is not as if we did not have bread in our home. It was on the top shelf of the pantry. But my father said the bread was for the farm worker and not for us. He told us that matzos we took to school were for the goyim. "Zoln zey zikh oyshtekhen di oygn" (Let them stare their eyes out), he would say with some passion. I did not like eating matzos so publicly because I felt it reminded the other children, who might otherwise have forgotten, that I was Jewish. And it reminded me, too.

For the seventh and eighth grade, we were transported to another one-room school in a different part of the township. Like the previous school, it had no plumbing or sanitary facilities, and the heat was provided by a potbellied stove in a corner. The discipline was even stricter than in the lower grades. One stern look from the teacher was enough to freeze the blood of even the most assertive of adolescents. But I do remember one creative activity. We built a model of a colonial home, and each of the students made a piece of furniture for it.

In December of my eighth grade, the Howell Township Consolidated School was opened, after a long struggle against those who fought for tradition. For the first time, school became interesting and exciting for me. The two-story building was on a grand scale, like my original New York school. There were water fountains in the hall, flush toilets, and a lunchroom. Seventh- and eighth-grade students moved to different classes and different teachers. I remember the feeling of freedom to be allowed to speak while classes were changing.

I was selected as the student representative to talk about the advantages of our new educational system at the formal dedication ceremonies. My father, very proud, took my assignment very seriously and insisted that I needed a new dress for the occasion. On the night of the dedication, I spotted him and my family from the stage, where I sat with the dignitaries. When I was about to speak, my father made sure everyone around him was absolutely quiet, and when I finished my delivery, he applauded the loudest and longest of anyone. I am not sure he understood what I was talking about, but he knew that I spoke well and that it was an important honor.

Before graduation, a counselor came to the Howell School from Free-

THE AUTHOR, FROM A
SCHOOL PHOTOGRAPH
AROUND 1934.

hold High to tell us to decide on one of three programs of study available: college preparatory, secretarial, and general. It was a crucial time of decision which, as far as I knew, was irrevocable. I tried to discuss plans for my future with my father, but he either (1) was too busy with the chickens, (2) could not take his daughter's education very seriously, or (3) did not understand anything about it. The only one left for me to talk to was my stepmother, who knew as little as my father, but had some very dogmatic ideas.

Ever since I learned that my natural mother had died of cancer, I wanted to be a doctor. Even before, as a very young child, I had fantasized ways of curing sick people. However, not knowing any women doctors and not being able to conceive of going to medical school from the farm, I did not even bring up the idea. I had a conviction that my wanting to be a doctor was a totally freakish thing. Instead, I offered the next best thing. I said I wanted to be a nurse. My stepmother responded with two words: "Bedpans. Feh!" The only other thing I could think of was to be a teacher. Again, two words spoken emphatically: "Old maids." She said I should study to be a nice secretary, to go into a nice clean office every day, to wear a nice dress with a white collar and cuffs and answer a phone. Or to be a bookkeeper and wear a nice dress and sit at a desk. Her main emphasis was on the nice dress and the clean office. My father, sitting nearby, nodded and smiled in agreement. So I was going into some office. And there I would stay until I married.

Although my father was not too interested in my education, he was interested in my marriage. When I was fourteen, he began thinking about his responsibility to see me married and suggested several young men—sons of businessmen in the nearby towns—as possible suitable choices. He was ready to start making arrangements with the boys' fathers. For the first meeting, he promised to buy me a new coat and hat. Upset and crying, I reminded him that we were in America and not in Europe and that I was not to be regarded as a piece of farm equipment to be traded off. He simply did not understand what I was talking about and was hurt by my anger.

High school was anything but a happy experience for me. My lack of grace and sophistication, my country manners, my farm background must have been immediately apparent to the town children, and I was mercilessly called a cow. The boys would start mooing as I appeared, and I had no way of stopping them. I could not even tell my father. He was too busy, and he probably would have been amused.

My high school program was not much of an improvement over my grade school. In addition to the personal social misery I experienced at Freehold High, I hated my courses: junior business, office practice, stenography, and typing—all of which seemed totally unchallenging and stultifying. But I persisted in training for my secretarial or accounting career. I chose as my life's goal to be a certified public accountant, the top of the line of work for which I was destined. I did not know that not many women became CPAs.

Nor were the Jewish children of Freehold much help. To them, we were the "chicken flickers," to be looked down upon. Our fathers were ignorant farmers; their fathers were shopkeepers. That made a big difference. Since they were so sure about our lower status, we mostly accepted it as true. As a result, one of my friends who had always loved the farm, field, and woods absolutely refused to go out with farm boys when she became of dating age.

There was no opportunity for me to take part in any of the after-school dances and clubs that might have made school more fun or introduced me to more friends. I depended on a school bus for transportation. Certainly my father could not leave his work to pick me up in Freehold. Besides, I had my job of packing eggs waiting for me when I came home.

In December of my junior year, America went to war, and changes came immediately, both in school and in my life. By my senior year, women were urgently needed for technical jobs which traditionally had been held by men. A federal agency, in cooperation with the schools, instituted intensive training programs for technicians and draftsmen. I entered the program and for the first time had some challenging courses in science and math, as well as in mechanical drawing.

When I finished school, I realized that I had capabilities that no one suspected or thought much about. I again began thinking of my future and tentatively approached my father with the idea of college. The stereotype that Jews are interested in education for their children and will sacrifice everything for it did not fit my father or many of the other Farmingdale fathers. Very few of my generation growing up in Farmingdale were encouraged to go to college. For my father, the highest value was to keep his family intact and in close proximity to him and to each other. The farm provided that opportunity. He had spent so much energy on it that he naturally envisaged his children continuing what he had started. And he had learned that education was not an essential ingredient for successful farming. Furthermore, while more and higher learning might be helpful to boys, it was totally frivolous for girls.

My father did not respond to my questions about college. He was outside, fixing the steps to the house. While I groped for the proper words, he kept working, not looking up at me at all. When I finished telling him I would like to go to college, he asked, as if talking to the cement, "What, to fold diapers you need a college education? To sweep floors you need a degree?"

Tears welled up in my eyes, and I was unable to say a word. My brother, sitting there, reassured me, "You're not a boy. It's only important for boys to go to college." He was attending Monmouth Junior College at night in nearby Long Branch. So college was out, or at least I was never again going to ask my father to send me.

Beyond School

Outside of school, the war had a tremendous effect on the lives of the young people in Farmingdale and elsewhere. If social opportunities had been limited for young girls before, they were even more limited after the draft. We could not meet Jewish boys from nearby towns because they went into the service; only the farm boys, who were exempt, were available. Of these, the Christians were automatically excluded from our social circles (no one I knew openly dated Christian boys), while the Jewish boys were rejected because they were farmers and we knew them too well. Besides there were not many among whom to pick.

The hotels in Lakewood, as a patriotic gesture, ran regular dances for servicemen. Some of my friends and I used to go to these. We never asked if the boys with whom we danced were Jewish, nor did we want to know. It did not seem to matter. But the dances were not happy events. I was overwhelmed by sadness, thinking about those sweet young men about to be shipped overseas. I remember how one young serviceman, whose name I do not know, took my face in his hands one night. He was no more than nineteen years old. Serious beyond his years, he looked directly into my eyes and said earnestly: "You are the last girl I will be dancing with for a very long time. I want to remember you as you are now, your lavender dress, the white flower in your hair, your beautiful eyes. Thank you so much for coming here." I still cry at the memory.

While the war limited our social lives, wartime needs also offered new opportunities, especially to women. Just before graduating from high school, I was among a group of participants selected to attend Rutgers University for an intensive summer training program in junior engineering.

For the first time, I lived away from home. The social experience and the sense of an expanded world away from Farmingdale were as important to me as were the studies. Urban people, aspiring to live in the country, often have romantic notions about nature and freedom, but I, who always knew about another world from which I was excluded, needed more contact with the city. Farmingdale had often seemed like a giant jail to me, from which there was no escape. My whole effort was to get out into the world. New Brunswick became my opening. I had to work hard at my studies to compensate for my deficient academic background, but I did very well.

At the end of the summer, I started my first job as a draftsman for Eastern Aircraft in Trenton. With the help of my father, I purchased a car and became a commuter. I was seventeen years old, earning a fairly good salary, paying off an automobile, and, at my insistence, contributing to the household. A year later, I took a drafting job with the Signal Corps, closer to home. When I had saved enough, I could afford to enroll in night classes at Monmouth Junior College, where some of my friends also attended. I never asked my father for tuition money; I paid my tuition out of my own earnings. For a year, I worked and studied.

But working full time and taking four college courses at night was exhausting. I slept in the car between classes; I did not have enough time to do homework and began to think it was not important. My schooling did not seem to be leading me anywhere; my work was giving me no satisfaction. The war was over; I was nineteen and terrified of being not even a teacher, just an old maid.

At the end of my second semester, before I was twenty years old, I married a childhood sweetheart, a farmer's son, and prepared to live on a farm. I felt resigned. If there was no way out of Farmingdale, then I had better do the best I could. My father was absolutely correct. To sweep floors or wash dishes or fold diapers, I did not need a college education.

17

Married Life and
the Community

When I married, it was not to one of the regular farm boys with whom I had grown up but to a city boy, Jack Dubrovsky, recently arrived from Boston and settled on a farm with his parents. Jack was very outgoing, rarely serious, joking and laughing all the time, and he had a kind of energy I found fascinating.

Since the war was over and the world more promising, I believed in a dream that my husband and I would move away from Farmingdale and explore together another part of the country. Though we never talked about it, I envisioned that he would enroll in some college and I would work to support him through it, and then we would reverse roles after he graduated. Many couples I knew did just that.

It never occurred to me that Jack would like the farm so much he would want to stay on it. I did not share his view of city life, which was colored by his experience in the small grocery store where his parents worked for fourteen to sixteen hours a day and never took a vacation together. All I thought about was that nobody in their right mind would elect to be stuck on a farm when there were so many fascinating possibilities in the larger world. After we married, I pleaded with Jack to consider moving someplace else, but he did not understand my need anymore than I understood his.

Instead of leaving Farmingdale, we moved into a bungalow on my parents' farm, one my father had built for hired help, and Jack began working for my family. I began to feel as if a tight net had been drawn over me and I had given up all control over my destiny. Finally, I stopped thinking about going away, and even found some comfort in the familiar pattern of life. I knew that my father's dearest wish was to have his children settled nearby. At least we were making him happy.

We were poor when we first married; our total income was the twenty-five dollars per week Jack earned from my father. But money, or lack of it, was not really a problem; we had both grown up in the depression and knew how to manage on very little. My biggest problem was boredom, and I solved it by getting a sales job in a department store in Asbury Park.

Finally, after all my high school preparation, I was working in a nice clean place and wearing a nice clean dress to work every day. And I loved the job. To me the excitement of the store was something like New York, with its constantly changing sights, smells, sounds, and colors. I worked there for a year and was two months into my first pregnancy when I left. Five months after my first son was born, I was again pregnant. Before I was twenty-two, I had two babies. Any additional work was unthinkable.

Jack and I decided that it was time for us to have our own farm. With my father's help and blessing, we bought some land, just down the road a piece from my family's, and less than two miles from Jack's. Although I was pleased we had our own place, I was where I had vowed never to be. Life for me was inevitable, immutable. My destiny was arranged for, my future clear. My only effective rebellion was a refusal to do any work whatsoever on the farm. I was not going to pack eggs, work in the chicken coops, put on farm clothes, or spend any time on the chicken range. Nor did I ever feel guilty about my refusal. Besides, with two babies to take care of, I was busy enough.

Our two sets of parents had signed notes for us to purchase the land and build a chicken coop with a capacity for two thousand layers—small enough for Jack to manage alone, and large enough to support us. Our parents agreed to meet the payments until the farm earned an income and we could pay them back. We were still living in the three-room bungalow on my father's farm.

Jack wanted to build a small apartment above the feed room of the chicken house. Many young city people moving then into Farmingdale did that for economy, but I saw no glamour in such a living arrangement. I pictured myself living for years with the smell of chickens, breathing in dust, and chasing rats and mice. I cried for my lost dreams, but I was adamant about not moving into the chicken house. I told Jack that if he was worried about the chickens, he could put up a cot in the coop and live there. I would continue to live with the babies in the bungalow until we could build a house. One year later, we negotiated a mortgage and put up a modest home. We now had a large debt, two small children, and two thousand chickens.

Jack, then twenty-five years old, began to feel he was too young to be saddled with so many responsibilities and began to talk about needing freedom and getting a divorce. I, even younger than he, was terrified at the prospect of what his freedom would mean to me. I was not prepared for anything except clerking in a store. With the war over, women were no longer seriously considered for well-paying jobs like drafting. I had lost my office skills; I did not remember my stenography or bookkeeping—and who was going to take care of my two little boys?

I saw myself going back to my father's house, working at the most unrewarding and unsatisfying of jobs to maintain myself and my children, becoming totally dependent on my father. My whole struggle for independence seemed to evaporate in front of me. My life was over; my potential was for naught. And to compound my difficulties, I thought of the shame I would feel in the small community, where all the Jews knew each other.

There was no privacy in Farmingdale. As the whole Jewish community had been invited to my wedding, they all knew about my private life. That's the way it was. In my mind's eye, I saw myself an object of pity and charity, my children in disgrace. In 1950, divorce, especially among Jewish people, was not common. I mustered my courage and told my husband that he might long for freedom, but I was not going to make it easy for him and would not give him the divorce he wanted. Nor did his anger shake my determination. He did not leave; we remained married.

We muddled along with our lives, each of us sensing that there was more in the world to do and to experience. I again began talking about leaving Farmingdale and starting all over again somewhere else. This time, we made some inquiries, and Jack actually went to see a farm in Indiana. At that time, farming was the only thing either of us could think of as a way of earning a living. But when I thought of what it might be like on a farm in Indiana, I got even more terrified. If I was stuck in Farmingdale, which was at least accessible to New York City, what would I feel like in the middle of America? I am not sure whether I voiced these fears or not. I told myself I needed the help and support of my family and stopped talking about Indiana.

Jack and I socialized a great deal with other young married couples who were married about the same time we were and who also had young children. Some of the people in our social set had grown up in Farmingdale, as I did: Celia Sokol Fisher; my brother Herbert; Sophia Peskin Dubrovsky, who married Jack's brother and became my sister-in-law; Max Levine, who was in the same class as I in public school and attended Yiddish *shule* with us. Others in our group were young city people settling on farms: George and Millie Brick, Harold and Esther Weiss, Penny Levine (who met Max when she and her family were summer boarders in nearby Bergerville), Sidney and Alice Boyarin. Sidney's relatives were the Peskins; his immediate family had settled on a farm thirteen or so years before he and his wife did.

We spent a great deal of time with each other, visiting in each other's homes, taking our children on outings together, attending center meetings, and working for the cooperative nursery school, where we all sent our children. My immediate family, my extended family, and my circle of friends kept me very busy, and living in Farmingdale was much easier. But for all that, something was missing in my life.

Jack and I gradually began participating in the life of the community by becoming involved in organizations—the nursery school, Ladies Club, the center board, the feed cooperative—and attending meetings. Since I had no Christian friends, it would have been difficult if not impossible for me to join anything but a Jewish organization. I never felt comfortable or at home in the PTA or the League of Women Voters, or even the women's committee of the Little League.

My need to feel accepted in a group was reinforced by incidents such as occurred on a day I accompanied my six-year-old son Steven to the birthday party of his Christian friend Billy. I joined a group talking about the upcoming township elections. "Can you imagine," announced one, "the Jews are now trying to run the township. They're trying to get their Jew elected." The women laughed; the hostess, uncomfortable, tried to engage me in conversation; I did not know where to turn.

There was never a question of acceptance at the Jewish Center. It was like a second home; the meetings provided an opportunity for intellectual sparring and stimulation. There was always a great deal of political excitement, tension, and commotion among the Jews of Farmingdale, and the meetings were as thoroughly unpredictable as they were interesting. At times, I felt as if I were participating in a "theatre of the absurd." But whatever else they were, for Jack and me they were a social experience, and we attended them together.

I do not remember when I became aware that politics were a crucial part of the doings at the Jewish Community Center. I knew that both at the center and at home the words *undz* (us) and *zey* (them) had special meanings. Early, they meant (us) Jews and (them) non-Jews. But the words took on political connotations and, depending on one's orientation, they meant *undz* (on the left) and *zey* (on the right), or vice versa.

Although *undz* and *zey* were part of my growing-up vocabulary, the first time I had heard them used in their political context was at a UJA fund-raising effort. At a special appeal evening at the center, one of *undz* presented a check as a donation. The chairman of the appeal—one of *zey*—thereupon tore it up, saying the donor could certainly give more. The donor was humiliated and left feeling persecuted, while *zey* started snickering. The left then went on strike, threatening to organize their own appeal. Finally, an uneasy compromise was worked out in which the right agreed that a portion of the money donated would go to the Russian colony of Birabijain, where Jewish farmers were establishing cooperatives.

Years later, the *undz-zey* fight became one of Communist versus non-Communist. It was in the early 1950s, when McCarthy was at the height of his power. People began seeing Communists everywhere, especially among the New York radicals who had settled in Farmingdale in the forties.

The cooperatives were especially suspect, which added to the high drama that occurred at the meetings, especially those of the FLF feed cooperative. The FLF was labeled a left-wing organization, and meetings were always intense. Our attendance was important, but more than that, we felt involved with issues, and a camaraderie with people who had a similar outlook. There was a sense that we could influence the government and the larger world in a meaningful way. The rhetoric, in English or in Yiddish, was on a high level, or, at the very least, high-flown, colorful, and full of images we could grasp. Who can forget Fanny Dubnick passionately exclaiming, "We are not chickens that can be separated at birth into hens and cockerels, one half to be exploited, the other to be discarded."

However, the leadership of the cooperative became more and more centered in one individual, Boris Schwartz, also called simply Berl. He was dynamic, charismatic, and, it must be said, dictatorial. An affirmed left-winger, he was always in the eye of the storm, while his *chaverim* (friends) gathered around him to present a solid front, an apparent unanimity of opinion. If any among them had troubling questions, they did not display them publicly. In doing my taped interviews twenty years or so later, I learned that the private meetings of the left were full of dissension and individuals identified themselves as pro- or anti-Schwartz. But in 1955, the public was not aware of what occurred in private.

At one FLF meeting at which Berl presided, a member began to question the managerial competence of the cooperative. The standing-room-only meeting was held in the public school auditorium, and microphones were set up so that the speakers could be heard. When a speaker antagonistic to Berl's position began speaking, Berl would bang his gavel in front of the microphone to drown out the questions. The dissenting group walked out of the meeting, and the business was then quickly concluded.

The Community Center meetings also had lively discussions. One concerned civil rights slogans that someone had put up around the walls of the room. The conservatives wanted them down, saying that we were a Jewish Community Center and not a political-action group. The radicals countered with the remark that civil rights were human rights and human rights could not be divorced from Judaism. The conservatives said the question was not human rights but political slogans. The radicals proposed: "OK, let's be consistent. We'll take everything off the walls, then." That included pictures of Chaim Weizmann and Theodore Herzl, as well as posters of Israel; the radicals insisted the pictures were Zionist slogans and thus also political. While the battle of the wall hangings raged, the slogans and pictures remained.

Then came the issue of the Doctor's Plot in the Soviet Union, mentioned above in chapter 12. The right wanted a resolution condemning the Soviet action in jailing Jewish intellectuals. The left said there was no proof; Jewish doctors were capable of committing crimes—in any event, the whole issue was political and not Jewish. This time, the left used the argument that politics do not have a place in the center: "We are a Jewish Community Center. Our interests should be focused on what affects our immediate Jewish community and not in playing into the Cold War, which in Farmingdale is becoming a red-hot one."

The right called for a vote on the resolution. The left called for tabling the motion. By the time another meeting was called specifically to deal with the tabled motion, every Jew and non-Jew in the area knew that there was "a big fight" at the Community Center. Word spread to surrounding communities and the press. The small center could not hold the people who came to the meeting. Someone said the vote should be by secret ballot. A mimeograph machine was brought from the FLF office, and the ballot was produced on the spot. The resolution was defeated, and a split resulted. People on the right decided it was time to start thinking about building another Jewish Community Center. They blamed their defeat on the FLF, which paid the Community Center dues of its members and thus, it was said, had a handy way of mobilizing a large group of voters.

Not everyone on the right walked out of the center. Some stayed and tried to change the leadership from within. When the next election of officers occurred, the right put up its slate, the left had a slate, and the moderates ran their candidates. The right voted as a solid block, while the left split its votes between the moderates and others. This time, the right won; but it was a Pyrrhic victory. Without support, the officers soon grew angry and frustrated and resigned.

Once I went to what was called a special meeting of the Women's Club, held suspiciously at someone's home rather than at the center. I had never seen most of the women at any previous club meeting I attended. Nor was the meeting chaired by the elected president. It soon became clear why.

The issue was that the Communists were in control of the club and had to be removed, not only from the club, but from the Jewish Center as well. I began to feel threatened by the proceedings and afraid that I or my family would be expelled from the community of Jews. I understood, then, why excommunication was such a powerful instrument of religions. I questioned the speaker, asking how one was to tell a Communist from a non-Communist, and I was told, authoritatively, "We know." Every head seemed to nod in agreement. The chairperson asked for and received a resolution to the effect that Communists were undesirable members of the Women's Club; their interests were incompatible with those of a Jewish Community.

I tried to speak against the motion by going into my own personal history. "The Community Center is a very important part of my life in Farmingdale. When my family first moved here, we met other Jewish people at the center. It was the place in which I grew up, where I had my first kiss." At that, I burst into tears, the first time in my life that I cried in public. I was ashamed of my lack of control and felt I had not presented a persuasive argument against the undemocratic procedures at hand. The room became quiet, totally quiet. As far as I know, no one was ever expelled from the Ladies Club.

One of my saddest memories of that time was the day a friend came to my house, a woman who had fought bravely and articulately for the causes to which she was committed. She said she just wanted to talk and have a cup of coffee. She talked around and around different subjects until I began to wonder why someone who could speak so clearly in front of groups should have so much difficulty talking to me in the privacy of my home. I could not understand what she was getting at until she suddenly said: "No one wants to play with my children. Their friends are being kept away from them because of my views. It's not fair to attack my kids like that." She started to cry, and I was not at all prepared for it. I sensed the vulnerability of even the most obdurate of believers. I did not know what to do to comfort her.

The problems in the community were exacerbated as the FBI became a more visible and ominous presence. An agent came to visit my father, who was dying of cancer. It did not make his last days any more pleasant, recalling as it did for him a different time in his life when he had lived through a pogrom. The agent wanted my father to tell him about the International Workers Orders. When he could get no information, he asked where the secretary of the local chapter lived. My bedridden father directed the agent to Asbury Park instead of to the secretary's home three farms away.

The ideological battle affected Jack and me personally in other ways. Our best friends were aligned with the so-called right and refused to attend meetings or social gatherings at the center. We could no longer discuss politics because the issues were too painful and a discussion might risk the friendship. But it became even worse.

Jack and a friend, Max Levine, had gone into a fuel oil business when the farm economy failed. The business was new and shaky; the money was all borrowed. Jack had been on the board of the Community Center and ran for reelection as a moderate, neither right nor left. Although he lost the election, he became identified in the minds of some as a left-wing sympathizer. A boycott of the new business was organized by some farmers—our former friends and neighbors—who canceled their fuel oil contracts. We survived the economic crisis, but the action left permanent emotional scars.

Our center life was in serious jeopardy, and I felt it was imperative to work in a constructive way to try to mend or heal some of the wounds. I headed the Youth Activities Committee and felt that if we could provide enough meaningful activities for young people, they, at least, would talk to each other and help the community survive. With the support and encouragement of other women, we instituted numerous creative activities. We arranged for cultural trips to museums, concerts, and parks in New York and New Jersey. We revived an arts-and-crafts program at the center. We set up a folk dance group and a summer day-camp. And people did, in fact, work together for these programs. But the split in the community never really healed.

In fact, the split was symptomatic of a much deeper malaise. The economics of poultry farming was slowly signing the death warrant of the community of Jewish farmers. My husband and I gave up farming, as did my brothers; our friends likewise began preparing for other work. People went back to school to pick up additional training or resume training in other careers. I enrolled full-time in Georgian Court College in nearby Lakewood.

Many continued living on their farms, and others had to sell them to pay off their debts. The younger people managed to go into other professions. My father died; the farm that he hoped would provide a future for his children was taken over by a creditor. My stepmother, together with other older people who had looked forward to a pleasant retirement on the farm, had to find new ways to live.

Growing
Up in
Farmingdale

18

Preparing to Leave

My attending Georgian Court College was not part of a carefully thought-out plan. Indeed, it came about almost by accident. My younger son left for his first day of school. After living with two battling boys for six years and feeling as if I were constantly on roller skates, I suddenly experienced the kind of quiet I could hardly remember. And I did not have anything to do. At twenty-seven, I was a displaced homemaker.

It was at this critical moment that my neighbor, Dorothy Hamburger, invited me to take a ride with her to Lakewood's Georgian Court College, where she was about to sign up for a music program. Having nothing to do, I went along for the ride.

I had never seen the campus, although it was very close to home, and I knew that my sister-in-law, Sophia, had graduated from the college. While we were driving, I realized that now I also had time to take a course. But I had been out of school for ten years, and I was not sure whether my brain would work or not. I decided it would be wise to take one course, whichever course would allow me to put the children on the school bus and to be home to greet them when they returned. I had no career plans; I did not know what I could or could not do. The registrar tried to explore with me what I wanted to do when I grew up. In answer to her questions, I simply said: "It doesn't matter what I take. I just need to be home at a certain time." When she asked if I liked literature, I answered that I enjoyed reading but did not have much time. Before the morning was up, I enrolled in a Shakespeare class, meeting two mornings a week. It was a thrilling awakening for me. The next year, I enrolled as a full-time student, majoring in English literature.

Georgian Court College is a Roman Catholic school staffed primarily by nuns. Growing up in a secular household, I had very little connection with organized religion of any kind, let alone that represented by Georgian Court. It was a foreign world for me.

When I became accustomed to the black-clothed figures and the ritual of prayers at the start of each class, I was enchanted by the quiet, orderly, serene, and contemplative place. All my tensions and anxieties left as soon as I entered the campus gates. For the first time, I really applied myself to studying, and I did very well. Learning was satisfying in a way that school and classes had never been before. I began to feel that I did not have to be bound by Farmingdale, that it was possible to explore the world of ideas and transcend, in this way, my immediate environment.

I tried to share my excitement about school with my acquaintances and friends. They were amused, but not interested. The following year, when I took on a full-time course of study, their amusement turned to hostility. I was the butt of all sorts of uncomplimentary jokes. The funny thing is that I thought my friends were right in considering me rather odd. After all, most women stayed at home happily, as far as I knew.

But my private history made it compelling for me to prepare to manage my life alone in the event I had to do so. I had learned more than I wanted to know about uncertainty. It became my utmost priority to finish school as soon as possible. Teaching was the career I chose because it offered the best working hours for a woman with children. By now, I was more mature and understood in a new way what the literature I was studying tried to express. My major became clear. In truth, I enjoyed all the courses I took: history, science, math, scholastic philosophy, even health. In every class, I experienced the excitement of discovery, the stimulation of discussing abstract concepts, the challenge of other students, and the making of new friends. I had broken out of jail. I looked forward to the challenges of the next step, working.

Jack could see that I was happy studying, and we both knew a second income would make life easier for us. We did not have much spare money, and by then farming was clearly going downhill. Jack borrowed money for my tuition from his business partner. By taking twenty-two and twenty-four credit hours a semester, I was able to finish three years of college in two years and two summers.

I worked constantly, keeping up with the housework, attending to my children's schedules, and writing papers until four o'clock in the morning. While Jack encouraged me, and even found ways to make it possible for me to attend school, he felt neglected by my rigorous schedule. His ambivalence was reinforced by our group of friends. He sometimes joined them when they teased me about my studies and he laughed at their pointed jokes, which hurt me and made me angry. But at the same time, I felt guilty about the pleasure I derived from my studies.

To compensate for my guilt, I kept up with the social commitments as best I could. I continued to make breakfast for Sidney and Alice, who dropped over practically every morning. The breakfast always made me late for Latin. The professor, assuming my lateness was related to my children's school-bus schedule, was sympathetic and arranged private study sessions so that she could help me keep up with the work. I did not correct her assumptions, but I had to get an A in her course. I played bridge every other night, continued going square dancing, had the usual parties, and accompanied my husband wherever he wanted to go. I managed to do it all. But the whole time, I kept wishing I did not feel so out of tune with the other people we knew.

I finished Georgian Court College in August and started teaching seventh- and eighth-grade English composition that September at Keyport. The school was on split session, and I taught from 12:00 noon to 4:30— six classes without a break in between. For a first-year's teaching assignment, the hours were dreadful, and the adolescent students, extremely demanding. My efforts to discipline them thoroughly exhausted me.

Jack's business was now doing fairly well, and money was no longer a pressing issue. I talked to Jack about doing graduate work in English at Rutgers University and, with his encouragement, left teaching after one year.

Graduate school was another liberating experience. At Georgian Court, I had made one good friend, an older woman returning to school as I had, but most of the students were young girls from affluent homes with whom I had very little in common outside of our studies. At Rutgers I met people of varying backgrounds and ages and had a completely different, and more satisfying, social experience. I eagerly invited some of these new friends to my home, but in doing this, I antagonized my Farmingdale friends and annoyed Jack. The old group felt betrayed, deserted by me in favor of new people. They began to make fun of my new friends.

I cannot speak authoritatively about social circles in small communities generally or about Jewish social groups. Mine, after all, was only one experience. But the group my husband and I were part of exercised a kind of dictatorial power. For ten years, we had socialized exclusively with the same ten couples. We went to movies together, to dinner, to each other's homes for parties, to meetings, to folk dancing and square dancing; we even went on vacations together. We considered ourselves the best, the liveliest, and the most imaginative people in the community. We often agreed that we were like one big family but were closer than family, closer than close. We even talked about sharing husbands and wives, but we, of course, never did. That would have been incestuous. We did share each other's most intimate secrets. To withhold information from the group was tantamount to treason. To have a party and not invite everyone was unthinkable.

As my personal horizons widened, I began to have the feeling that my home, my husband, and my children were not my own but group property. People (my friends, of course) were free to comment on my children's behavior, to participate in discussions about when and where my husband and I were to go on our vacations, and to analyze our general life patterns. People felt free to walk into my home, open my refrigerator, and prepare food for themselves. One person even felt it his right to scan the mail that came. I did not feel free to break out of this make-believe family life when it became repressive.

Once I put up a weak, and ultimately ineffectual, protest. Our house was very near the Community Center, where many meetings were still being held. After a center meeting, the group typically went to someone's house for coffee and cake. At the end of a busy day, I often had little energy to prepare food and cope with the mountain of dishes after the guests left. Finally, I said I would happily give them each a drink, if they wanted it, but I was not going to serve coffee and cake. The group was taken aback. First, I had rarely ever been that assertive—most women in Farmingdale were not—and second, I was breaking a tradition. Finally, they figured out a way to prove that I could not unilaterally make such a decision.

One night they descended en masse after a meeting, bringing a big urn of coffee and some cake and setting it up in the study while I was in the living room, unaware of what they were doing. One by one, they poured themselves coffee and helped themselves to cake. They thought it a hilarious joke, but it made me sick. When everyone left, I threw up and then had a noisy fight with my husband, whom I accused of participating in the cruel hoax, while he accused me of favoring my new friends over the old ones who were "closer than family." He berated me for forgetting my obligations because I was selfishly involved with other interests.

It was an accusation I heard over and over again, made by different people in the group. Sometimes it was directly expressed; sometimes it was clearly implied. It seemed that every step I tried to take away from the proscribed rituals of Farmingdale met with an incredible amount of passion.

And yet, in spite of all, I liked the people in my Farmingdale group. There was a certain warmth and camaraderie I valued. Regardless of their quirks, I felt that when push came to shove and I, or anyone else, needed real emotional support, we could depend on each other. Had it not been proven in times of sickness and tragedy? Had we not prepared each other's meals of condolence and taken care of each other's psychic wounds? I rationalized that if some people were mildly unthinking and sometimes cruel, it was not important. Would my new friends, whom I recently met and with whom I enjoyed passionate intellectual conversations, be able to meet critical life needs? Although the Farmingdale parties became very predictable—we knew exactly who would get drunk, who would tell corny jokes, what they would be, who would start an argument—there was security in being together.

Years later, when my marriage dissolved and I had serious needs, I realized that the group, which was "closer than family" and "better than any other," did not exist outside of my mind. The group was not responsible for my divorce, but their pressure in getting me to conform made my life much more difficult.

After receiving an M.A. degree, I started teaching in a high school closer to home and at more regular hours. The work was very satisfying: I no longer had the discipline problems I had before; the courses and the students were interesting, and every day was exciting. I probably gave my students too many writing assignments, but their dramatic improvement in communication skills was gratifying and justified the time it took me to correct their papers. I was working harder than ever and feeling less tired.

Two years later I left teaching to wait for my third baby; it was a lovely period of rest and anticipation. We were still living on the farm but did not farm. The child brought joy unbounded to me and the whole family. We delighted in having a baby to play with and to cuddle. But I missed the classroom. When Benjamin was two and a half years old, I accepted an adjunct teaching position at Fairleigh Dickinson University, and when he was three and a half years old, I was offered a full-time teaching position at Trenton State College. I could hardly believe my good fortune; college teaching was a dream to which I had aspired.

But this opportunity put strains on the relationship with my husband, who could not accept my professional status. And as soon as I started teaching, our friends, perhaps to reassure themselves that everything was the same, besieged us with a constant stream of invitations: Mondays, square dancing; Tuesdays, bridge; weekends, parties and visits. I was teaching four courses, involving three new preparations. I needed time to prepare, and I also needed time to spend with my children, particularly with Benjamin.

Irrationally, I tried to keep up the socializing, hoping in this way to make my husband happier. Late at night and on weekends, I tried to prepare for the following day's or week's teaching.

By the time summer came, I felt as if I never had been so tired in my life. Grading eggs and working on the farm seemed like child's play in comparison to what I was doing. I needed a vacation, to get away; I needed to leave Farmingdale as much as I needed a rest. Because school had previously been so therapeutic for me, I enrolled in a summer course at the University of Edinburgh and arranged with Jack that Benjamin and I would go to Scotland and he would come with the two older boys sometime later for all of us to have a European vacation together.

In Scotland, it was a great relief to be free of pressures, to listen to lectures at the university, and to meet students from all over the world. An unemployed schoolteacher took care of Benjamin, and after my classes we explored the city and the countryside together. I made notes on places to revisit with Jack and the boys when they came.

Jack never arrived. He was so upset and angry when Benjamin and I actually left—he had encouraged me but always felt I would not go—that he decided not to meet us. "What woman in Farmingdale has done what you have done?" he demanded.

While I was gone, he had entertained "the group" without me. "It was just like old times," one of them said to me when I returned. "We had great parties. Too bad you missed them."

At the end of August, I had a gall-bladder attack and needed morphine for the pain. I became progressively sicker, and by the time school started, I had already lost considerable weight. By December, I had lost twenty-five more pounds, and the doctors urged me to have surgery before I became too debilitated. I waited for the Christmas break, went into the hospital on December 19, and came out ten days later.

During my illness, my Farmingdale friends ignored me. No one came to visit, no one called to ask how I was feeling, no one visited me in the hospital. On New Year's Eve, less than two weeks after my major surgery, Max and Penny stopped in to remind Jack of the annual community party. "You come too," they said to me. "All you have to do is sit. After all, that's what you are doing at home." When I said I was not up to partying, they told me I was thoughtless. I was not doing myself or my husband a favor by keeping him down.

At 10:30 P.M., Jack decided he was going to celebrate the coming of the New Year with his close friends. When he left, I locked the door, locked my bedroom, and tried to go to sleep. I had never felt so gloomy and so alone in my life.

I returned to work for the spring semester but resigned my job for the following year. My marriage was clearly on the rocks; I was still weak from my recent surgery; I had a four-year-old child to take care of and two rebellious adolescents at home. As soon as the semester was over, Jack left.

Outside of my mother's death, it was the most traumatic thing that had ever happened in my life. I experienced deep grief, dislocation, and depression. One day my friend Alice asked if I would like to have lunch with her. I ate very little, as my eyes kept filling up with tears. "I knew you'd be upset, but I certainly did not anticipate this type of grief," she said. I felt guilty even about my grief.

Another friend, Anna, with whom I had commuted regularly to school when we were students at Rutgers, called to say that as far as she was concerned, Jack and I were both to blame, and that's that. My brother Herbert wondered why I was upset. "What did you expect?" he asked. "After all, look at the kind of mother you have been." The family of community friends, no doubt not knowing how to handle their own feelings, left me completely alone.

Although mine was not the first divorce in the Jewish community, it was the first in my group. My old reliable friends were not supportive; they were not kind; they were not even interested in what I was doing or how I was managing. They held me responsible for the marriage breakup, and they were angry that the solidarity of the group was now destroyed. "You are a threat to all of us," was one woman's rather candid comment.

Once, in desperation, I called a friend with whom I had shared much and asked her to invite me to dinner because I was terribly lonely. "Well, you know," she said without apology, "we have had to make other friends. You will have to do the same."

Yet, some were kind in a way that I will never forget, people I'd known from childhood but who were not in my social group of married adults. Dorothy Hamburger suggested a picnic in the nearby woods. We went, just the two of us, talked about wildflowers and birds, splashed our feet in a stream, ate sandwiches, and respected each other's silences. It was more therapeutic than I can express. Florence, my friend from high school days, living quite a distance from Farmingdale, called to invite me to a day's outing in New York, suggesting we take a tour of the shops as we used to do when we were both growing up. Blanche Friedman bought two tickets for *The Man of La Mancha* and asked me to go with her.

The friends I had made at Rutgers tried to help me over this sad period of my life. For my birthday, two visited me from Richmond, Virginia, bringing a birthday cake, guests, gifts, and good cheer. They stayed with me for a week, helping me during an exceptionally painful time. Another, teaching in San Jose, called every week, urging me to visit him and his wife. They invited me to come alone or with my children for the summer. I did not go that first year, but I did the following, when I could better enjoy their warm hospitality.

The details of my divorce are not important. Divorces are unpleasant, no matter where they occur or to whom. Later, in women's groups, I learned that some of my experiences in Farmingdale were shared by others. Women in divorce almost universally feel that society blames them and holds them responsible for the dissolution of the marriage and for whatever bad happens to the children. Other women experienced the isolation of former friends, who sympathized with the poor lonely husband and invited him to their social gatherings. They too found that friends were not supportive and concluded it was because of the complexity of the situation.

But in a small community like Farmingdale, the isolation was almost total. There was no choice of groups to which to belong, no social functions for the single adult, and no privacy.

I have made my peace with that period of my life, with Farmingdale, and with those old friends. When I remarried, I invited the old group to my wedding. By then, I was researching and recording my own community, and the wedding was videotaped. One woman, looking into the camera, was honest about her feelings. In response to a question by my friend and coworker, she volunteered, "Now that she is married, we can let her back into the group again." She meant no harm; she is a kind and thoughtful person, but she summed up the group morality and the group norm.

I still enjoy seeing my former friends once in a while, which I do. I enjoy the old familiarity and nonchalance. But I no longer live in the community, nor am I the same person.

19

Leaving Farmingdale

If my parents, in settling on a farm, had hoped to become rooted to America, the roots took in me. Although I was not consulted when they made their initial decision and although I lived in Farmingdale for many years against my will, I loved it, in spite of all my efforts to leave. When my horizons widened with studies and work, I no longer viewed the small community as a jail from which I wanted to escape, but as a secure and welcome home to return after a journey away.

After our third child was born, Jack and I enlarged our house, adding a separate dining room and a spacious family room with windows that extended our space to the outdoors. When our family became fragmented and seemed to disappear, the house was too large for me and too small for all the ghosts it contained. Benjamin and the ghosts and memories in every room were my only companions. I felt that if I stayed, I would start talking to the walls. Yet, I did not leave. I thought I would wake from my nightmare, Jack would return, and our family would be intact. My mission was to keep the hearth warm. I lived like this for four and a half years, until it became clear to me that Jack had no intention of returning, at least not in the foreseeable future, and that I would have to begin life over again for myself and Benjamin in some other place, leaving the ghosts behind.

I went back to graduate school, commuting to Columbia University, where I worked toward my doctorate, spending much time traveling.

Weekends, when Benjamin was with his father, were especially difficult, and I would travel to Princeton to work at the Firestone Library. I began making friends in Princeton and decided it was where I wanted to live. It was the right transition between a small community and a city, with easy access to public transportation to New York and Philadelphia.

Finding a house was no easy task, but I finally located one I could afford and put a deposit on it. Jack refused to sign the mortgage, and I had no property in my own name with which to secure the loan. But even if I had, women could not get mortgage money independently in 1969. I lost the house. Eventually, in May 1970, I found an apartment and signed a lease for occupancy as of July first. But then, on reflection, I thought it would be crazy to leave the shore during the summer to move to hot Princeton, so I sublet the apartment I had just rented until September 1. I then decided I did not want to stay in Farmingdale for the summer either.

Benjamin and I left for Israel, where we spent two months exploring Jerusalem. It was a necessary interim for me. I was breaking away in stages, getting my distance, testing how I could manage by myself in a totally new environment. I returned on August 30 and called movers to pick up our things on September eighth, so Benjamin could start school on the ninth.

I had little spare time to think about my departure and what it meant to me. I selected the furniture I could use in a four-room apartment and gave everything else away. It was unthinkable for me to sell anything, to reduce the objects of my life to the marketplace and assign a dollars-and-cents value to them. What I could not give away or take, I left exactly where it was on the farm. Our sit-down lawn mower remained in an out-building; our lawn furniture, under the trees near the swings and sandbox; all our farm tools, in the shed. I left quickly, taking only a brief farewell tour to look at the trees I had planted and the flower bed I had put in that spring, just after I signed my lease and bought my plane ticket for Israel. I had to put the flowers in, even though I knew there would be no one to tend them. I packed up a lifetime in a week. On September 8, Benjamin, carrying our cat, Smokey, and I got into the car, and we drove away, leading the moving van to our new address.

Although I knew I was going to make it, that first night under a roof that was not yet home to us was hard for me. I kept hearing the traffic on Harrison Street and thinking of the soothing quiet on the farm. In the morning, I felt an intense longing for the smell of new-mown grass. I thought I would never again awake to such a smell, and I mourned for the grass. The birds that used to call to me in the dawn were silent now; I would never again hear those familiar birds. I wondered if they would miss me as I missed them. And I mourned for the birds. I thought of the seasons I had slowly become accustomed to watching. Autumn would surely turn to winter in Princeton, but would I ever again see winter turn to spring?

Fortunately, I did not have too much time to spend mourning. I had to get Benjamin to his new school.

After we moved, Jack found a tenant for the house and turned the income over to me. Under our agreement, I acquired sole ownership of the farm. Jack did not care what became of it, but I thought of it as belonging to our family, and of myself as the interim caretaker. I wanted the children to inherit it.

I felt the most meaningful inheritance my children could get from me was the sense of tradition related to a specific place. I could hear them telling their children, "This is where I used to ride my horse; this is where your grandmother went to school; this is the home your grandmother and grandfather moved into when they first married; this is the home they built for us all." Richard, Steven, and Benjamin would become a part and parcel of the land which would be theirs, as it had been Charlie Hulick's. They would not be strangers in the way my father and I were. The farm would ensure that.

But the state put an end to that dream. The farm was situated on a tract designated as the site of a reservoir. All the farms within the designation were condemned and purchased by the state. Instead of the farm, I eventually received a sum of money. It seemed as if all my ties to Farmingdale were being cut. I considered all the things I could do with the money, all the ways in which I could invest it so that I could derive an income. But then I wondered what I would have to pass on to my children. Money is the least valuable of all inheritances. It comes, it goes, it means nothing. The land is solid and stable. Without it, I felt not only bereft but also robbed of my dreams.

Farmingdale was the beginning; I wanted it to be the ending. I took all the money I received from the sale of our farm and purchased an abandoned farm across the way from both the old Jewish Community Center property (also condemned by the state) and from Bierstein's woods, which I loved so much. Instead of my deriving an income from the money, I paid taxes every year on the property. When my older son Richard married, I carved out a piece of land on which a house stood and sold it to him. He lives there now with his family and plants a lovely garden every summer. My middle son, Steven, also lives on a farm with his family, but not in New Jersey. My youngest son, Benjamin, a computer engineer, lives in Boston.

It has given me some comfort to think that I can eventually go back to Farmingdale, although I am not sure, anymore, that I ever will. The area has changed completely. The new Jewish Center, built with the funds received from the sale of the old, is no longer my place. The large Bingo sign in the front of the property offends me. The people I knew and loved are almost all gone; no one is farming anymore. My own future is not secure financially, and I may have to sell my property for an income after all. I hope not. I still want to hold it in trust for my sons.

My father was at his happiest bringing in string beans and tomatoes from the garden he planted. He loved working outdoors, building a new room on the chicken coop, mixing cement for a new walk. He was always building and rebuilding. He built a home, a farm, and a future for his children. I want to hold on to my inheritance from him and pass it on to my children.

I still belong to Farmingdale; I have never left it.

Notes

Introduction

1. Theodore Saloutos, "The Immigrant Contribution to American Agriculture," *Agricultural History* 5 (January 1976): 45.

2. Hans Lamm, "The So-Called Letter of a German Jew to the President of the Congress of the United States of America of 1783," *Publications of the American Jewish Historical Society* (hereafter referred to as *PAJHS*) 37 (1947): 171–84.

3. Quoted in Morris U. Schappes, *A Documentary History of the Jews in the United States* (New York: Schocken Books, 1971), pp. 141–47. See also Lee M. Friedman, *Pilgrims in a New Land* (Philadelphia: Jewish Publication Society of America, 1948), pp. 233–47.

4. Schappes, *Documentary History,* pp. 142–43.

5. Ibid., p. 147.

6. *Niles Weekly Reader,* October 21, 1820, p. 114.

7. W. Kisch, "Nordamerikanische Kolonizationgesellschaft," *PAJHS* 34, (1937): 26–27.

8. *The Second Report of the American Society for Meliorating the Condition of the Jews* (Princeton, N.J., 1824), p. 34.

9. A. E. Thompson, *A Century of Jewish Missions* (Chicago: Fleming H. Revell, 1902), p. 228.

10. Lee Friedman, *Early American Jews* (Cambridge: Harvard University Press, 1934), p. 105.

11. Thompson, *Century of Jewish Missions,* p. 229.

12. Schappes, *Documentary History,* p. 158.

13. Ibid., pp. 159–60.

14. Ibid., p. 247. See also Solomon Grayzel, *A History of the Jews* (Philadelphia: Jewish Publication Society of America, 1963), p. 590.

15. Leo Shpall, "Jewish Agricultural Colonies in the United States," *Agricultural History* 24, no. 3 (July 1950): 120.

16. H. Eliassof, "The Jews of Chicago," *PAJHS* 11 (1903): 119. See also B. Felsenthal, "On the History of the Jews of Chicago," ibid. 2 (1894): 21–27.

17. Schappes, *Documentary History,* pp. 346–47.

18. *Occident* 3 (February 1845): 562, quoted in Shpall, "Jewish Agricultural Colonies," p. 122.

19. Schappes, *Documentary History,* p. 343.

20. For a complete discussion, see Esther L. Panitz, "The Polarity of American Jewish Attitudes towards Immigration (1870–1891): A Chapter in American Socio-Economic History," in *The Jewish Experience in America,* vol. 4, ed. Abraham Karp (New York: Ktav, 1969), pp. 31–62.

21. "The Board of Delegates of American Israelites, Final Report," *PAJHS* 29 (1925): 100–103.

22. Ibid., p. 102.

23. Shpall, "Jewish Agricultural Colonies," p. 125.

24. Gilbert Osofsky, "The Hebrew Emigrant Aid Society of the United States (1881–1883)," in *The Jewish Experience in America,* vol. 4, ed. Abraham Karp (New York: Ktav, 1969), pp. 75ff.

25. Shpall, "Jewish Agricultural Colonies," p. 127.

26. See Robert Alan Goldberg, *Back to the Soil: The Jewish Farmers of Clarion, Utah, and Their World* (Salt Lake City: University of Utah Press, 1986).

27. Moritz Ellinger, *Report on the European Conference on Emigration* (New York, 1887), pp. 103–7, quoted in Shpall, "Jewish Agricultural Colonies," p. 128.

28. George E. Barnett, "A Method of Determining the Jewish Population of the Large Cities in the United States," *PAJHS* 10 (1902): 44.

29. *Abstract of the Eleventh Census, 1890* (Washington, D.C.: U.S. Government Printing Office, 1896), Table 14, pp. 50–51.

30. Barnett cities evidence from reports of the commissioner of immigration that the Russian immigration consisted almost entirely of Jews. For the year ending June 30, 1900, he finds 37,000 Hebrew and only 1,165 other Russians ("Method," p. 45).

31. *American Israelite,* November 17, 1882, quoted in Shpall, "Jewish Agricultural Colonies," p. 128.

32. "Board of Delegates, Final Report," p. 101.

33. *Jewish Messenger,* August 28, 1882, quoted in Osofsky, "Hebrew Emigrant Aid Society," p. 83.

34. *Yiddische Volkzeitung,* June 6, 1882, quoted in Shpall, "Jewish Agricultural Colonies," p. 128.

35. Shpall, "Jewish Agricultural Colonies," p. 133.

36. "Bilu" is an acronym from the Hebrew phrase "Beit Ya'akov lekhu ve nelkhah." This phrase appears in Isaiah 2:5 and is translated, "House of Jacob,

come ye, let us go." The Hebrew phrases "Am Olam" and "Erez Israel" mean "Eternal People" and "Land of Israel."

37. "The Hebrew Emigrant Aid Society's Dissatisfied Applicants for Aid," *New York Times*, August 8, 1882.

38. "The Memoir of Dr. George M. Price," *PAJHS* 29 (1925): 101.

39. *Encyclopedia Judaica* claims that Am Olam established four colonies. Mark Wischnitzer says that sixteen colonies were established by these young Russian idealists of Am Olam (*To Dwell in Safety* [Philadelphia: Jewish Publication Society, 1948], pp. 61ff.). *Jews in American Agriculture*, a history of Jewish farming in the United States, credits the Am Olam with establishing twenty-five colonies in eight states [New York: Jewish Agricultural Society, 1954], p. 24).

40. Allan duPont Breck, *The Centennial History of the Jews of Colorado* (Denver: Hirschfeld Press, 1960), p. 77.

41. Quoted in ibid., p. 79.

42. Gabriel Davidson, *Our Jewish Farmers* (New York: L. B. Fischer, 1943), p. 218.

43. Martha Thal, "Early Days: The Story of Sarah Thal," *Pioneer Stories Written by People of Nelson County, North Dakota* (n.d.), p. 15.

44. *American Israelite*, August 22, 1884, quoted in Shpall, "Jewish Agricultural Colonies," p. 138.

45. See Abraham Cahan, *Bleter fun mayn leben*, vol. 2 (New York: Forward, 1926), p. 123, for a description of Frey.

46. *American Israelite*, October 3, 1884.

47. Ibid.

48. Shpall, "Jewish Agricultural Colonies," p. 131.

49. *Jewish Gazette*, November 25, 1886, quoted in Shpall, "Jewish Agricultural Colonies," p. 138.

50. Davidson, *Our Jewish Farmers*, p. 207.

51. Ibid., p. 232.

52. Cahan, *Bleter*, pp. 123–38 and 296–305.

53. See Joseph Brandes, *Immigrants to Freedom* (Philadelphia: University of Pennsylvania Press, 1971), for a complete discussion of the early South Jersey colonies.

54. Baron de Hirsch, "My Views on Philanthropy," *North American Review*, no. 416 (July 1891). See also Samuel Joseph, *History of the Baron de Hirsch Fund* (Philadelphia: Jewish Publication Society, 1935), p. 276.

55. The National Farm School is now the Delaware Valley College of Agriculture and Technology.

56. Toms River file, Farmingdale Collection. This collection is an archive of documents, including taped and filmed interviews, reflecting the total history of Farmingdale, New Jersey, spanning the years from 1895 to 1975. All subsequent quoted remarks and documents of farmers and others connected with Farmingdale are in the archive, currently in the author's possession.

57. *A Bintel Brief: Sixty Years of Letters from the Lower East Side to the Daily Forward,* ed. Isaac Metzker (New York: Doubleday, 1971), pp. 92–93.

58. Theodore Norman, *An Outstretched Arm: A History of the Jewish Colonization Association* (London: Routledge & Kegan Paul, 1985), pp. 108–11.

59. Before any definitive statement can be made about the similarities and differences among the scattered Jewish farm communities, more community studies need to be undertaken.

60. Interview in Trenton, New Jersey, April 10, 1987.

61. "Cultural pluralism" was first defined by Horace Kallen in an article in the *Nation* (February 18, 1915) and then expanded in *Culture and Democracy in the United States* (New York: Boni & Liveright, 1924) and *Cultural Pluralism and the American Idea* (Philadelphia: University of Pennsylvania Press, 1956). See Sidney Ratner, "Horace M. Kallen and Cultural Pluralism," *Modern Judaism* 4 (May 19, 1984): 185–200.

62. For some of these thoughts, the writer is indebted to Jonathan Boyarin, anthropologist, and a great-nephew of one of the earliest of the Farmingdale farmers ("Memory and Farmingdale," remarks at Symposium, "New Americans— New Farmers," held at Princeton University, April 8, 1984). Boyarin was born in Farmingdale, a member of the youngest generation in the farming community.

Part One: Beginnings

1. Howell Township was formed in 1801. Included in its large land areas were all the boroughs along the Atlantic Ocean from Barnegat Inlet to the Shark River Inlet at Belmar, New Jersey. By 1903, several municipalities and townships were carved out from its original borders, including the borough of Farmingdale in the central part of Howell. See Wollman and Rose, *Historical and Biographical Atlas of N.J. Coast* (1878), quoted in *History of Howell* (Howell, N.J.: Ardena School, [1970]), p. 21.

2. West Farms, originally known as New Bargaintown, is located about two miles from the borough of Farmingdale and is near the center of the township. The first Jewish families bought their farms in West Farms and later donated a piece of property for a Jewish community center, known both as the West Farms Jewish Community Center and the Farmingdale Jewish Community Center.

3. Annual Reports of the JAS reveal that twenty families settled in Farmingdale in 1925 and 1926 with JAS help, and an equal number without it. These are approximate figures, for no census was taken (Archives, American Jewish Historical Society, Waltham, Mass.).

Part Two: The People

1. See Joseph, *History,* pp. 171–72. See also Davidson, *Our Jewish Farmers.*

2. When a chicken has difficulty laying an egg, she sometimes bleeds.

Chickens, being cannibalistic, are attracted to the blood and pick the unfortunate bird to death. Shielding, specking, and debeaking were devices to prevent such behavior. A metal or a rubber shield was pinned to the chicken's vent, or specs were put on their beaks allowing only peripheral vision, or the beaks were blunted to prevent pecking. Each of these methods was labor intensive, as each chicken had to be handled by two people for a few moments.

3. A book of death certificates was found among material discarded when the Farmingdale Jewish Community Center did housecleaning. Of the ninety-five certificates, four list the cause of death as gunshot wounds, presumably self-inflicted. Suicides among the farmers obviously occurred, and the phenomenon is noted, although not fully researched for this study. Five more suicides that I know about were not among those represented by the available certificates. In addition, a large number of farmers were involved in automobile accidents resulting in fatalities.

4. Morris Freedman, "The New Farmers of Lakewood," in *Commentary on the American Scene: Portraits of Jewish Life in America,* ed. Elliot Cohen (New York: Knopf, 1953), p. 137.

5. The Hebrew word *aliya* literally means "ascending." The Torah reading is divided into portions, and it is a special honor for a congregant to "ascend," or approach, the *bimah* (usually a raised reading platform) or reading table to participate in the service by reading a few lines or reciting the blessing before the portion is read.

Part Three: The Life

1. The Arbitration Committee is discussed more fully in chapter 12, "Coping with Problems."

2. Hebrew is written without letter vowels. Yiddish is more phonetic in that each sound has a letter equivalent. Hebrew words in the texts used by the Sholem Aleichem Folk Shules were rendered in Yiddish spellings.

3. Files, Sholem Aleichem Folk Institute Archives, YIVO Institute for Jewish Research, New York.

4. "Howell Township School," in *History of Howell* (Howell, N.J.: Ardena School, [1970]), pp. 42–45.

5. In 1939, all the schools in the township were consolidated into one large modern building.

6. In the early 1970s, in an avant-garde school system such as that in Princeton, New Jersey, there was a "revolutionary" educational development known as "multi-age" classrooms, where grades were grouped together so that younger children could learn from older ones, and slower learners could benefit from faster ones. Its model, of course, was rural schools, which were multi-age by necessity.

7. Although most of the Jewish farmers did not observe all the dietary rules of the religion, they did not eat nonkosher meat or fish or allow it in their homes.

8. Printed in souvenir journal, 1955, Ladies Club file, Farmingdale Collection.

9. Freedman, "New Farmers," p. 138.

10. Ibid., p. 137.

11. Both Christian and Jewish farmers in rural communities within a fifty-mile radius of cities rented out rooms in their homes to city people looking for inexpensive vacations.

12. It is ironic that today, the area of the lake is incorporated into the thousands of acres in Howell Township which were taken over by the state for the Manasquan River Reservoir. It looks like the beautiful, bountiful lake the farmers envisioned when they organized the West Farms Lake Association.

13. Copy of chattel mortgage in the Economics file, Farmingdale Collection.

14. Joseph, *History*, pp. 171–72.

15. Salomon J. Flink, ed., *The Economy of New Jersey* (New Brunswick, N.J.: Rutgers University Press, 1958), p. 518.

16. Ibid.

17. *The Mixer,* November 15, 1945, p. 1, in the Farmingdale Collection.

18. The story of exactly how the U.S. Department of Agriculture and other vested interests in Washington were covertly involved in the collapse of poultry farming in New Jersey, and of small family farming all over the country, has yet to be researched and told. It is behind the demise of the Jewish farm community of Farmingdale and the disappearance of other such communities.

19. Howell-Jackson file, Farmingdale Collection.

20. The Farmingdale Jewish Community Center was incorporated as the West Farms Community Center because it was in a section of the township called West Farms.

21. The FBI files on the Farmingdale Jewish Community were requested under the Freedom of Information Act. When they arrived, they were incomplete and heavily censored.

22. Farmers from Farmingdale, Lakewood, and Freehold testified in support of a price-support program at hearings before the U.S. Senate Committee on Agriculture and Forestry, November 19, 1955, in Utica, New York. They asked that grain purchased by the government and stored in silos be released to desperate farmers in the Northeast. Irving Berger, poultryman of Lakewood, said, "Part of the problem confronting the poultry industry today is created by [the poultry] consumption of price-supported feeds as raw material to the production of a non-supported egg-product. Consideration is requested of the proposition that eggs are as much a basic commodity as any product and should be considered in the same light with other price-supported items" (*Hearings before the Committee on Agriculture and Forestry, United States Senate, Eighty-Fourth Congress,* part 7 [Washington, D.C.: U.S. Government Printing Office, 1956], p. 3232). Clarence Althouse, representing the National Poultry Farmers Association, urged that "eggs and poultry must have the same parity level of support as wheat and corn" (p. 3260). Berger and others also suggested that FHA loans to commercial poultry farmers be extended and liberalized, that the Department of Agriculture purchase eggs for domestic and foreign relief programs, and that state universities be given grants

to develop additional uses and needs of poultry products. With the exception of Althouse, the witnesses, who reflected the feelings of many farmers, were regarded as representing their own views.

23. Records of the Office of the Secretary of Agriculture, Record Group 16, Box 2523, National Archives, Washington, D.C.

Part Four: Growing Up in Farmingdale

1. Gittel is my Yiddish name. Gittele is a diminutive form generally used affectionately. Tenenbaum's use of it indicates not only that he knew me but also that he was fond of me.

2. The idiom is difficult to translate. *Blaybt* means "remains." *Pintele* means "small dot" and also refers to the diacritical marks used in Hebrew writing. *Dos pintele yid* is a metaphor for a small spark of Judaism. An underlying meaning of the expression refers to the need to pay attention to the dots, the pointing, when reading texts in order to gain greater understanding.

3. While collecting the Farmingdale archives, I found his name in the daybooks of Michael Hamburger. Evidently, Cherkiss enjoyed intellectual meetings at the Hamburger home, where book discussions and meetings of the Spinoza Society were held. He made his money doing odd jobs. Hamburger writes in 1937 that he gave Cherkiss a half-day's work painting and fixing the flower beds. No one I interviewed knew what happened to him.

4. Whenever my father had enough of the relatives, he always turned off the water to the house, saying the well was running low and the water had to be preserved for the chickens. This meant that the indoor bathroom could not be used, and the relatives, not happy with our outhouse, soon beat a hasty retreat back to New York City. However, when he became a rooming-house entrepreneur, we seemed to have enough water for everything but bathing. He built an outdoor shower which depended on solar heating, for the benefit of the roomers.

5. In 1975, when I interviewed surviving farmers, many reminded me of how much they enjoyed my performances and how exciting the programs were. I felt then the same satisfaction I felt as a child listening to the audience applauding.

Bibliography

Barnett, George E. "A Method of Determining the Jewish Population of the Large Cities in the United States." *Publications of the American Jewish Historical Society* 10 (1902): 37–45.

Brandes, Joseph. *Immigrants to Freedom.* Philadelphia: University of Pennsylvania Press, 1971.

Breck, Allan duPont. *The Centennial History of the Jews of Colorado.* Denver: Hirschfeld Press, 1960.

Cahan, Abraham. *Bleter fun mayn leben.* Vol. 2. New York: Forward, 1926.

Davidson, Gabriel. *Our Jewish Farmers.* New York: L. B. Fischer, 1943.

Dobin, Abraham. *Fertile Fields: Recollections and Reflections of a Busy Life.* Cranbury, N.J.: A. S. Barnes, 1975.

Dubrovsky, Gertrude. *The Farmingdale Collection.* New York: Yivo Institute for Jewish Research, 1976.

———. "Farmingdale, New Jersey: A Jewish Farm Community." *American Jewish Historical Quarterly* 66 (June 1977): 485–97.

———. "The Rural Experience of Jews in Farmingdale, New Jersey." In *New Jersey's Ethnic Heritage,* ed. Paul Stellhorn, pp. 36–58. Trenton: New Jersey Historical Commission, 1978.

———. "Growing Up in Farmingdale." *American Jewish History* 71 (December 1981): 239–55.

———. "Jewish Agriculture in America." In *The American Jewish Farmer,* ed. Abraham Peck, pp. 3–7. Cincinnati, Ohio: American Jewish Archives, 1986.

———. "In Search of America: Lexington, Ky., and Farmingdale, N.J." *Midstream* 34, no. 7 (October 1988): 29–33.

———. "Down on the Farm." *Lilith* 14, no. 2 (Spring 1989/5749): 27–29.

———. "Der Yiddisher Farmer." *Reform Judaism* 18, no. 1 (Fall 1989): 5–7.

———. "The Soil and the Star." *Midstream* 35, no. 6 (August/September 1989): 36–40.

Eliassof, H. "The Jews of Chicago." *Publications of the American Jewish Historical Society* 11 (1903): 117–30.

Felsenthal B. "On the History of the Jews of Chicago." *Publications of the American Jewish Historical Society* 2 (1894): 21–27.

Freedman, Morris. "The New Farmers of Lakewood." In *Commentary on the American Scene: Portraits of Jewish Life in America,* ed. Elliot Cohen, pp. 127–46. New York: Knopf, 1953.

Friedman, Lee M. *Pilgrims in a New Land.* Philadelphia: Jewish Publication Society of America, 1948.

Goldberg, Robert A. *Back to the Soil: The Jewish Farmers of Clarion, Utah, and Their World.* Salt Lake City: University of Utah Press, 1986.

Goldhaft, Arthur D. *The Golden Egg.* New York: Horizon Press, 1957.

Grayzel, Solomon. *A History of the Jews.* Philadelphia: Jewish Publication Society of America, 1963.

Hamburg, Alice. *Sam Hamburg: Agricultural Pioneer in California and Israel.* Berkeley, Calif.: Western Jewish History Center, 1989.

Herscher, Uri D. *Jewish Agricultural Utopias in America, 1880–1910.* Detroit: Wayne State University Press, 1981.

Joseph, Samuel. *History of the Baron de Hirsch Fund.* Philadelphia: Jewish Publication Society, 1935.

Karp, Abraham, ed. *The Jewish Experience in America.* Vol. 4. New York: Ktav, 1969.

Kisch, W. "Nordamerikanische Kolonizationgesellschaft." *Publications of the American Jewish Historical Society* 44 (1937): 11–49.

Levine, Herman J., and Benjamin Miller. *The American Jewish Farmer in Changing Times.* New York: Jewish Agricultural Society, 1966.

Meckler, Brenda Weisberg. *Papa Was a Farmer.* Chapel Hill, N.C.: Algonquin Books, 1988.

Norman, Theodore. *An Outstretched Arm: A History of the Jewish Colonization Association.* London: Routledge & Kegan Paul, 1985.

Purmell, Bluma B. R., and F. L. Rovner. *A Farmer's Daughter: Bluma.* Marina del Rey, Calif.: Havenhurst Publishers, 1981.

Saloutos, Theodore. "The Immigrant Contribution to American Agriculture." *Agricultural History* 5 (January 1976): 45–67.

Schappes, Morris U. *A Documentary History of the Jews in the United States.* New York: Schocken Books, 1971.

Sher, Eva. *Life with Farmer Goldstein.* New York: Funk & Wagnalls, 1967.

Shpall, Leo. "Jewish Agricultural Colonies in the United States." *Agricultural History* 24, no. 3 (July 1950): 120–46.

Thal, Martha. "Early Days: The Story of Sarah Thal." In *Pioneer Stories Written by People of Nelson County, North Dakota.* Cincinnati: American Jewish Archives, n.d.

Trupin, Sophie. *Dakota Diaspora: Memoirs of a Jewish Homesteader.* Berkeley, Calif.: Alternative Press, 1984.

245

Index

250

Index

Yiddish, 33, 44, 55, 56, 57, 61, 77, 78–79, 107–108, 113–17, 178. *See also* Schools: Yiddish

(Der) Yiddisher Farmer, 21, 48

Zelnick, Joseph, 67, 73, 156–57

About the Author

Gertrude Wishnick Dubrovsky grew up in Farmingdale, New Jersey, and lived there for thirty-eight years. She holds a doctorate from Columbia University. She is instructor of Yiddish at the B'nai B'rith Hillel Foundation at Princeton University. She also serves as president of DOCUMENTARY III, a non-profit corporation that works to preserve ethnic rural history.